13.75

$13\frac{75}{N}mc.$

Essay Ind

P9-AFK-607

STORIES OF AUTHORS

GEOFFREY CHAUCER

From a portrait in Occleve's Poems in the British Museum

Stories of Authors

British and American

BY

EDWIN WATTS CHUBB

Professor of English Literature
in the Ohio University.

NEW EDITION

ILLUSTRATED

Essay Index Reprint Series

Essay Index

Originally published by:

THE MACMILLAN COMPANY

 BOOKS FOR LIBRARIES PRESS
FREEPORT, NEW YORK

New Edition First Published 1926
Reprinted 1968

LIBRARY OF CONGRESS CATALOG CARD NUMBER:

68-54338

MANUFACTURED
BY
HALLMARK LITHOGRAPHERS, INC.
IN THE U.S.A.

PREFACE

THE purpose of this book is to help in making literature and the makers of literature alive and interesting. Few schools have libraries including the bound volumes of the magazines of the past quarter of a century. But what an aid such a collection is to the appreciation of literature! The dignified and abbreviated history of literature cannot indulge in such delightful gossip as is found in the freer essay and fuller biography. To show the excellences of the art and the lovableness of the artist rather than to hunt for defects is the duty and the delight of the teacher of literature. This does not mean, however, that one dare never see the weaker side, the foibles and eccentricities of the man of genius.

I like Macaulay none the less because his cocksureness and loquacity came dangerously near to making him a bore; Dr. Johnson grows in interest when I learn that he found it a continual and almost hopeless struggle to become an early riser, that he feared death, and could drink tea as long as the housekeeper could brew it; that Tennyson was a slave to tobacco and acted like a yokel when the newly-wedded Müllers entertained him at breakfast does not detract from my enjoyment of the exquisite pathos of *Tears, Idle Tears;* that the marriage of the Brownings was a runaway romance is a whole commentary of explanation when I read their poems of romantic love; that

Longfellow is said to have declined an invitation to the Adirondacks because he was told that Emerson was to carry a gun is really far more delightful, and I may add valuable, information than to know the exact date of the birth of either. Of knowledge such as this is the kingdom of literary interest. It is not well to place our literary lights upon a pedestal so lofty that the radiating warmth and light never reach our hearts.

While many of the articles may be somewhat gossipy in tone, the serious phase has not been overlooked. The sketches have been gathered from many sources. Some have been written by myself, others have been gathered from magazines and books. I wish to acknowledge the kindness of *Scribners' Magazine,* of the *Bookman,* and of the *New England Magazine* in permitting me to use articles originally appearing in these respective magazines. To all who have wittingly or unwittingly made it possible for me to gather my material I wish to acknowledge my indebtedness. Every article has been written, selected, or adapted because of some special value. In these pages the reader may find what Lamb earned during the years of his famous clerkship, or the exciting details of Shelley's death. How many times have we heard of Sir Philip Sidney's immortal act of chivalry as he *lay* on the field at Zutphen! But definite information has it otherwise. To learn of the prodigious industry of the youthful Mill, the perseverance of Darwin, the heroic struggle of Scott, the gentleness of Stevenson, the modesty of Browning, the lifelong consecration of Motley,—is not the leaven of inspiration made of knowledge such as this?

I have an unshaken conviction that the highest art of the teacher is manifested in the awakening of such an interest that the pupil shall forever after be an eager learner. Am I wrong in hoping that no one, though with but a meager knowledge of literature, can read these sketches without a desire to know more of the men and women who are the glory of England and America? Here is but a taste of a more sumptuous feast.

Dreams, books are each a world; and books, we know,
Are a substantial world, both pure and good:
Round these, with tendrils strong as flesh and blood,
Our pastime and our happiness will grow.

EDWIN WATTS CHUBB.

CONTENTS

ENGLISH WRITERS

CONTENTS

AMERICAN WRITERS

ILLUSTRATIONS

STORIES OF AUTHORS

I

THE ANCIENT TABARD INN

THE picture we see here is that of an inn whose fame is as widespread as the love of English poetry, for it is at the Tabard Inn that Chaucer more than five hundred years ago assembled his nine and twenty pilgrims who were preparing to visit the tomb of Thomas à Becket at Canterbury. The witchery of the springtime had stirred the blood of these Londoners who, perhaps, were enticed from home more by the soft April showers and the melody of the birds than by their need of spiritual consolation. This, at least, is the impression we receive as in imagination we join these immortal pilgrims at the Tabard. Our guide is

> Dan Chaucer, the first warbler, whose sweet breath
> Preluded those melodious bursts that fill
> The spacious times of great Elizabeth
> With sounds that echo still,—

and as he moves among his motley group, let us take a glance at the Tabard.

The picture we have is that of the typical old English inn. "As late as 1870 the ruins of the famous Tabard could be found. It was near St. Saviour in the Borough High Street. Turning from the street into one of those courtyards

which abound in the east of London, the visitor
comes upon the ruins of the once famous inn the
very name of which has been transformed by
time. It is now known as the 'Talbot,' but the
inscription above the doorway contradicts the
modern signboard and proclaims the house to be
'The Ancient Tabard Inn.' The whole yard is
redolent of dilapidation. Facing the visitor on
entering is an interesting block of old buildings,
forming part of the left side, and the bottom of
what once was an ample courtyard. This part
of the building contains not improbably the shell
of the corresponding portion of the original inn.
The doors of the first floor all open into one of
the wide balustraded galleries or verandas so
common in the genuine old English hostelry.
Until recently the landlord of the Talbot, then a
small public-house, and still forming part of the
modern mass of brick building that blocks up the
right side and part of the center of the courtyard, rented the rooms by which this balustraded
gallery was, and still is, surrounded. They were
then let as bedrooms, and kept in good repair;
and are supposed to occupy the site of the very
rooms once tenanted by the Canterbury pilgrims;
the gallery probably differing but little in appearance from what it was when Chaucer frequented
it in search of good wine. The landlord eventually became insolvent; the paltry tavern was
shut up, and the bedrooms were dismantled. In
that plight they might be seen some years ago,
may still possibly be seen—empty, dusty, dreary
—ranged above ground-floor premises which do
duty as a parcels' conveyance office, and abutting
on a mean, ill-kept yard. Until within the last

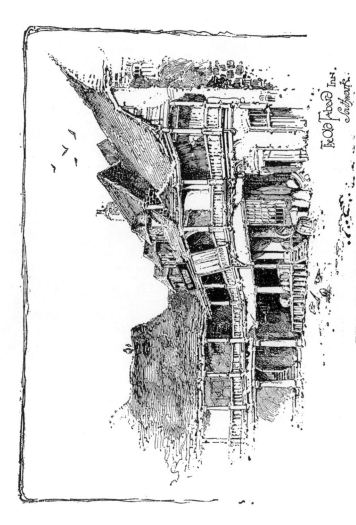

THE OLD TABARD INN

From a drawing by Herbert Railton

few years the coigne of the old balustraded gallery was connected on the right with the modern brick mass by an ancient wood-work bridge, coeval at least with the oldest portion of the building as it stands. But the bridge is gone, and the lust of gold and the pride of life have so destroyed that spirit of reverence and refined superstitious love for the venerable which should characterize an advanced civilization, that it is greatly to be feared the rest of the structure will soon follow. Yet it was in this courtyard, and before this very inn, that Chaucer and his nine-and-twenty pilgrims stood in picturesque confusion in the early dawn of that spring morning, long, long ago; and agreed for their common amusement on the road each one of them should tell at least one tale in going to, and another in returning from Canterbury; the best story teller to be treated to a supper by his fellow travelers on their return to the Tabard Inn. The company comprises representatives from all classes of society except the two extremes; there is neither a prince nor a beggar. The characters are taken from middle-class life, of which they may be accepted as fair and truthful types; being described with a vigorous fidelity which has never been surpassed in the whole range of art. Every figure stands out from the canvas sharp and clear like pictures seen through a stereoscope. Not a touch, not a line is wanting; each trick of speech and peculiarity of feature or of dress, is photographed with Preraphaelite fidelity.''

II

WHENEVER the name of Sir Philip Sidney is mentioned one involuntarily thinks of noble generosity and knightly gentleness and self-sacrifice. And here is the story of the act that forever united his name with the highest ideals of chivalry:

In August, 1586, Leicester assembled his troops at Arnheim, which he made his headquarters. After reducing Doesburg, he prepared to besiege Zutphen, an important town on the Yssel. The garrison was in sore need of provisions, which Parma, before marching to its relief, determined to supply. A convoy of corn, meat, and other necessaries, sufficient to victual the place for three months, was accordingly collected, and on the twenty-second of September left the Spanish camp. So high was Parma's estimate of the importance of preserving Zutphen, that the escort despatched with the convoy numbered twenty-nine hundred foot and six hundred horse. Leicester was informed of the enemy's movement, but not of the force which protected it. An ambuscade of five hundred men, under Sir John Norris, was held sufficient to intercept the convoy. About fifty young officers volunteered to add their services. This gallant band was composed of the flower of the English army. . . . It was indeed "an incredible extravagance to send a handful of such heroes against such an army," but Leicester can scarcely be blamed for failing to restrain the impulsive ardor which animated his entire staff. Sidney's characteristic magnanimity betrayed him that day into a fatal excess. He had risen at the first sound of the trumpet and left his tent completely armed, but observing that Sir William Pelham, an older soldier, had not protected his legs with cuishes, returned and threw off his own.

The morning was cold and densely foggy, as the little company galloped forth to join their comrades in ambush. Just as they came up, Sir John Norris had caught the first sounds of the approaching convoy. Almost at the same moment the fog cleared off and revealed at what terrible odds the battle was to be fought that day. Mounted arquebusiers, pikemen and musketeers on foot, Spaniards, Italians, and even, it is said, Albanians, to the number of thirty-five hundred, guarded the wagons before and behind. The English were but five hundred and fifty men. Yet among them all, the historian has the right of blood to say with confidence, "There was no thought of retreat." The indomitable national spirit embodied itself in the war-cry of young Essex: "Follow me, good fellows, for the honor of England and England's queen!" At the word a hundred horsemen, Sidney in the midst, with lance in hand and curtel-axe at saddle-bow, spurred to the charge. The enemy's cavalry broke, but the musketeers in the rear fired a deadly volley, under cover of which it formed anew. A second charge re-broke it. In the onset Sidney's horse was killed, but he remounted and rode forward. Lord Willoughby, after unhorsing and capturing the Albanian leader, lost his own horse. Attacked on all sides, he must have fallen and yielded, when Sidney came to the rescue and struck down his assailants. Individual valor, however, proved unavailing against the might of numbers. After nearly two hours' desperate opposition, the convoy still made way. Charge succeeded charge in the vain effort to prevent its effecting a junction with the garrison, two thousand of whom were waiting for the right moment to sally forth. In the last of these onsets, Sir Philip's impetuosity carried him within musket-shot of the camp. A bullet struck his unprotected leg, just above the knee, and shattered the bone. He endeavored to remain on the field, but his horse became unmanageable, and in agonies of pain and thirst he rode back to the English quarters, a mile and a half distant. An incident of that ride, as told in the quaint language of Lord Brooke, retains the immortal charm of pathos which commands our tears, how often soever repeated:

In which sad progress, passing along by the rest of the army, where his uncle the general was, and being thirsty with excess of bleeding, he called for drink, which was presently brought him, but as he was putting the bottle to his mouth, he saw a poor soldier carried along who had eaten his last at that same feast, ghastly, casting up his eyes at the bottle, which Sir Philip perceiving, took it from his head before he drank, and delivered it to the poor man with these words, "Thy necessity is greater than mine." And when he had pledged this poor soldier, he was presently carried to Arnheim.

The golden chain of heroic actions, Christian and pagan. may contain examples of self-denial sublimer and more absolute than this; but in the blended grace and tenderness of its knightly courtesy, we know not where to find its parallel.

Leicester met his nephew as he was borne back to the camp, and burst into a genuine passion of sorrow. Many a rough soldier among those who, in returning from the failure of their impossible enterprise, now came up with their comrade, was unmanned for the first time that day. Sir William Russell, as tender-hearted as he was daring, embraced him weeping, and kissed his hand amid broken words of admiration and sympathy. But Sidney needed no consolation. "I would," said Leicester, in a letter to Sir Thomas Heneage, "you had stood by to hear his most loyal speeches to her Majesty, his constant mind to the cause, his loving care over me, and his most resolute determination for death; not one jot appalled for his blow, which is the most grievous that ever I saw with such a bullet."

The English surgeons at first gave hopes of his speedy restoration to health, and the favorable news was sent to England. Lady Sidney, who had followed him to Flushing some months before, at once hastened to him, but with no idea of his danger. The nation at large thought him convalescent. He himself, however, never expected to recover, although submitting with fortitude to whatever systems of treatment were proposed. Nothing was left untried that affection could suggest or the imperfect science of the age effect. His wife tenderly nursed him, and his two younger brothers were constantly at his side. His quondam foe, Count Hohenlo, though himself dangerously wounded, sent off his own physician,

Adrian Van den Spiegel, to his aid. After examining the injuries Adrian pronounced them mortal, and then hastened back to the Count, whose case was not so desperate. "Away, villain!" cried the generous soldier in a transport of wrath; "never see my face again till thou bring better news of that man's recovery, for whose redemption many such as I were happily lost!"

From the first to the last moment of his suffering Sir Philip's temper was calm and cheerful. During the three weeks that he lingered at Arnheim he occupied himself with the thoughts befitting a death-bed. . . . On the 17th of October he felt himself dying, and summoned his friends to say farewell. His latest words were addressed to his brother Robert: "Love my memory; cherish my friends; their faith to me may assure you they are honest. But, above all things, govern your will and affections by the will and word of your Creator; in me beholding the end of this world with all her vanities." When powerless to speak, he replied to the entreaty of friends, who desired some token of his trust in God, by clasping his hands in the attitude of prayer, and a few moments afterwards had ceased to breathe.

—Adapted from the *Edinburgh Review.*

WILLIAM SHAKSPERE
From the portrait by Martin Droeshout

III

WHAT would we not give to be able to relate a half-dozen good anecdotes about Shakspere? It is true there are traditions, the best known of which is the story that he poached deer in the park of Sir Thomas Lucy. Men have discussed the pros and cons of this deer-stealing tradition with a gravity and fulness worthy of a weightier cause. Suppose he did engage in the exciting sport of worrying a nobleman who had a game preserve. Does that fact blacken the youth's character? It is said the students at Oxford were the most notorious poachers in the kingdom, although expulsion was the penalty. Dr. Forman relates how a student who afterwards became a bishop was more given to poaching than to study.

What do we know about the life of Shakspere? We know that he was born at Stratford-on-Avon in 1564, that he died there in 1616, April 23. Some years ago I stood in the house which is reputed to be the place of his birth; over 20,000 pilgrims from all lands each year pay their shilling for the privilege of going through that house; the town corporation has purchased the property and controls it; the place has been photographed until

the reading world is familiar with the picture,—
and yet we do not positively know that Shakspere
was born in that house. For Shakspere's father
owned two houses at the time of the son's birth;
in which of the two he lived at this time we can
but guess. We suppose he lived in the Henley
Street house, for it was the better of the two
houses and the Shakspere family was prospering
when William was born. The house itself has
been remodeled. I think it is Sidney Lee who
says that the only thing that remains as it was in
Shakspere's time is the cellar. We do not know
the day of Shakspere's birth. In Holy Trinity
Church one may look into the book containing
the baptismal record of the babe, William. He
was baptized April 26 and as children were usually baptized three days after their birth we infer
he was born April 23. We know that he married
Anne Hathaway, a woman eight years his senior;
that in early manhood he went to London; that
he became actor, dramatist, manager of a theater;
that in 1597 he bought New Place, the stateliest
residence in Stratford; that he lived in Stratford
during the last years of his life as a highly es-
teemed and worthy man, and that he died in 1616
and was buried in Trinity Church. These are the
facts in the records of Shakspere's life. They,
however, are not the important facts. The main
fact in his life is his work, the matchless collection of literary masterpieces that bear the im-
print of his genius. It is also well to keep in
mind that our paucity of definite documentary
records is not characteristic of Shakspere alone.
We may know little of Shakspere, but we know
less of Marlowe, his most brilliant competitor.

It is because we know so little of fact in the life of Shakspere that we delight to let fancy paint its charming pictures. We are led into the old Grammar School which Shakspere in all probability attended. Tradition points out the desk at which he used to sit. We can infer what he studied. The name of the Latin grammar then used we can deduce from his quoting a Latin sentence just as it was misquoted in Lilly's grammar. Artists have painted from imagination the picture of the boy Shakspere. Poets have wandered over the Warwickshire region and in their mind's eye have seen the youthful bard as he walked over the same picturesque region. In *Midsummer-Night's Dream* we read

> I know a bank where the wild thyme blows,
> Where oxlips and the nodding violet grows,
> Quite over-canopied with luscious woodbine,
> With sweet musk-roses and with eglantine.—

and we see the young Shakspere, keen-eyed, observant, reveling in the beauty of nature. In *Macbeth* we read

> This castle hath a pleasant seat; the air
> Nimbly and sweetly recommends itself
> Unto our gentle senses.—

and we recall that Kenilworth and Warwick Castles are near Stratford and we see the boyish Shakspere as he walks about these magnificent testimonies to the might and power of feudal England, or perhaps mingling with the crowd when Royalty has come to Kenilworth to be entertained by the lavish Leicester. So, too, when we find in *Much Ado About Nothing*

> The pleasant'st angling is to see the fish
> Cut with her golden oars the silver stream,
> And greedily devour the treacherous bait,—

we have a picture before us of the boy standing on the banks of the placid Avon, enjoying the sports of boyhood and unconsciously receiving impressions that shall later be reproduced to adorn with freshest imagery the poetry of the world's greatest genius.

After years of labor the scholars of the world have scraped together enough definite information to make the Life of Shakspere, as Mr. Raleigh puts it, "assume the appearance of a scrap-heap of respectable size." But to us the great fact in the life of Shakspere is that he has given us his masterpieces. Perhaps it is just as well that we know so little about the facts in his life. We have all the more time to study his works. About their quality there is little of disagreement. Three hundred years ago Ben Jonson wrote

> . . . I confess thy writings to be such
> As neither man nor muse can praise too much,—

and the critic of to-day is saying the same thing, only he uses two volumes instead of two lines to say it. It is true an occasional voice, like that of Tolstoy's, will be heard in protest, but the protest and the critic are both likely to be forgotten before the consensus of three centuries shall be set aside.

Shakspere lives and shall live as long as the human race shall delight in the study of the human heart, not because of the chastity and clearness of his diction, not because of the supremacy of his imagination, nor because of the variety of his melodious verse,—not even because of the matchless combination of all these charms; but the Bard of Stratford lives and shall live because his sanity enabled him to see the "God of things as they are,'' and his passion penetrated into the deepest sorrows and rose to the highest aspirations of the human heart,—and throughout all this sympathizing with goodness and while despising the depraved yet pitying with a heart of love.

No system-maker or formula-builder can account for Shakspere. Genius is ever a miracle. However, we can study the environment in which genius moves and has its being. When we ask ourselves how does it happen that the plays of Shakspere breathe such a wholesome and vigorous morality, we are led to two conclusions,—first, that the England of Shakspere's time was a wholesome and vigorous England; second, that the man Shakspere was sound to the core.

The close of the sixteenth century is one of the most remarkable periods in the history of the world. Indeed, so striking is the intellectual activity of this age that lately an eminent scientist advanced the hypothesis that some electric influence, some magnetic current must have let itself loose to work upon the destinies of the world in the production of great men. For in that period in Italy we find Tasso, the greatest of modern epic poets; then too lived Galileo and Kepler, the astronomers; in France we find the philosophic essayist, Montaigne; in Spain the world-renowned Cervantes, the author of the immortal Don Quixote; in England both Bacon and Shakspere, beside a host of other writers, generals, admirals and artists. This same age is the most flourishing period in Mahometan India; so, too, in China, in Japan, and even in far away Persia we find an unusual degree of intellectual activity.

The England of Shakspere! The phrase suggests a train of associations that kindle the imagination. The age of literature, war, conquest, adventure, and achievement. The era of Edmund Spenser, "called from faeryland to struggle 'gainst dark ways;" of Sir Philip Sidney, the scholar, the courtier, the gentleman; of Sir Walter Raleigh, author, knight, and explorer; of Bacon, "the wisest, meanest, brightest of mankind." It is the time when in the *Golden Hind* Drake is circumnavigating the globe; when Hawkins is exploring the Indies, and Frobisher is becoming the hero of the Northwest passage; the age of marvelous tales told by intrepid explorers and adventurers returning from America, a land whose fountains renewed youth and whose rivers flowed over sands of gold. It is the era of English sea-dogs pillaging Spanish provinces in spite of imperial manifestos,—above all, it is the age of the Spanish Armada.

To recall what this means it is necessary to remember that Spain was the great dominating empire of the sixteenth century. Philip II, the Duke of Alva, the horrors of the Spanish inquisition, condemn Spain's power in this period. But one midsummer morn all England awoke to the glorious news that the Invincible Armada lay at the bottom of the sea. England had triumphed, and now for the first time national life dreamed of the possibility of leadership in the great game of world-politics. The atmosphere was electric with new life. In rural England along lanes flanked with green hedges Englishmen walked with bosoms swelling with new pride, in bustling London vigorous burghers strode the city's streets with hearts pulsating with new warmth, and everywhere the eyes of all Englishmen flashed with new fire.

Could a soul so sensitive as Shakspere's live in such an atmosphere and not be influenced by it? Listen to him as he pays his beautiful, patriotic tribute to England's national glory:

> This other Eden, demi-paradise,
> This fortress built by Nature for herself,
> This precious stone set in the silver sea,
> This blessed plot, this earth, this realm, this England,
> This land of such dear souls, this dear, dear land,
> Dear for her reputation through the world.

And the second cause, we say, is the personality of the man himself. Shakspere wrote pure and lofty poetry because his was a pure and lofty nature. I know the disparagers of Shakspere and the advocates of the Baconian theory make much of the traditional wildness of Shakspere's youth. The common argument is that a man who is charged with the poaching of deer in his youth is too bad to write good poetry, therefore Bacon wrote Shakspere. Was Bacon an angel? By the same process of reasoning Burns could not have written the Cotter's Saturday Night. But I deny that Shakspere was profligate, and in making this denial I need not prove the impeccability of Shakspere. But his life was essentially pure, his heart good, because the influence of the life is sane and wholesome.

Not alone the greatest intellect of his time, of all times, but also the greatest heart, was that possessed by this Warwickshire poet. As a man thinketh in his heart so he is. As Shakspere was, so he wrote. This crystalline wholesome water dashing over this rocky cliff did not have its origin in yonder pool. Pure water does not flow from a mud-puddle. Here is a man who in twenty years writes in round numbers forty productions —the task of Hercules. The product of the man attests the nobility of his soul. No man can labor for twenty years without putting his stamp upon his work. Shakspere was no bar-room brawler, no prodigal spender of time and substance in riotous living. He lived to the mature age of fifty-two and died a well-to-do man. The prodigals of the world do not retire with a competency. I repeat that Shakspere was not impeccable; he was no Puritan; but we cannot think of the creator of Hamlet, Ophelia, Othello, Desdemona, Cordelia, Portia, Rosalind, Miranda, and Prospero as other than a man of a contrite spirit and a pure heart. As he surpassed his contemporaries in breadth and loftiness of intellect, so too he surpassed them in the reach and vigor of his moral feeling.

We cannot believe that this man who penetrated deeper than others into the mystery of life missed the meaning of his own life. Let us hear the conclusion of the whole matter—the power that moves the world is not brilliancy of intellect; it is purity of heart. Nobility of character is the essence of powerful personality. Lincoln is greater than Webster, Washington than Jefferson, not through greater mental grasp, but because of a purer spiritual essence. The world without takes its meaning and color from the world within. Shakspere saw a world of pure passion and wholesome sanity because his world within was pure and sane.

JOHN MILTON

From a miniature by Faithorne, painted in 1667

IV

IN 1623, when Milton was a boy of fifteen, John Heminge and Henry Condell, "only to keep the memory of so worthy a friend and fellow alive as was our Shakspere," had given to the world the folio edition of Shakspere's works, very anxious that the said folio might commend itself to "the most noble and incomparable pair of brethern," William, Earl of this, and Philip, Earl of that, and exceedingly unconscious that, next to the production of the works themselves, they were doing the most important thing done, or likely to be done, in the literary history of the world. Milton read Shakspere, and in the lines which he wrote upon him in 1630, there seems to be the due throb of transcendent admiration....

As Shakspere is the supreme name in this order of poets, the men of sympathy and of humor, Milton stands first in that other great order which is too didactic for humor, and of which Schiller is the best recent representative. He was called the lady of his college not only for his beautiful face, but because of the vestal purity and austerity of his virtue. The men of the former class are intuitive, passionate, impulsive; not steadily conscious of their powers; fit-

17

ful, unsystematic. Their love is ecstasy; their
errors are the intoxication of joy; their sorrows
are the pangs of death. . . .

Milton, the poet of Puritanism, stands out in
bold contrast to these imperfect characters. From
his infancy there was nothing unregulated in his
life. His father, clearly a superior man, of keen
Protestantism, successful in business, well skilled
in music, soon perceived that one of the race of
immortals had been born in his house. He began,
apparently with the conscious and delighted as-
sent of his son, to give the young Apollo such an
education as Plato might have prescribed. An
eminently good education it proved to be; only
not so good, with a view to the production of a
world-poet, as that which nature, jealous of the
Platos and pedagogues, and apt to tumble them
and their grammatical appurtenances out of the
window when she has one of her miraculous children in hand, had provided for that Stratford
lad who came to London broken in character and
probably almost broken in heart, some forty years
earlier, to be a hanger-on of the theaters and to
mount the intellectual throne of the world. No
deer-stealing expeditions late o' nights when the
moon silvered the elms of Charlecote chase; no
passionate love affairs and wild boy-marriage.

Milton, carefully grounded in the tongues, went
in due course to Cambridge University, and during those years when the youthful mind is in its
stage of richest recipiency, lived among the kind
of men who haunt seats of learning,—on the
whole, the most uninteresting men in existence,
whose very knowledge is a learned ignorance; not
bees of industry, who have hoarded information

by experience, but book-*worms*. . . . It is important, also, that Milton was never to any distracting
extent in love. If Shakspere had been a distinguished university man, would he have told us
of a catch that could "draw three souls out of one
weaver?" And if the boy of eighteen had not
been in a fine frenzy about Anne Hathaway, could
he have known how Juliet and Romeo, Othello and
Desdemona, loved?

. . . It is a proof of the fiery and inextinguishable nature of Milton's genius that it triumphed
over the artificiality of his training; that there is
the pulse of a true poetical life in his most highly
wrought poems, and that the whole mountain of
his learning glows with the strong internal flame.
His inspiration was from within, the inspiration
of a profound enthusiasm for beauty and an impassioned devotion to virtue. The district in which
he lived during much of his most elaborate self-
education is not marked enough to have disturbed,
by strong impressions from without, the develop-
ment of his genius from within. Horton lies
where the dead flat of southeastern Buckingham
meets the dead flat of southwestern Middlesex.
Egham Hill, not quite so high as Hampstead, and
the chalk knoll on which Windsor Castle fails to
be sublime, are the loftiest ground in the immediate neighborhood. Staines, the Pontes of the
Romans, and Runnymede with its associations,
are near the parish church of Horton, in which
Milton worshiped for five or six years, and in
which his mother is buried, has one of the Norman
porches common in the district, but is drearily
heavy in its general structure, and forms a notable contrast to that fine example of the old Eng-

lish church in which, by the willows of Avon, lie
Shakspere's bones. The river Colne breaks itself, a few miles to the north, into a leash of
streams, the most considerable of which flows by
Horton. The abounding watercourses are veiled
with willows, but the tree does not seem to have
attracted Milton's attention. It was reserved for
the poet-painter of the *Liber Studiorum* to show
what depths of homely pathos, and what exquisite
picturesqueness of gnarled and knotted line, could
be found in a pollard willow, and for Tennyson
to reveal the poetic expressiveness of the tree as
denoting a solemn and pensive landscape, such as
that amid whose "willowy hills and fields" rose
the carol

> . . . mournful, holy,
> Chaunted loudly, chaunted lowly,
> Till her blood was frozen slowly,
> And her eyes were darkened wholly,

of the Lady of Shalott. . . .

    Milton's bodily appearance at this time was in
brilliant correspondence with the ideal which
imagination might form of a youthful poet. Perfect in all bodily proportions, an accomplished
fencer, with delicate flowing hair, and beautiful
features through which genius, still half in slumber, shed its mystic glow, he was all that the imagination of Greece saw in the young Hyperion or
Apollo.

    . . . His three daughters, Anne, Deborah, and
Mary, were the children of his first wife. He was
twice married after her death in 1653, but had no
more children. So early as 1644 his sight began
to fail, and when his little girls were left motherless, they could be known to him, as Professor

Masson touchingly says, "only as tiny voices of complaint going about in the darkness." The tiny voices did not move him to love or pity. His impatient and imperious nature had doubtless undergone exquisite misery from the moaning discontent of his wife; the daughters took the mother's part so soon as they were able to understand her sorrows; and the grave Puritan displeasure with which Milton regards the mother seems to have been transferred to the children. His austerity as a Puritan and a pedagogue, and the worse than old Hebrew meanness of his estimate of women, appear to the greatest disadvantage in connection with his daughters. Had they been sons, he would have thrown all his ardor into the enterprise of their education. The training of boys was one of his enthusiasms; but his daughters were taught nothing except to read, and were ordered to read aloud to him in languages of which they did not understand a word. Naturally they never loved him; his fame, which they were not able to appreciate, cast on them no ray of comforting light; and they thought probably in sad and scared bewilderment of the relations between their unhappy wraith-like mother, and their Titan father. How different the warm and tender relations between Shakspere and his children! In that instance it was the daughter, the pet Judith, that was the demure sweet Puritan, yet with a touch of her father's wit in her, and able to enjoy all the depth of his smile when he would ask her whether cakes and ale were to be *quite* abolished when the reign of the saints came in.

. . . To the man himself we turn, for one brief glance before laying down the pen. In the evil times of the Restoration, in the land of the Philistines, Agonistes but unconquerable, the Puritan Samson ended his days. Serene and strong; conscious that the ambition of his youth had been achieved, he begins the day with the Hebrew Bible, listens reverently to words in which Moses or David or Isaiah spake of God. But he attends no church, belongs to no communion, and has no form of worship in his family; notable circumstances which we may refer, in part at least, to his blindness, but significant of more than that. His religion was of the spirit, and did not take kindly to any form. Though the most Puritan of the Puritan, he had never stopped long in the ranks of any Puritan party, or given satisfaction to Puritan ecclesiastics and theologians. In his youth he loved the night; in his old age he loves the sunlight of early morning as it glimmers on his sightless eyes. The music which had been his delight since childhood has still its charm, and he either sings or plays on the organ or bass-violin every day. In his gray coat, at the door of his house in Bunhill Fields, he sits on clear afternoons; a proud, ruggedly genial old man, with sharp satiric touches in his talk, the untunable fiber in him to the last. Eminent foreigners come to see him; friends approach reverently, drawn by the splendor of his discourse. It would range, one can well imagine, in glittering freedom, like "arabesques of lightning," over all ages and all literatures. He was the prince of scholars; a memory of superlative power waiting, as submissive handmaid, on the queenliest imagination. The whole spectacle of ancient civilization, its cities, its camps, its landscapes, was before him.

There he sat in his gray coat, like a statue cut in granite. England had made a sordid failure, but he had not failed. His soul's fellowship was with the great Republicans of Greece and Rome, and with the Psalmist and Isaiah and Oliver Cromwell. —From Peter Bayne in the *Contemporary Review.*

V

THE author of the *Essays of Elia* and *Tales Founded on the Plays of Shakspere* worked for the greater part of his life in the employ of the Honorable East India Company. He received his appointment in 1792, the year of the birth of Shelley. He had been trained at Christ's Hospital for a university career; this gave him a good classical education but not especially good preparation for his new work. Had he been obliged to pass a civil service examination he would hardly have received the appointment. Of geography and arithmetic he knew little. The schoolboy of to-day will be surprised to learn that a boy a hundred and more years ago might reach the age of fifteen in a good grammar school of that period and yet not be able to use the multiplication table. As late as 1823 Lamb writes: "I think I lose a hundred pounds a year owing solely to my want of neatness in making up accounts: how I puzzle 'em out at last is the wonder!" There is no evidence, however, to show that Lamb did not overcome his lack of preparation. The contrary impression sometimes prevails, due, perhaps, to his supposed apology for his late arrival by his representation that he made up for it by a correspondingly early departure. His industry must have been appreciated, for his salary rose from nothing to a fair figure.

The modern young man, desirous of earning a good salary at once, will be surprised at the statement that Lamb worked for nothing at first. He will be still more surprised to learn that in those days a clerk in the employ of the great India Company worked three years for nothing. This period evidently was considered as the apprenticeship. It is true a gratuity of 30 pounds was given, and by extra work one might earn small sums. In April, 1795, three years having ended, he received a salary of 40 pounds a year. The next year it rose to 70. By 1799 it had advanced to 90, and from then on to 1814 he received an increment of ten pounds every two years. He also received a gratuity each year. The gratuity by 1814 had amounted to 80 pounds. After a reorganization of the company in 1815 Lamb seems to have progressed in salary, for he then received 480 pounds, and in 1821 it was 700; and at the time of his retirement it was 730.

On the whole, one can say that Lamb's lot was not a hard one. No doubt, many of his fellow-authors had reason to envy him his assured income. His work was hard and not always pleasant, but he knew, with all his half-pretended grumbling, that it would not be wise to rely on his pen for a livelihood. He once remonstrated with the poetical Quaker, Bernard Barton, who proposed to give up a bank-clerkship, in this wise: "Trust not the public; I bless every star that Providence, not seeing good to make me independent, has seen it next good to settle me down

on the stable foundation of Leadenhall. . . .
Henceforth I retract all my fond complaints of
mercantile employments; look upon them as lovers' quarrels. I was but half in earnest. Welcome, dead timber of a desk that makes me live!
a little grumbling is a wholesome medicine for
the spleen; but in my inner heart do I improve
and embrace this our close but unharassing way
of life."

That his work was no sinecure can be gathered
from this letter of about 1815: "On Friday I was
at office from ten in the morning (two hours dinner excepted) to eleven at night; last night till
nine. My business and office business in general
have increased so; I don't mean I am there every
night, but I must expect a great deal of it. I never
leave till four, and do not keep a holiday now
once in ten times, where I used to keep all red-let-
ter days and some five days besides, which I used
to dub nature's holidays. . . . I had formerly little to do. . . . Hard work and thinking about it
taints even the leisure hours—stains Sunday with
workday contemplations."

After thirty-three years of service he was
granted by his company a pension of 450 pounds.
On the minutes of the Court of Directors can be
found the following resolution: "that the resignation of Mr. Charles Lamb, of the accountant-gen-
eral's office, on account of certified ill-health be
accepted, and it appearing that he has served the
company faithfully for thirty-three years . . .
he be allowed a pension of 450 pounds annually."

When the resolution was communicated to him
he went home to enjoy one long holiday of leisure
and literary study and authorship. "I am Re-

tired Leisure. . . . I have worked task work, and have the rest of the day to myself.'' But his day did not last many years. ''Lamb was but fifty when he quitted the service of the company; yet less than ten years of life were left to him. Not only so, but the happiness he had expected to find proved more and more elusive. The increasing frequency of his sister's aberration was a heavy burden for a back which grew daily less able to bear the strain. The leisure to which he had looked forward so eagerly was spent in listening to incoherent babblings, that rambling chat which was to him 'better than the sense and sanity of this world.' In her lucid intervals they played picquet together, or talked gravely but firmly of the inevitable separation looming nearer and nearer. In 1830 Hazlitt died. Four years later that 'great and dear spirit,' Coleridge, passed away after long suffering. The blow to Lamb was stunning in its severity; and the loss of this earliest and best-loved friend possibly accelerated his own decease. Towards the close of the year a fall while walking caused a trifling wound. No harm was expected to result; but the general feebleness of his health brought on erysipelas, and upon Saturday, January 3, 1835, he was borne to his rest in a quiet corner of Edmonton Church-yard, there to await the coming, twelve years later, of the sister who had been throughout his life at once his greatest joy and his chiefest care.''

VI

DR JOHNSON AND CHARLES LAMB

BETWEEN Johnson and Lamb there would seem to be little in common. The ponderous old philosopher, "tearing his meat like a tiger, and swallowing his tea in oceans," presents a picture very dissimilar to that of the stammering Lamb whom Coleridge has well called the "gentle-hearted Lamb." And yet there are many points of similarity.

Perhaps the most striking resemblance is in respect to their generosity. The unfailing testimony of all their friends is that neither could restrain the impulse to give. The celebrated De Quincey is led to characterize Lamb's munificence as *princely,* while Procter, one of his younger friends, simply says, "he gave away greatly." On the other hand, the testimony in regard to the generosity of Johnson is equally strong. He was so open-hearted that he could not trust himself to go upon the street with much money in his purse. Neither Lamb nor Johnson believed in the modern methods of attending to charitable giving through the mediation of boards and committees. Each violated the commonest precepts of a cold-blooded political economy. If want and suffering were depicted upon the face of the mendicant, that

was enough to call for the open purse. What if
the beggar did look like a thief or drunkard? He
might spend the money for gin or tobacco, but
what of that? "Why should they be denied such
sweeteners of their existence?" was Johnson's
indulgent plea. This stern moralist so much enjoyed giving that he doubtless would have regretted the passing of laws prohibiting the beggar
from plying his vocation in public. So too would
the genial Elia, who obeyed his own precept of
"give and ask no questions."

While returning to his lodgings after midnight
Johnson would often drop pennies into the hands
of poor children sleeping on the thresholds and
stalls, to furnish them with the means for a breakfast. This was done at a time when he was living
on pennies himself. "Reader," pleads Elia in his
Praise of Chimney Sweepers, "if thou meetest one
of these small gentry in thy early rambles, it is
good to give him a penny—it is better to give him
a twopence." And then Lamb describes the
choice and fragrant drink, *Saloop,* the delight of
the sweep, a basin of which together with a slice
of delicate bread and butter will cost but a twopence. As we read the description we have no
hesitancy in believing that the "unpennied sweep"
frequently became a pennied sweep after the
gentle Elia had passed by.

Goldsmith once remarked that to be miserable
was enough to insure the protection of Johnson.
This generous quality of mind filled the house of
Johnson with a queer assortment of pensioners.
Had Lamb's home life permitted, equally full of
the needy and homeless would it have been. In
1796 occurred the terrible tragedy that we may

permit Lamb himself to describe in his letter to Coleridge,—''White, or some of my friends, or the public papers by this time may have informed you of the terrible calamities that have fallen on our family. I will only give you the outlines: My poor, dear, dearest sister, in a fit of insanity, has been the death of her own mother. I was at hand only time enough to snatch the knife out of her grasp. She is at present in a madhouse, from which I fear she must be moved to an hospital. . . . My poor father was slightly wounded, and I am left to take care of him and my aunt. . . . God Almighty have us well in his keeping!'' Lamb assumed the tender care of his sister, and his watchfulness and loving care are more beautiful than the most charming essay he ever wrote. But this condition at home prevented that generous open-hearted hospitality so characteristic of Johnson. As it was he contributed to the support of several. For a long period he gave thirty pounds a year to his old schoolmistress. Telfourd relates that when Lamb saw the nurse who had waited on Coleridge during his last illness, he forced five guineas on her. Equally impulsive was his manner toward Procter, whom he one time noticed to be in low spirits and imagined the cause to be lack of money. ''My dear boy,'' said he suddenly turning toward his friend, ''I have a quantity of useless things, I have now in my desk a—a hundred pounds—that I don't *know* what to do with. Take it.''

Some years ago when comparing these two men a Mr. Roose wrote in concluding his paper: ''We are all familiar with Johnson's huge, ungainly form, arrayed in brown suit more or less dilapi-

dated, singed, bushy wig, black stockings, and
mean old shoes. A quaint little figure, Lamb
comes before our vision, in costume uncontempo-
rary and as queer as himself, consisting of a suit
of black cloth (they both affected dark colors),
rusty silk stockings shown from the knees, thick
shoes a mile too large, shirt with a wide, ill-plaited
frill, and tiny white neckcloth tied in a minute
bow.''

It is pleasant to fancy these two originals being
brought into personal contact. Nor is it hard,
for all the tokens to the contrary, to imagine Elia
taking the grand, humane old doctor into his embrace (a huger armful than his beloved folios),
sitting up with him o' nights, as he did with them,
delighting in the humor of his conversation, which
was said by a contemporary to be unequaled except by the old comedians, in whom Lamb's spirit
found diversion; piercing to heights and depths in
his nature which Boswell never revealed to him;
while Johnson, it may safely be inferred, would
have loved this ''poor Charles,'' in whom Carlyle
could perceive but so slender a strain of worth.
But had they met at all, it would have been on
equal terms. Goldsmith maintained with difficulty, though he did maintain, his attitude of independence towards the colossus of his age.
Charles Lamb, without any difficulty and without
the show of assertiveness, would have maintained
it better. Lamb, who from earliest manhood refused to knock under to the threatening intellectual arrogance of Coleridge; who shook Wordsworth by the nose instead of by the hand with the
greeting, ''How d'ye do, old Lake Poet!''—his
stammering voice might have broken with impu-

nity on the doctor's weightiest utterances with the absurdest quips and twists of speech of which even he was capable. Yet both were of wayward nature, and had they met might not have coalesced.

Lamb would have understood Johnson better than Johnson would have understood the whimsicalities of the witty clerk. At one time while discussing authors with friends Lamb said,— "There is Dr. Johnson: I have no curiosity; no strange uncertainty about him."

Johnson's restraint in the use of alcoholic drinks is in contrast with Lamb's indulgence. But Johnson's intemperate tea-drinking makes him one with Lamb in his struggle with tobacco. In writing to Coleridge for advice on smoking, Lamb asks: "What do you think of smoking? I want your sober *average noon opinion* of it. . . . May be the truth is, that *one* pipe is wholesome, *two* pipes toothsome, *three* pipes noisome, *four* pipes fulsome, *five* pipes quarrelsome; and that's the *sum* on't. But that is deciding rather upon rhyme than reason." And Telfourd tells us that when Parr saw Lamb puffing like some furious enchanter, he asked how he had acquired the power of smoking at such a rate. Lamb replied, "I toiled after it, sir, as some men toil after virtue."

VII

THE DEATH OF DR. JOHNSON

BY common consent Boswell's *Life of Johnson*
takes first place as a biography. Some
critics go so far as to say that the excellence
of the biography is to be accounted for by the
deficiency in the character of Boswell; that Boswell was such a blind and whole-souled worshiper
of Johnson that he exposed the faults of his subject with the same zeal with which he published
the virtues. This may be true. Whether true or
not, it is not an altogether bad quality. Many of
us think that the biographies of our modern men
of letters would have more vivacity and lifelike-
ness were they to contain an occasional glimpse of
the hero when he is not on the parade ground.
The biography of Tennyson by his son, Lord Hallam, would be far more convincing had the son
given us occasional pictures of the poet when he
was not at his best. But, perhaps, it is too much
to hope that a reverent and admiring son can give
the world a vital, impartial, and comprehensive
life of his father.

Boswell has given us a full account of Johnson's
last days. The gruff old lexicographer had lived
a robust life; he had faced many temptations, and
had not always retired from the conflict victorious.

On the whole, however, he had lived an exemplary life, but like many another good man he had a dread of dying; he feared he might not meet the last foe as worthily as a man of his character and reputation should. But this was a groundless fear. For when the last illness was upon him, he asked his physician to tell him plainly whether there was any hope of his recovery. The doctor first asked his patient whether he could bear the whole truth, whatever it might be. Upon hearing an affirmative reply, the physician declared that in his opinion nothing short of a miracle would restore health.

"Then," said Johnson, "I will take no more physic, not even my opiates; for I have prayed that I may render up my soul unclouded."

A brother of Boswell's wrote the following letter concerning the last hours of Johnson:

"The Doctor, from the time that he was certain his death was near, appeared to be perfectly resigned, was seldom or never fretful or out of temper, and often said to his faithful servant, who gave me this account, 'Attend, Francis, to the salvation of your soul, which is the object of greatest importance:' he also explained to him passages in the Scripture, and seemed to have pleasure in talking upon religious subjects.

"On Monday, the 13th of December, the day on which he died, a Miss Morris, daughter to a particular friend of his, called, and said to Francis, that she begged to be permitted to see the doctor, that she might earnestly request him to give her his blessing. Francis went into the room, followed by the young lady, and delivered the message. The doctor turned himself in the bed, and said,

'God bless you, my dear!' These were the last words he spoke. His difficulty of breathing increased till about seven o'clock in the evening, when Mr. Barber and Mrs. Desmoulins, who were sitting in the room, observed that the noise he made in breathing had ceased, went to the bed, and found he was dead.''

This account, together with several others given by various friends, assures us that the death of Johnson was trustful and tranquil. It is another illustration of that beautiful dispensation of nature which, as a rule, makes death a mere slipping away, a falling asleep. The Francis who is mentioned in the letter is the faithful negro servant whom Johnson so generously provided for in his will. In making his will the doctor had asked a friend how much of an annuity gentlemen usually gave to a favorite servant, and was told that in the case of a nobleman fifty pounds a year was considered an adequate reward for many years of faithful service:

''Then,'' said Johnson, ''shall I be *nobilissimus*, for I mean to leave Frank seventy pounds a year, and I desire you to tell him so.''

This generosity was too much for the equanimity of Sir John Hawkins, one of the executors of the will, who, when he found that this negro servant would receive about fifteen hundred pounds, including an annuity of seventy pounds a year, grumbled and muttered ''a caveat against ostentatious bounty and favor to negroes.'' But however much the Sir Johns may grumble, we cannot think the less of Johnson for his kindness in remembering a faithful and deserving servant.

Johnson's refusal to take either wine or opiates

recalls that in an age in which the use of alcoholic drinks was very common he was an uncompromising foe to wine, and that he was, in his latter years, loud in his praise of water. ''As we drove back to Ashbourne,'' says Boswell, ''Dr. Johnson recommended to me, as he had often done, to drink water only. 'For,' said he, 'you are then sure not to get drunk; whereas if you drink wine, you are never sure.' '' And this was not the only matter in which he was in advance of his contemporaries, and of most of ours too. Johnson liked satisfying food, such as a leg of pork, or veal pie well stuffed, with plum pie and sugar, and he devoured enormous quantities of fruit, especially peaches. His inordinate love of tea has almost passed into a proverb,—he has actually been credited with twenty-five cups at a sitting, and he would keep Mrs. Thrale brewing it for him till four o'clock in the morning. The following impromptu, spoken to Miss Reynolds, points its own moral:

> For hear, alas, the dreadful truth,
> Nor hear it with a frown:
> Thou can'st not make the tea so fast
> As I can gulp it down.

VIII

GRAY WRITES THE ELEGY

RECENTLY I was conversing with a practical man of affairs who had just returned from his first visit to Europe. Art galleries had proved tiresome and Westminster Abbey had bored him. But there was one place that he had determined to see and see it he did.

"What place was that?" I asked.

"Stoke Pogis," was the reply.

Is not this answer indicative of the attitude of thousands who can never forget the exquisite charm cast over their youth by the melancholy beauty of the *Elegy in a Country Church-yard?* If fame was the end of General Wolfe's ambition, he was wise in saying that he would rather have written the *Elegy* than be able to take Quebec on the morrow; for of all English poems the *Elegy* is the most popular and widely known; it is the flower of the "literature of melancholy." The *Elegy* is the glorification of the obscure; therein lies its popularity. The most of us are obscure. The *Elegy* flatters us by suggesting that we might have swayed the rod of empire or "waked to ecstasy the living lyre," if we had had the chance, —or, what we think is more likely the explanation, if we had not had a saner insight into the values of life than the Miltons and Cromwells.

37

Stoke Pogis is always associated with the name of Gray. It is a village, if such it may be called, between London and Windsor Castle. The church is "on a little level space about four miles north of the Thames at Eton. From the neighborhood of the church no vestige of hamlet or village is visible, and the aspect of the place is slightly artificial, like a rustic church in a park on a stage. The traveler almost expects to see the grateful peasantry of an opera, cheerfully habited, make their appearance, dancing on the greensward."

Gray and his mother, the father having died in 1741, went to Stoke Pogis in 1742. At West End House, a simple farmhouse of two stories, Gray lived for many years. In the autumn of 1742 was begun the *Elegy in a Country Church-yard*. The common impression is that the whole poem was written at Stoke Pogis, but this is not the truth. It is better to say that it was begun in October or November at Stoke Pogis, continued seven years later at the same place and at Cambridge, and finished at Stoke Pogis on June 12th, 1750. It is interesting to note that in each case an impetus was given to the composition of the poem by the death of a friend. Several months before the poem was begun in 1742, West, a friend whose death made a very deep impression upon the sensitive nature of Gray, had passed away; and on October 31 Jonathan Rogers, an uncle of Gray's, died at Stoke Pogis; and when the poem was next taken up Gray was mourning the death of his aunt. In commenting on this subject Mr. Gosse writes,—"He was a man who had a very slender hold on life himself, who walked habitually in the Valley of the Shadow of Death, and whose periods

of greatest vitality were those in which bereave-
ment proved to him that, melancholy as he was,
even he had something to lose and to regret."

On the 12th of June, 1750, Gray wrote to his
friend, Horace Walpole,—"Having put an end to
a thing whose beginning you have seen long ago,
I immediately send it to you. You will, I hope,
look upon it in the light of a thing with an end to
it: a merit that most of my writings have wanted,
and are like to want." Walpole was naturally
delighted with the poem—so delighted, in fact,
that he handed it about from friend to friend and
even made manuscript copies of it. This caused
some embarrassment to the poet. In February,
1751, he was annoyed to find that the publisher of
the *Magazine of Magazines* was actually printing
his *Elegy* in his periodical. So Gray immediately
wrote to Walpole: "As I am not at all disposed to
be either so indulgent or so correspondent as they
desire, I have but one bad way to escape the honor
they would inflict upon me: and therefore am
obliged to desire you would make Dodsley print
it immediately (which may be done in less than a
week's time) from your copy, but without my
name, in what form is most convenient for him,
but on his best paper and character; he must cor-
rect the press himself, and print it without any
interval between the stanzas, because the sense is
in some places continued without them." On the
16th of February, only five days after this letter
was received, *An Elegy wrote in a Country
Church-yard* appeared as a large quarto pamphlet, anonymous, price sixpence.

From the very first it achieved great popularity.
Magazine after magazine published it without giv-

ing the author any compensation. Gray was soon hit upon as the author. Unfortunately, the success of the poem gave no increased income to the poet. Dodsley, the publisher, is said to have made about a thousand pounds from the various poems of Gray, but Gray had the impractical idea that it was not dignified for a poet to make money from poetry.

In view of this lack of compensation for his poetic writings, it is very gratifying to know that during the latter days of his life Gray enjoyed the emolument arising from his holding the chair of Modern Literature and Modern Languages at Cambridge. This paid him 400 pounds a year, and did not require much work, as the office was a sinecure.

One of the biographers points out that this promotion was brought about inadvertently through the riotous living of Gray's great enemy, Lord Sandwich. Professor Lawrence Brockett, the incumbent of the chair of Literature at Cambridge, dined with Lord Sandwich at Hinchinbroke. He became so drunk that in riding home to Cambridge he fell from his horse and broke his neck. At once five obscure dons made brisk application for the vacant place, and Gray, sensitive and lacking the arts of the politician, did not expect the place. But the author of the *Elegy* was no longer to be neglected. He soon received a letter highly complimenting his work and offering him the professorship. Gray accepted and was summoned to court to kiss the hand of the monarch, George III. The king made several complimentary remarks to Gray. Afterwards when the poet's friends asked Gray

to tell them what the king had said he replied that
the room was so hot and he so embarrassed that
he really did not know what the king had said.

Large was his bounty, and his soul sincere;
  Heaven did a recompense as largely send:
He gave to misery—all he had—a tear,
  He gained from Heaven—'twas all he wished—a friend.

No farther seek his merits to disclose,
  Or draw his frailties from their dread abode,—
There they alike in trembling hope repose,—
  The bosom of his Father and his God.

IX

COWPER AS A LETTER WRITER

WILLIAM COWPER is well known as a poet, having written one of the most popular hymns in the English language, and he is also one of the best of letter writers. It is commonly said that we have lost the gentle art of writing a good letter. When a man can send a postal card from Boston to San Francisco for one cent and one from New York to Paris for two cents, he is not likely to be so choice in his use of language as when he paid a shilling for the privilege of getting a letter. In the first letter which is here quoted we find Cowper writing an urgent invitation to his cousin, Lady Hesketh, to visit him at Olney:

"And now, my dear, let me tell you once more that your kindness in promising us a visit has charmed us both. I shall see you again. I shall hear your voice. We shall take walks together. I will show you my prospects, the hovel, the alcove, the Ouse and its banks, everything that I have described. Talk not of an inn! Mention it not for your life! We have never had so many visitors but we could accommodate them all, though we have received Unwin and his wife, and his sister, and his son, all at once. My dear, I will not let you come till the end of May, or beginning of June, because before that time my greenhouse will not be ready to receive us, and it is the only pleasant room belonging to us. When the plants go out, we go in. I line it with mats, and spread the floor with mats; and there you shall sit with a bed of mignonette at your side, and a hedge of honeysuckles, roses, and jasmine; and I will make you a bouquet of myrtle every day. Sooner than the time I mention the country will not be in complete beauty; and I will tell you what you shall find at your first entrance. Imprimis, as soon as you have entered the vestibule, if you cast a look on either side of you, you shall see on the right hand a box of my making. It is the box in which have been lodged all my hares, and in which lodges Puss (Cowper's pet hare) at present. But he, poor fellow, is worn out with age and promises to die before you can see him. On the right hand stands a cupboard, the work of the same author; it was once a dove-cage, but I transformed it. Opposite to you stands a table, which I also made. But a merciless servant having scrubbed it till it became paralytic, it serves no purpose now but of ornament, and all my clean shoes stand under it. On the left hand, at the farther end of this superb vestibule, you will find the door of the parlor, into which I will conduct you, and where I will introduce you to Mrs. Unwin, unless we should meet her before, and where we will be as happy as the day is long. Order yourself, my cousin, to the *Swan* at Newport and there you shall find me ready to conduct you to Olney. My dear, I have told Homer what you say about casks and urns, and have asked him whether he is sure that it is a cask in which Jupiter keeps his wine. He swears that it is a cask, and that it will never be anything better than a cask to eternity. So if the god is content with it, we must even wonder at his taste, and be so too.—Adieu! my dearest, dearest cousin,—W. C.''

Cowper's letters are not interesting because they treat of the great men and important affairs of his day. They are interesting because he lived a quiet life and was able in his own way to paint a picture treating of the common doings of an apparently unimportant life. Here is a picture of an election in the country, or rather of the candidates' methods in the old days:

''We were sitting yesterday after dinner, the two ladies and myself, very composedly, and without the least apprehension of any such intrusion, in our snug parlor, one lady knitting, the other netting, and the gentleman winding worsted, when, to our unspeakable surprise, a mob appeared before the window, a smart rap was heard at the door, the boys halloed, and the maid announced Mr. Grenville. Puss was unfortunately let out of her box, so that the candidate, with all his good friends at his heels, was refused entrance at the grand entry, and referred to the back door, as the only possible way of approach. Candidates are creatures not very susceptible to affronts, and would rather, I suppose, climb in at a window than be absolutely excluded. In a minute the yard, the kitchen, and the parlor were filled. Mr. Grenville, advancing toward me, shook me by the hand with a degree of cordiality that was extremely seducing. As soon as he and as many more as could find chairs were seated, he began to open the intent of his visit. I told him I had no vote, for which he readily gave me credit. I assured him I had no influence, which he was not equally inclined to believe, and the less, no doubt, because Mr. Ashburner, the drapier, addressing himself to me at that moment, informed me that I had a great deal. Supposing that I could not be possessed of such a treasure without knowing it, I ventured to confirm my first assertion by saying that if I had any I was utterly at a loss to imagine where it could be, or wherein it consisted. Thus ended the conference. Mr. Grenville squeezed me by the hand again, kissed the ladies, and withdrew. He kissed likewise the maid in the kitchen, and seemed upon the whole a most loving, kissing, kind-hearted gentleman.''

X

GIBBON AND HIS VISIT TO ROME

I N that celebrated literary club founded by Dr.
Johnson and Sir Joshua Reynolds were Burke,
Goldsmith, Garrick, Fox, Gibbon, and Sheri-
dan. Of these Gibbon is not the least distinguished. He is an illustrious example of what
an ordinary personality can accomplish by reason
of an extraordinary devotion to one purpose.
Some few men achieve fame by their brilliant
versatility; some, as in the case of Samuel Johnson, by their commanding personal force; Gibbon
has won a permanent place in literary history by
spending his life in doing one thing. That one
thing he did so well that E. A. Freeman, one of
the prominent historians of the nineteenth century, has truthfully said,—"He remains the one
historian of the eighteenth century whom modern
research has neither set aside nor threatened to
set aside."

In his memoirs Gibbon reveals himself as a
man with little dignity or heroism. There is a
droll story that is apt to suggest itself when one
thinks of Gibbon. At one time, when asking a
dignified lady for her hand in marriage, he fell
upon his knees in proper lover-like manner. Unfortunately Gibbon was so stout that upon her

refusal he found himself in the embarrassing need of calling in a servant to help him to his feet again. Memories such as these, however, cannot blind us to the essential worth in the character of the great historian. In the light of his consecration to a worthy purpose his life is not without its heroism. To write *The History of the Decline and Fall of the Roman Empire* is a monumental achievement. To bend every energy to the fulfilling of a high resolve is heroic. From 1764 to 1787 his one aim in life was to write a scholarly history that should cover the vast field that he had chosen. He may lack that spiritual insight which enables one to estimate world movements in the upper regions of religion, but he did not lack unfaltering devotion to his purpose. So well did he do his work that his six volumes can be found in the library of every student of the past. The story is told of a great German who learned English in order to read Gibbon in the original.

In the following extract from his Autobiography is found his own explanation of the circumstances under which he conceived his vast project "amid the ruins of the Capitol," in 1764:

"My temper is not very susceptible of enthusiasm; and the enthusiasm which I do not feel, I have ever scorned to affect. But, at the distance of twenty-five years, I can neither forget nor express the strong emotions which agitated my mind as I first approached and entered the eternal city. After a sleepless night, I trod, with a lofty step, the ruins of the Forum; each memorable spot where Romulus stood, or Tully spoke, or Cæsar fell, was at once present to my eye; and several days of intoxication were lost or enjoyed before I could descend to a cool and minute investigation. My guide was Mr. Byers, a Scotch antiquary of experience and taste; but in the daily labor of eighteen weeks, the powers of attention were sometimes fatigued, till I was myself qualified, in a last review, to select and study the capital works of ancient and modern art. Six weeks were borrowed for my tour of Naples, the most populous of cities, relative to its size, whose luxurious inhabitants seem to dwell on the confines of paradise and hell-fire. I was presented to the boy-king by our new envoy, Sir William Hamilton, who, wisely diverting his correspondence from the Secretary of State to the Royal Society and British Museum, has elucidated a country of such inestimable value to the naturalist and antiquarian. On my return, I fondly embraced, for the last time, the miracles of Rome. . . . In my pilgrimage from Rome to Loretto I again crossed the Apennine; from the coast of the Adriatic I traversed a fruitful and populous country, which could alone disprove the paradox of Montesquieu, that modern Italy is a desert. . . .

"The use of foreign travel has been often debated as a general question; but the conclusion must be finally applied to the character and circumstances of each individual. With the education of boys, where or how they may pass over some juvenile years with the least mischief to themselves or others, I have no concern. But after supposing the previous and indispensable requisites of age, judgment, a competent knowledge of men and books, and a freedom from domestic prejudices, I will briefly describe the qualifications which I deem most essential to a traveler. He should be endowed with an active, indefatigable vigor of mind and body, which can seize every mode of conveyance, and support, with a careless smile, every hardship of the road, the weather, or the inn. The benefits of foreign travel will correspond with the degrees of these qualifications; but, in this sketch, those to whom I am known will not accuse me of framing my own panegyric. It was at Rome, on the 15th of October, 1764, as I sat musing amidst the ruins of the Capitol, while the bare-footed friars were singing vespers in the temple of Jupiter, that the idea of writing the decline and fall of the city first started to my mind.''

XI

WHEN Robert Burns and his brother were working hard on the Mount Oliphant farm, Robert fell in love. This experience, alas, in after years became too frequent an occurrence to occasion much comment, for the ease with which the poet fell in and out of love was the chief fault in a faulty life. But when this episode occurred the boy was still an innocent country lad in his fifteenth year, a lad perhaps somewhat rude and clownish, at least such is an unfounded tradition. Out of the monotony of this life of prosaic toil and drudgery, Burns is lifted by the romance which fortunately he has himself described.

"You know," he says, "our country custom of coupling a man and woman together as partners in the labors of the harvest. In my fifteenth summer my partner was a bewitching creature, a year younger than myself. My scarcity of English denies me the power of doing her justice in that language, but you know the Scottish idiom. She was a bonnie, sweet, sonsie lass. In short, she, altogether unwittingly to herself, initiated me in that delicious passion, which in spite of acid disappointment, gin-house prudence, and book-worm philosophy, I hold to be the first of human joys here below! How she caught the contagion I cannot tell. . . . Indeed, I did not know myself why I liked so much to loiter behind with her, when returning in the evening from our labors; why the tones of her voice made my heartstrings thrill like an Æolian harp; and especially why my pulse beat such a furious ratan when I looked and fingered over her little hand, to pick out the cruel nettle-stings and thistles. Among her love-inspiring qualities, she sung sweetly; and it was her favorite reel to which I attempted giving an embodied vehicle in rhyme. I was not so presumptuous as to imagine that I could make verses like printed ones, composed by men who read Greek and Latin; but my girl sung a song which was said to be composed by a country laird's son, on one of his father's maids, with whom he was in love; and I saw no reason why I might not rhyme as well as he; for, excepting that he could shear sheep and cast peats, his father living in the moorlands, he had no more scholar-craft than myself. Thus with me began love and poetry.''

The song that was due to this boyish passion is called ''Handsome Nell,'' and is said to be the first he wrote. It can be found in any complete edition of the poet's work. In after years he himself calls it puerile and silly, but, while lacking the exquisite perfection of Burns' later lyrics, it is far superior to the usual first attempts of poets. The last two stanzas run thus:

> A gaudy dress and gentle air
> May slightly touch the heart;
> But it's Innocence and Modesty
> That polishes the dart.

> 'Tis this in Nelly pleases me,
> 'Tis this enchants my soul!
> For absolutely in my breast
> She reigns without control.

"I composed it," says Burns, "in a wild enthusiasm of passion, and to this hour I never recollect it but my heart melts, my blood sallies at the remembrance."

Poor Burns! How much happier he would have been had all his loves been as innocent as this first experience! In one of Tennyson's most vigorous passages in the *Idylls* we read,

> . . . for indeed I knew
> Of no more subtle master under heaven
> Than is the maiden passion for a maid,
> Not only to keep down the base in man,
> But teach high thoughts, and amiable words
> And courtliness, and the desire of fame,
> And love of truth, and all that makes a man.

Perhaps, if Burns in a later love affair had been successful in his suit, his life and reputation would not have suffered as they have, for the most culpable trait in the character of the famous Scotch poet is the ease with which he abandoned one lover for another. He was forever falling in love, and there is some evidence to the effect that he loved two or three at the same time. There is only too much truth in Burns' own lines,

> Where'er I gaed, where'er I rade,
> A mistress still I had aye.

But perhaps all this would have been different had Ellison Begbie, the daughter of a small farmer, smiled favorably upon the advances of the young farmer from Lochlea. She is said to have been a young woman of great charm and liveliness of mind, though not a beauty. In after years Burns always spoke of her with the greatest of respect and as the one woman, of the many upon whom he had lavished his fickle affection, who most likely would have made a pleasant partner for life.

His love affair with this young lady took place near the close of his twenty-second year. Her refusal seems to have had a malign influence upon the career of our poet. Up to this time his love affairs, although numerous, were innocent. As his brother Gilbert says, they were "governed by the strictest rules of virtue and modesty." But henceforth there is a change in the character of Burns. Shortly after the fair Ellison had turned a deaf ear to the letters and love-songs of the importunate wooer, Robert and his brother Gilbert went to Irvine, hoping that in this flax-dressing center they could increase their income by dressing the flax raised on their own farm. Here Burns, always very susceptible to new influences, —he would not be the poet he is had he not been keenly alive and susceptible,—fell under the malignant charm of a wild sailor-lad whose habits were loose and irregular. "He was," says Burns, "the only man I ever knew who was a greater fool than myself, where woman was the presiding star; but he spoke of lawless love with levity, which hitherto I had regarded with horror. *Here his friendship did me a mischief.*"

XII

BURNS was in trouble; he had failed as a
farmer, and as a young man he had wounded
the sensibilities of his family. It seemed
best to try a new life in a new land, so he promised a Mr. Douglas to go to Jamaica and become
a bookkeeper on his estate there. But where
should he get the money to pay his passage?
There were the poems lying in his table-drawer—
might they not be published and money be raised
by the sale? His friends encouraged him to publish them, and what is more to the point, they
subscribed in advance for a number of the copies.
John Wilson of Kilmarnock was to do the printing. During May, June, and July of 1786 the
printer was doing his work. At the end of July
the volume appeared, and soon the fame of the
Ayrshire Plowman was established. Let us hear
Burns himself give his account of the venture:

"I gave up my part of the farm to my brother,
and made what little preparation was in my
power for Jamaica. But, before leaving my
native country forever, I resolved to publish my
poems. I weighed my productions as impartially
as was in my power; I thought they had merit;
and it was a delicious idea that I should be called

a clever fellow, even though it should never reach
my ears—a poor negro-driver, or perhaps a victim to that inhospitable clime, and gone to the
world of spirits! I can truly say that *pauvre
inconnu* as I then was, I had pretty nearly as
high an idea of my works as I have at this
moment, when the public has decided in their
favor. . . .

"I threw off about six hundred copies, of which
I got subscriptions for about three hundred and
fifty. My vanity was highly gratified by the
reception I met with from the public; and besides,
I pocketed, all expenses deducted, nearly twenty
pounds. This sum came very seasonably, as I
was thinking of indenting myself, for want of
money, to procure a passage. As soon as I was
master of nine guineas, the price of wafting me
to the torrid zone, I took a steerage passage in
the first ship that was to sail from the Clyde, for

'Hungry ruin had me in the wind.'

"I had been for some days skulking from covert
to covert, under all the terrors of a jail, as some
ill-advised people had uncoupled the merciless
pack of the law at my heels. I had taken the last
farewell of my friends; my chest was on the way
to Greenock; I had composed the last song I
should ever measure in Caledonia, '*The gloomy
night is gathering fast*,' when a letter from Dr.
Blacklock to a friend of mine overthrew all my
schemes, by opening up new prospects to my
poetic ambition."

The success of the first edition of his poems was
so pronounced that Burns soon gave up the idea
of going away to Jamaica. Ayrshire was flat-

tered to discover that within its borders lived a genuine poet. Robert Heron, a young literary man living in that neighborhood, gives us an account of the reception of the little book of poems: "Old and young, high and low, grave and gay, learned or ignorant, were alike delighted, agitated, transported. I was at that time resident in Galloway, contiguous to Ayrshire, and I can well remember how even plowboys and maidservants would have gladly bestowed the wages they earned most hardly, and which they wanted to purchase necessary clothing, if they might procure the works of Burns."

When Burns wished a second edition of his poems, he had a very poor offer from his printer. So he went to Edinburgh to see whether he could not make a more advantageous bargain in the Scottish capital. He reached that famous city on the 28th of November, 1786. Here he was feted and banqueted, admired and criticised. In April, 1787, the second edition appeared. The volume was a handsome octavo. The Scottish public had subscribed very liberally, and eventually Burns received 500 pounds, but Creech, his publisher, was so slow in making payments that Burns had to wait a long time before he received his due.

Walter Scott was among the many who met Burns during his stay in Edinburgh. Scott was but a boy of fifteen, but he never forgot the glance of approval bestowed upon him by the poet. We are especially fortunate in having Scott's own account of the incident: "As for Burns, I may truly say, *'Virgilium vidi tantum.'* I was a lad of fifteen when he came to Edinburgh. I saw him

one day at the late venerable Professor Adam
Fergusson's. Of course we youngsters sat silent,
looked, and listened. The only thing I remember
which was remarkable in Burns' manner, was the
effect produced upon him by a print of Bun-
bury's, representing a soldier lying dead on the
snow, his dog sitting in misery on one side—on
the other his widow, with her child in her arms.
These lines were written beneath:

> Cold on Canadian hills, or Minden's plain,
> Perhaps that parent wept her soldier slain—
> Bent o'er the babe, her eye dissolved in dew,
> The big drops mingling with the milk he drew,
> Gave the sad presage of his future years,
> The child of misery baptized in tears.

"Burns seemed much affected by the print: he
actually shed tears. He asked whose the lines
were, and it chanced that nobody but myself
remembered that they occur in a half-forgotten
poem of Langhorne's, called by the unpromising
title of *The Justice of Peace*. I whispered my
information to a friend present, who mentioned
it to Burns, who rewarded me with a look and a
word, which though of mere civility, I then received with very great pleasure. His person was
strong and robust; his manner rustic, not clownish; a sort of dignified plainness and simplicity.
His countenance was more massive than it looks
in any of the portraits. I would have taken the
poet, had I not known who he was, for a very
sagacious country farmer of the old Scotch school
—the *douce gudeman* who held his own plow.
There was a strong expression of sense and
shrewdness in all his lineaments; the eye alone,
I think, indicated the poetical character and

temperament. It was large, and of a dark cast, which glowed (I say literally, glowed) when he spoke with feeling or interest. I never saw such another eye in a human head, though I have seen the most distinguished men of my time."

XIII

SAMUEL TAYLOR COLERIDGE IN SCHOOL AND COLLEGE

THE following affecting narrative, written in Coleridge's person by the tender-hearted Elia, gives the best view possible of Coleridge's scanty and suffering commencement of life. At that time, it may be premised, the dietary of Christ's Hospital was of the lowest: breakfast consisting of a "quarter of penny loaf, moistened with attenuated small beer in wooden piggins, smacking of the pitched leathern jack it was poured from," and the weekly rule giving "three banyan-days to four meat days."

"I was a poor, friendless boy; my parents, and those who should have cared for me, were far away. Those few acquaintances of theirs, whom they could reckon upon being kind to me in the great city, after a little forced notice, which they had the grace to take of me on my first arrival in town, soon grew tired of my holiday visits. They seemed to them to recur too often, though I thought them few enough. One after another they all failed me, and I felt myself alone among six hundred playmates. Oh the cruelty of separating a poor lad from his early homestead! The yearnings which I used to have towards it in those unfledged years! . . . The warm, long days of summer never return but they bring with them a gloom from the haunting memory of those *whole days' leave,* when, by some strange arrangement, we were turned out for the livelong day, upon our own hands, whether we had friends to go to or none. I remember those bathing excursions to the New River which Lamb recalls with so much relish, better, I think, than he can— for he was a home-seeking lad, and did not care much for such water-parties. How we would sally forth into the fields, and strip under the first warmth of the sun, and wanton like young dace in the streams, getting appetites for the noon; which those of us that were penniless (our scanty morning crust long since exhausted) had not the means of allaying—while the cattle and the birds and the fishes were at feed about us, and we had nothing to satisfy our cravings; the very beauty of the day and the exercise of the pastime, and the sense of liberty setting a keener edge upon them! How faint and languid, finally, we would return toward nightfall to our desired morsel, half rejoicing, half reluctant, that the hours of uneasy liberty had expired!

"It was worse in the days of winter, to go prowling about the streets objectless, shivering at cold windows of printshops, to extract a little amusement; or haply, as a last resort, in the hope of a little novelty, to pay a fifty-times-repeated visit (where our individual faces would be as well known to the warden as those of his own charges) to the lions in the Tower, to whose *levée,* by courtesy immemorial, we had a prescriptive right of admission."

This melancholy and harsh life was, however,

ameliorated by some curious personal incidents. Once, for example, the solitary boy, moving along the crowded streets, fancied, in the strange vividness of his waking dream, that he was Leander swimming across the Hellespont. His hand "came in contact with a gentleman's pocket" as he pursued this visionary amusement, and for two or three minutes Coleridge was in danger of being taken into custody as a pickpocket. On finding out how matters really stood, however, this stranger—genial, nameless soul—immediately gave to the strange boy the advantage of a subscription to a library close by, thus setting him up, as it were, in life. On another occasion, one of the higher boys, a "deputy-Grecian," found him seated in a corner reading Virgil. "Are you studying your lesson?" he asked. "No, I am reading for pleasure," said the boy, who was not sufficiently advanced to read Virgil in school. This introduced him to the favorable notice of the head-master Bowyer, and made of the elder scholar, Middleton by name, a steady friend and counselor for years. Yet at this time Coleridge was considered by the lower-master, under whom he was, "a dull and inept scholar who could not be made to repeat a single rule of syntax, although he would give a rule in his own way." The life, however, of this great school, with all its injudicious liberties and confinements, must have been anything but a healthy one. Starved and solitary, careless of play as play, and already full of that consuming spiritual curiosity which never left him, Coleridge's devotion to the indiscriminate stores of the circulating library gave the last aggravation to all the unwholesome particulars of his life. "Conceive what I must have been at fourteen," he exclaims. "I was in a continual low fever. My whole being was, with eyes closed to every object of present sense, to crumple myself up in a sunny corner and read, read, read; fancy myself on Robinson Crusoe's island finding a mountain of plum-cake, and eating a room for myself, and then eating it into the shapes of tables and chairs—hunger, and fancy!" . . .

A droll incident occurred about this period of his life, which shows . . . his absolute want of ambition. The friendless boy had made acquaintance with a shoemaker and his wife, who had a shop near the school, and who were kind to him; and thereupon he conceived the extraordinary idea of getting himself apprenticed to his friend, whom he persuaded to go to the head-master to make this wonderful proposal. "Od's, my life, man, what d'ye mean?" cried the master, with not unnatural indignation mingling with his amazement; and notwithstanding Coleridge's support of the application, the shoemaker was turned out of the place, and the would-be apprentice chosen, "against my will," he says, "as one of those destined for the university." The same irascible yet excellent master flogged the boy severely on hearing that he boasted of being an infidel. . . .

His next stage in life was not a shoemaker's shop in Newgate Street, but Jesus College, Cambridge, which he entered in 1791 at the age of nineteen—the object of many high prophecies and hopes on the part of his school and schoolfellows, who had unanimously determined that he was to be great and do them honor. The first thing he did, however, was alas! too common an incident: he got into debt, though not, it would appear, for an overwhelming sum, or in any discreditable way. So long as his friend of Christ's Hospital, Middleton, remained in Cambridge, Coleridge pursued his studies with a great deal of regularity and in his first year won the prize for a Greek ode. But after awhile his industry slackened, and a kind of dreamy idleness—implying no languor of the soul or common reluctance to mental work, but rather, it would seem, a disinclination to work in the usual grooves, and do what was expected of him—took possession of the young scholar. "He was very studious, but his reading was desultory and capricious," writes a fellow-student. "He was ready at any time to shed his mind in conversation, and for the sake of this his rooms were a constant rendezvous of conversation-loving friends. What evenings I have spent in these rooms! What little suppers, or *sizings,* as they were called, have I enjoyed; when Aeschylus and Plato and Thucydides were pushed aside with a pile of lexicons and the like, to discuss the pamphlets of the day! Ever and anon a pamphlet issued from the pen of Burke. There was no need of having the book before us; Coleridge had read it in the morning and in the evening he would repeat whole pages *verbatim.*"

—Adapted from *Blackwood's Magazine.*

XIV

IN 1858 Trelawney published his *Recollections of the Last Days of Shelley and Byron*. In many ways this is a remarkable book. It is the one source of information as to the last days of Shelley; concerning Byron's, others have furnished material. Trelawney is suspected of mingling some fiction with his truth, but the general tendency nowadays is to place confidence in these *Recollections*. He may not always give us a literal report, but he has likely reproduced the spirit. He is much more sympathetic in his treatment of Shelley than he is in his account of Byron. Trelawney himself was a remarkable character. He lived far into the time of a new generation, dying in his eighty-ninth year in 1881. Mary Shelley, in a letter to Maria Gisborne, February, 1822, describes him as "A kind of half-Arab Englishman. . . . He is clever: for his moral qualities I am yet in the dark. He is a strange web which I am endeavoring to unravel."

In the *Recollections* occurs this interesting account of Byron:

Byron has been accused of drinking deeply. Our universities, certainly, did turn out more famous drinkers than scholars. In the good old

LORD BYRON
From the portrait by T. Phillips

times, to drink lustily was the characteristic of all Englishmen, just as tuft-hunting is now. Eternal swilling, and the rank habits and braggadocio manners which it engendered, came to a climax in George IV's reign. Since then, excessive drinking has gone out of fashion, but an elaborate style of gastronomy has come in to fill the void; so there is not much gained. Byron used to boast of the quantity of wine he had drunk. He said, "We young Whigs imbibed claret, and so saved our constitutions: the Tories stuck to port, and destroyed theirs and their country's."

He bragged, too, of his prowess in riding, boxing, fencing, and even walking; but to excel in these things feet are as necessary as hands. It was difficult to avoid smiling at his boasting and self-glorification. In the water a fin is better than a foot, and in that element he did well; he was built for floating,—with a flexible body, open chest, broad beam, and round limbs. If the sea was smooth and warm, he would stay in it for hours; but as he seldom indulged in this sport, and when he did, over-exerted himself, he suffered severely; which observing, and knowing how deeply he would be mortified at being beaten, I had the magnanimity when contending with him to give in.

He had a misgiving in his mind that I was trifling with him; and one day as we were on the shore, and the *Bolivar* at anchor, about three miles off, he insisted on our trying conclusions; we were to swim to the yacht, dine in the sea alongside of her, treading water the while, and then to return to the shore. It was calm and hot, and seeing he would not be fobbed off, we started.

I reached the boat a long time before he did; ordered the edibles to be ready, and floated until he arrived. We ate our fare leisurely, from off a grating that floated alongside, drank a bottle of ale, and I smoked a cigar, which he tried to extinguish,—as he never smoked. We then put about, and struck off towards the shore. We had not got a hundred yards on our passage, when he retched violently, and, as that is often followed by cramp, I urged him to put his hand on my shoulder that I might tow him back to the schooner.

"Keep off, you villain, don't touch me. I'll drown ere I give in."

I answered as Iago did to Roderigo:

" 'A fig for drowning! drown cats and blind puppies.' I shall go on board and try the effects of a glass of grog to stay my stomach."

"Come on," he shouted, "I am always better after vomiting."

With difficulty I deluded him back; I went on board, and he sat on the steps of the accommodation-ladder, with his feet in the water. I handed him a wineglass of brandy, and screened him from the burning sun. He was in a sullen mood, but after a time resumed his usual tone. Nothing could induce him to be landed in the schooner's boat, though I protested I had had enough of the water.

"You may do as you like," he called out, and plumped in, and we swam on shore.

He never afterwards alluded to this event, nor to his prowess in swimming, to me, except in the past tense. He was ill, and kept to his bed for two days afterwards.

To return to his drinking propensities, after this digression about his gymnastic prowess: I must say, that of all his vauntings, it was, luckily for him, the emptiest—that is, after he left England and his boon companions, as I know nothing of what he did there. From all that I heard or witnessed of his habits abroad, he was and had been exceedingly abstemious in eating and drink ing. When alone, he drank a glass or two of small claret or hock, and when utterly exhausted at night, a single glass of grog; which when I mixed it for him I lowered to what sailors call "water bewitched," and he never made any remark. I once, to try him, omitted the alcohol; he then said, "Tre, have you not forgotten the creature comfort?" I then put in two spoonfuls, and he was satisfied. This does not look like an habitual toper. His English acquaintances in Italy were, he said in derision, all milksops. On the rare occasion of any of his former friends visiting him, he would urge them to have a carouse with him, but they had grown wiser. He used to say that little Tommy Moore was the only man he knew who stuck to the bottle and put him on his mettle, adding, "But he is a native of the damp isle, where men subsist by suction."

Byron had not damaged his body by strong drinks, but his terror of getting fat was so great that he reduced his diet to the point of absolute starvation. He was of that soft, lymphatic temperament which it is almost impossible to keep within a moderate compass, particularly as in his case his lameness prevented his taking exercise. When he added to his weight, even standing was painful, so he resolved to keep down to eleven stone, or shoot himself. He said everything he swallowed was instantly converted into tallow and deposited on his ribs.

He was the only human being I ever met with who had sufficient self-restraint and resolution to resist this proneness to fatten: he did so, and at Genoa, where he was last weighed, he was ten stone and nine pounds, and looked much less. This was not from vanity about his personal appearance, but from a better motive; and as, like Justice Greedy, he was always hungry, his merit was the greater. Occasionally he relaxed his vigilance, when he swelled apace.

I remember one of his old friends saying, "Byron, how well you are looking!" If he had stopped there it had been well, but when he added, "You are getting fat," Byron's brow reddened, and his eyes flashed—"Do you call getting fat looking well, as if I were a hog?" and, turning to me, he muttered, "The beast, I can hardly keep my hands off him." The man who thus offended him was the husband of the lady addressed as "Genevra," and the original of his "Zuleika," in the *Bride of Abydos*. I don't think he had much appetite for his dinner that day, or for many days, and never forgave the man who, so far from wishing to offend, intended to pay him a compliment.

Byron said he had tried all sorts of experiments to stay his hunger, without adding to his bulk. "I swelled," he said, "at one time to fourteen stone, so I clapped the muzzle to my jaws, and, like the hibernating animals, consumed my own fat."

He would exist on biscuits and soda-water for

days together, then, to allay the eternal hunger gnawing at his vitals, he would make up a horrid mess of cold potatoes, rice, fish, or greens, deluged in vinegar, and gobble it up like a famished dog. On either of these unsavory dishes, with a biscuit and a glass or two of Rhine wine, he cared not how sour, he called feasting sumptuously. Upon my observing he might as well have fresh fish and vegetables, instead of stale, he laughed and answered:

"I have an advantage over you, I have no palate; one thing is as good as another to me."

"Nothing," I said, "disagrees with the natural man; he fasts and gorges, his nerves and brain don't bother him; but if you wish to live?—

"Who wants to live?" he replied, "not I. The Byrons are a short-lived race on both sides, father and mother; longevity is hereditary: I am nearly at the end of my tether. I don't care for death a——; it is her sting! I can't bear pain."

His habits and want of exercise damaged him, not drink. It must be borne in mind, moreover, that his brain was always working at high pressure. The consequences resulting from his way of life were low or intermittent fevers; these last had fastened on him in his early travels in the Levant; and there is this peculiarity in malarial fevers, that if you have once had them, you are ever afterwards susceptible to a renewal of their attacks if within their reach, and Byron was hardly ever out of it. Venice and Ravenna are belted in with swamps, and fevers are rife in the autumn. By starving his body Byron kept his brains clear; no man had brighter eyes or a clearer voice; and his resolute bearing and prompt replies, when excited, gave to his body an appearance of muscular power that imposed on strangers. I never doubted, for he was indifferent to life, and prouder than Lucifer, that if he had drawn his sword in Greece, or elsewhere, he would have thrown away the scabbard.

PERCY BYSSHE SHELLEY

From a chalk drawing after the original painting by Miss Curran

XV

SHELLEY AS A FRESHMAN

IF one were to name ten of the greatest English poets beginning with Chaucer and ending with Tennyson, the name of Shelley would be included, although he died before he was thirty years old. Hogg, a friend of Shelley's, has given us an interesting account of their meeting when both were freshmen at Oxford.

"At the commencement of Michaelmas Term," writes Hogg, "that is, at the end of October in the year 1801, I happened one day to sit next a freshman at dinner; it was his first appearance in hall. His figure was slight, and his aspect remarkably youthful, even at our table, where all were very young. He seemed thoughtful and absent. He ate little and had no acquaintance with any one. I know not how we fell into conversation, for such familiarity was unusual, and, strange to say, much reserve prevailed in a society where there could not possibly be occasion for any." This conversation led into a heated discussion of the merits of German and Italian literature. When the time for leaving the dining hall had come, Hogg invited his new acquaintance over to his rooms. During the transit the thread of the argument was lost, and while Hogg was lighting the candles Shelley frankly said that he was not competent to argue the point, as he had little knowledge of either German or Italian literature. Then Hogg with equal ingenuousness confessed that he knew but little of Italian and nothing of German literature.

So the talk went merrily on. Shelley said it made little difference whether Italian or German literature were the more worthy, for all literature, what was it but vain trifling? What is the study of language but the study of words, of phrases, of the names of things? How much better and wiser to study things themselves!

"I inquired," says Hogg, "a little bewildered, how this was to be effected. He answered, 'Through the physical sciences, and especially through chemistry,' and raising his voice, his face flushing as he spoke, he discoursed, with a degree of animation that far outshone his zeal in defense of the Germans, of chemistry and chemical analysis." While this is going on Hogg studies the youthful speaker. What manner of man is this brilliant guest? "It was a sum of many contradictions. His figure was slight and fragile, and yet his bones were large and strong. He was tall, but he stooped so much that he seemed of low stature. His clothes were expensive and made after the most approved mode of the day; but they were tumbled, rumpled, unbrushed. His gestures were abrupt, and sometimes violent, occasionally even awkward, yet more frequently gentle and graceful. His complexion was delicate and almost feminine, of the purest red and white; yet he was tanned and freckled by exposure to the sun, having passed the autumn, as he

said, in shooting. His features, his whole face
and particularly his head, were, in fact, unusually
small, yet the last appeared of a remarkable bulk,
for his hair was long and bushy, and in fits of
absence, and in the agonies (if I may use the
word) of anxious thought, he often rubbed it
fiercely with his hands, or passed his fingers
quickly through his locks unconsciously, so that
it was singularly wild and rough. In times when
it was the mode to imitate stage-coachmen as
closely as possible in costume, and when the hair
was invariably cropped, like that of our soldiers,
this eccentricity was very striking. His features
were not symmetrical (the mouth, perhaps, excepted), yet was the effect of the whole extremely
powerful. They breathed an animation, a fire,
an enthusiasm, a vivid and preternatural intelligence, that I never met with in any other
countenance. Nor was the moral expression less
beautiful than the intellectual, for there was a
softness, a delicacy, a gentleness, and especially
(though this will surprise many) that air of profound religious veneration that characterizes the
best works, and chiefly the frescoes of the great
masters of Florence and Rome.''

The next day Hogg pays a visit to Shelley's
rooms. The furniture was new and the walls
were freshly papered, but everything in the room
was in confusion. ''Books, boots, papers, shoes,
philosophical instruments, clothes, pistols, linen,
crockery, ammunition, and phials innumerable,
with money, stockings, prints, crucibles, bags, and
boxes, were scattered on the floor in every place,
as if the young chemist, in order to analyze the
mystery of creation, had endeavored first to re-

construct the primeval chaos. The tables, and especially the carpet, were already stained with large spots of various hues, which frequently proclaimed the agency of fire. An electrical machine, an air pump, the galvanic trough, a solar microscope, and large glass jars were conspicuous amidst the mass of matter. Upon the table by his side were some books lying open, several letters, a bundle of new pens, and a bottle of japan ink, that served as an ink-stand, a piece of deal, lately part of the lid of a box, with many chips, and a handsome razor that had been used as a knife. There were bottles of soda-water, sugar, pieces of lemon, and the traces of an effervescent beverage. Two piles of books supported the tongs, and these upheld a small glass retort above an argand lamp. I had not been seated many minutes before the liquor in the vessel boiled over, adding fresh stains to the table, and rising in fumes with a disagreeable odor. Shelley snatched the glass quickly, and dashing it in pieces among ashes under the grate, increased the unpleasant and penetrating effluvium."

Hogg and Shelley soon became fast friends and met every evening. "I was enabled," writes Hogg, "to continue my studies in the evening in consequence of a very remarkable peculiarity. My young and energetic friend was then overcome by extreme drowsiness, which speedily and completely vanquished him; he would sleep from two to four hours, often so soundly that his slumbers resembled a deep lethargy; he lay occasionally upon the sofa, but more commonly stretched upon the rug before a large fire, like a

cat, and his little round head was exposed to
such fierce heat, that I used to wonder how he
was able to bear it. Sometimes I have interposed
some shelter, but rarely with any permanent
effect, for the sleeper usually contrived to turn
himself, and to roll again into the spot where the
fire glowed the brightest. His torpor was generally profound, but he would sometimes discourse incoherently for a long while in his sleep.
At six he would suddenly compose himself, even
in the midst of an animated narrative or of earnest discussion, and he would lie buried in entire
forgetfulness, in a sweet and mighty oblivion,
until ten, when he would suddenly start up, and
rubbing his eyes with great violence, and passing
his fingers swiftly through his long hair, would
enter at once into a vehement argument, or begin
to recite verses, either of his own composition or
from the works of others, with a rapidity and an
energy that were often quite painful. During
the period of his occultation I took tea, and read
or wrote without interruption. He would sometimes sleep for a shorter time, for about two
hours, postponing for the like period the commencement of his retreat to the rug, and rising
with tolerable punctuality at ten, and sometimes,
though rarely, he was able entirely to forego the
accustomed refreshment.''

After supper, which Shelley would take upon
awaking at ten, the two friends would talk and
read together until two o'clock.

XVI

IN the Protestant cemetery at Rome one can find in an obscure place a plain stone bearing record of Percy Bysshe Shelley, and these lines from Shakspere's Tempest:

> Nothing of him that doth fade,
> But doth suffer a sea-change
> Into something rich and strange.

And this is the story of how Shelley happens to have a memorial in the Roman cemetery:

Shelley was a revolutionist in religion and politics, and revolutionists are seldom popular at home. Shelley's lyric poetry is unsurpassed, but his theories in some respects will never meet with the approval of common-sense humanity. England proved uncomfortable and so he left his country to live in other lands. In 1822 we find him with his family and a Mr. and Mrs. Williams in Casa Magni, a Roman villa in a cove on the bay of Spezzia. Here the poet and his friends became very fond of sailing in a boat which had been made for them. The boat, which they called the Ariel, was twenty-eight feet long and eight feet broad, and this with the assistance of a lad they learned to manage fairly well. To Shelley, whose health had been failing, the out-of-door life gave renewed vigor.

On the eighth of July, Shelley and Williams, accompanied by a sailor-lad, left the harbor of Leghorn to go home to their wives, from whom they had been absent for several days. They had gone to Pisa to welcome Leigh Hunt to Italy, to meet other friends (among the number was Byron), and to do some business. Neither Shelley, Williams, nor the lad, was ever seen alive after that day. As we are indebted to Hogg for the best pen-pictures of the boy Shelley, so we are indebted to Trelawney for the best description of the closing scene. So we shall follow Trelawney's account in the main.

Trelawney was in Leghorn and intended to accompany his friends out of the harbor in a separate boat, but owing to the refusal of the health officer of the harbor he was not allowed to go. As from his own vessel he watched the Ariel, containing the small party happy in the thought that in seven short hours they should be at home with their loved ones, his Genoese mate turned to him and said: "They are standing too much in-shore; the current will set them there." "They will soon have the land-breeze," replied Trelawney. "Maybe," said the mate, "she will soon have too much breeze; that gaff topsail is foolish in a boat with no deck and no sailor on board." Then he added as he pointed to the southwest, "Look at those black lines and dirty rags hanging on them out of the sky; look at the smoke on the water; the devil is brewing mischief."

"Although the sun was obscured by mists," Trelawney writes, "it was oppressively sultry. There was not a breath of air in the harbor. The heaviness of the atmosphere and an unwonted stillness benumbed my senses. I went down into the cabin and sank into a slumber. I was roused up by a noise overhead, and went on deck. The men were getting up another chain-cable to let go another anchor. There was a general stir amongst the shipping; shifting berths, getting down yards and masts, veering out cables, hauling in of hawsers, letting go anchors, hailing from the ships and quays, boats sculling rapidly to and fro. It was almost dusk, although only half-past six o'clock. The sea was of the color and looked as solid and smooth as a sheet of lead, and covered with an oily scum. Gusts of wind swept over without ruffling it, and big drops of rain fell on its surface, rebounding, as if they could not penetrate it. There was a commotion in the air, made up of many threatening sounds, coming upon us from the sea. Fishing craft and coasting vessels, under bare poles, rushed by us in shoals, running foul of the ships in the harbor. As yet the din and hubbub was that made by men, but their shrill pipings were suddenly silenced by the crashing voice of a thunder-squall that burst right over our heads. For some time no other sounds were to be heard than the thunder, wind, and rain. When the fury of the storm, which did not last for more than twenty minutes, had abated and the horizon was in some degree cleared, I looked to sea anxiously, in the hope of descrying Shelley's boat amongst the many small craft scattered about. I watched every speck that loomed on the horizon, thinking that they would have borne up on their return to the port, as all the other boats that had gone out in the same direction had done."

Then followed a period of painful suspense. Were they safe or had they gone down? On the third day Trelawney went to Pisa to ascertain whether any one had heard anything of Shelley. "I told my fears to Hunt," he writes, "and then went upstairs to Byron. When I told him his lip quivered, and his voice faltered as he questioned me."

And what of the wives at Casa Magni awaiting the return of their husbands? Let one of the two tell the story. Mary is the wife of Shelley, and Jane is Mrs. Williams.

"Yet I thought when he, when my Shelley returns, I shall be happy—he will comfort me; if my boy be ill, he will restore him and encourage me. . . . Thus a week passed. On Monday, 8th, Jane had a letter from Edward dated Saturday; he said that he waited at Leghorn for Shelley, who was at Pisa; that Shelley's return was certain; 'but,' he continued, 'if I should not come by Monday, I will come in a felucca, and you may expect me on Thursday evening at furthest.'

"This was Monday, the fatal Monday, but with us it was stormy all day, and we did not at all suppose that they could put to sea. At twelve at night we had a thunder-storm. Tuesday it rained all day and was calm—the sky wept on their graves. On Wednesday, the wind was fair from Leghorn, and in the evening several feluccas arrived thence. One brought word they had sailed Monday, but we did not believe them. Thursday was another day of fair wind, and when twelve at night came, and we did not see the tall sails of the little boat double the promontory before us, we began to fear, not the truth, but some

illness, some disagreeable news for their deten-
tion.''

"Jane got so uneasy that she determined to
proceed the next day to Leghorn in a boat to see
what was the matter. Friday came and with it
a heavy sea and bad wind. Jane, however, resolved to be rowed to Leghorn, since no boat could
sail, and busied herself in preparation. I wished
her to wait for letters, since Friday was letter-
day. She would not, but the sea detained her;
the swell rose so that no boat would endure out.
At twelve at noon our letters came; there was one
from Hunt to Shelley; it said, 'Pray write to tell
us how you got home, for they say that you had
bad weather after you sailed on Monday and we
are anxious.' The paper fell from me. I trembled all over. Jane read it. 'Then it is all over,'
she said. 'No, my dear Jane,' I cried, 'it is not
all over, but this suspense is dreadful. Come
with me—we will go to Leghorn, we will post, to
be swift and learn our fate.'

"We crossed to Lerici . . . we posted to Pisa.
It must have been fearful to see us—two poor,
wild, aghast creatures, driving (like Matilda)
towards the sea to learn if we were to be forever
doomed to misery. I knew that Hunt was at
Pisa, at Lord Byron's house, but I thought that
Lord Byron was at Leghorn. I settled that we
should drive to Casa Lanfranchi, that I should
get out and ask the fearful question of Hunt, 'Do
you know anything of Shelley?' On entering
Pisa, the idea of seeing Hunt for the first time for
four years under such circumstances and asking
him such a question was so terrific to me that it
was with difficulty that I prevented myself from

going into convulsions. My struggles were dreadful. They knocked at the door and some one called out, 'Chi e?' It was the Guiccioli's maid. Lord Byron was in Pisa. Hunt was in bed, so I was to see Lord Byron instead of him. This was a great relief to me. I staggered upstairs; the Guicciola came to meet me smiling, while I could hardly say, 'Where is he—Sapete alcuna cosa di Shelley?' They knew nothing; he had left Pisa on Sunday; on Monday he had sailed; there had been bad weather Monday afternoon; more they knew not.''

XVII

I N the village of Enfield, in Middlesex, ten miles on the North Road from London, my father, John Clarke, says Charles Cowden Clarke in *The Gentleman's Magazine,* kept a school. The house had been built by a West India merchant in the latter end of the seventeenth or beginning of the eighteenth century. It was of the better character of the domestic architecture of that period, the whole front being of the purest red brick, wrought by means of molds into rich designs of flowers and pomegranates, with heads of cherubim over niches in the center of the building. The elegance of the design and the perfect finish of the structure were such as to procure its protection when a branch railway was brought from the Ware and Cambridge line to Enfield. . . .

Here it was that John Keats all but commenced, and did complete, his school education. He was born on the twenty-ninth of October, 1795, and he was one of the little fellows who had not wholly emerged from the child's costume upon being placed under my father's care. It will be readily conceived that it is difficult to recall from the "dark backward and abysm" of seventy-odd years the general acts of perhaps the youngest indi-

vidual in a corporation of between seventy and
eighty youngsters; and very little more of Keats's
child-life can I remember than that he had a
brisk, winning face, and was a favorite with all,
particularly my mother. . . .

Keats's father was the principal servant at the
Swan and Hoop stables—a man of so remarkably
fine a common-sense, and native respectability,
that I perfectly remember the warm terms in
which his demeanor used to be canvassed by my
parents after he had been to visit his boys. John
was the only one resembling him in person and
feature, with brown hair and dark hazel eyes.
The father was killed by a fall from his horse in
returning from a visit to the school. This detail
may be deemed requisite when we see in the last
memoir of the poet the statement that "John
Keats was born on the twenty-ninth of October,
1795, in the upper rank of the middle class."
His two brothers—George, older, and Thomas,
younger than himself—were like the mother, who
was tall, of good figure,with large oval face and
sensible deportment. The last of the family was
a sister—Fanny, I think, much younger than all,
—and I hope still living (in 1874)—of whom I remember, when once walking in the garden with her
brothers, my mother speaking of her with much
fondness for her pretty and simple manners. . . .

In the early part of his school-life John gave
no extraordinary indications of intellectual character; but it was remembered of him afterwards,
that there was ever present a determined and
steady spirit in all his undertakings: I never knew
it misdirected in his required pursuit of study.
He was a most orderly scholar. The future rami-

fications of that noble genius were then closely
shut in the seed, which was greedily drinking in
the moisture which made it afterwards burst forth
so kindly into luxuriance and beauty.

My father was in the habit, at each half-year's
vacation, of bestowing prizes upon those pupils
who had performed the greatest quantity of vol-
untary work; and such was Keats's indefatigable
energy for the last two or three successive half-
years of his remaining at school, that, upon each
occasion he took the first prize by a considerable
distance. He was at work before the first school
hour began, and that was at seven o'clock, almost
all the intervening times of recreation were so
devoted, and during the afternoon holidays, when
all were at play, he would be in the school—almost the only one—at his Latin or French translation, and so unconscious and regardless was he
of the consequences of so close and persevering
an application that he never would have taken the
necessary exercise had he not been sometimes
driven out for the purpose by one of his masters.

It has just been said that he was a favorite with
all. Not the less beloved was he for having a
highly pugnacious spirit, which, when roused, was
one of the most picturesque exhibitions—off the
stage—I ever saw. One of the transports of that
marvelous actor, Edmund Kean—whom, by the
way, he idolized—was its nearest resemblance;
and the two were not very dissimilar in face and
figure. Upon one occasion, when an usher, on
account of some impertinent behavior, had boxed
his brother Tom's ears, John rushed up, put himself in the received posture of offense, and, it was
said, struck the usher—who could, so to say, have

put him into his pocket. His passion at times
was almost ungovernable, and his brother George,
being considerably the taller and stronger, used
frequently to hold him down by main force, laughing when John was in "one of his moods," and
was endeavoring to beat him. It was all, however, a wisp-of-straw conflagration, for he had an
intensely tender affection for his brothers and
proved it upon the most trying occasions. He
was not merely the "favorite of all," like a pet
prize-fighter, for his terrier courage; but his high-
mindedness, his utter unconsciousness of a mean
motive, his placability, his generosity, wrought so
general a feeling in his behalf, that I never heard
a word of disapproval from any one, superior or
equal, who had known him.

In the latter part of the time—perhaps eighteen
months—that he remained at school, he occupied
the hours during meals in reading. Thus, his
whole time was engrossed. He had a tolerably
retentive memory, and the quantity that he read
was surprising. He must in those last months
have exhausted the school library, which consisted
principally of abridgments of all the voyages and
travels of any note; Mavor's collection, also his
Universal History; Robertson's histories of Scotland, America, and Charles the Fifth; all Miss
Edgeworth's productions, together with many
other works equally well calculated for youth.
The books, however, that were his constantly
recurring sources of attraction were Tooke's
Pantheon, Lemprière's *Classical Dictionary,* which
he appeared to *learn,* and Spence's *Polymetis.*
This was the store whence he acquired his intimacy with the Greek mythology; here was he

"suckled in that creed outworn;" for his amount of classical attainment extended no farther than the *Æneid,* with which epic, indeed, he was so fascinated that before leaving school he had *voluntarily* translated in writing a considerable portion. And yet I remember that at that early age —mayhap under fourteen—notwithstanding, and through all its incidental attractiveness, he hazarded the opinion to me (and the expression riveted my surprise), that there was feebleness in the structure of the work. He must have gone through all the better publications in the school library, for he asked me to lend him some of my books, and, in my "mind's eye" I now see him at supper (we had our meals in the school-room), sitting back on the form, from the table, holding the folio volume of Burnet's *History of His Own Time* between himself and the table, eating his meal from beyond it. This work, and Leigh Hunt's *Examiner*—which my father took in, and I used to lend to Keats—no doubt laid the foundation of his love of civil and religious liberty. He once told me, smiling, that one of his guardians, being informed what books I had lent him to read, declared that if he had fifty children he would not send one of them to that school. Bless his patriot head!

When he left Enfield at fourteen years of age, he was apprenticed to Mr. Thomas Hammond, a medical man, residing in Church Street, Edmonton, and exactly two miles from Enfield. This arrangement evidently gave him satisfaction, and I fear it was the most placid period of his painful life; for now, with the exception of the duty he had to perform in the surgery—by no means an onerous one—his whole leisure hours were employed in indulging his passion for reading and translating. During his apprenticeship he finished the *Æneid*.

The distance between our residences being so short, I gladly encouraged his inclination to come over when he could claim a leisure hour; and in consequence I saw him about five or six times a month on my own leisure afternoons. He rarely came empty-handed; either he had a book to read, or brought one to be exchanged. When the weather permitted, we always sat in an arbor at the end of a spacious garden, and—in Boswellian dialect—"we had a good talk." . . .

XVIII

WHEN Carlyle wrote and lectured on *Heroes and Hero Worship,* he would have made no mistake in selecting one of his contemporary countrymen as a fine example of the man of letters as hero. But it is one of the characteristics of human nature to see the heroic in the remote in time and place rather than in the near. Carlyle, had he closely examined the life of his Scotch neighbor, would have been forced to acknowledge that no knight battling with chivalric valor in the fiction of Sir Walter ever displayed more nobility of soul than that displayed by Walter Scott in his adversity. Critics may find flaws in Scott's style, but as time reveals more fully the character of the man they are unable to find fault with the man himself. Some years ago was published Scott's journal. Parts of this had been published before, but, owing to the nature of some of the information, much of this had been suppressed until sixty years after the death of the writer. To quote from this journal is, perhaps, the best method of giving a first-hand impression of the real man. He is his own revealer. Scott called the big book in which he from time to time records for several years his thoughts his "Gurnal," because his daughter Sophia had once spelled the word in that way. This book could be closed with a lock and key. On the title-page was written:

As I walked by myself,
I talked to myself,
And thus myself said to me.

(Old Song.)

Scott's poems and novels brought him much revenue. This he spent in purchasing land. He became a Scotch "laird" owning many acres, and a most beautiful home, Abbotsford. But unfortunately he formed a bad business partnership. When the firm through mismanagement and speculation, in which Scott had no part, went down in ruin, Scott found to his surprise that he owed a vast sum. In his "Gurnal" of September 5, 1827, he wrote: "The debts for which I am legally responsible, though no party to this contraction, amount to £30,000." But although his legal responsibility was for so great a sum, he felt that morally he was responsible for a far greater amount. When the printing house of James Ballantyne & Co., the publishing house of Constable, and Hunt and Robinson, failed, they failed for upwards of half a million pounds. Of this enormous total, Scott could be held morally responsible for one hundred and thirty thousand pounds.

For several weeks after intimations of failure had reached Scott, he lived in a state of uncertainty. On the 18th of December, 1825, he wrote a long account in his journal. It was published lately for the first time, appearing in the *Quarterly Review*. What a revelation of the man it is!

"Ballantyne called on me this morning. *Venit illa suprema dies.* My extremity is come. Cadell has received letters from London which all but positively announce the failure of Hurst and Robinson, so that Constable and Co. must follow, and I must go with poor James Ballantyne for company. I suppose it will involve my all. . . . I have been rash in anticipating funds to buy lands, but then I made from £5,000 to £10,000 a year, and land was my temptation. I think nobody can lose a penny—that is my one comfort. Men will think pride has had a fall. Let them indulge their own pride in thinking that my fall makes them higher, or seems so at least. I have the satisfaction to recollect that my prosperity has been of advantage to many, and that some at least will forgive my transient wealth on account of the innocence of my intentions, and my real wish to do good to the poor. This news will make sad hearts at Darnick, and in the cottages of Abbotsford, which I do not cherish the least hope of preserving. It has been my Delilah, and so I have often termed it; and now the recollection of the extensive woods I planted, and the walks I have formed, from which strangers must derive both the pleasure and profit, will excite feelings likely to sober my gayest moments. I have half resolved never to see the place again. How could I tread my hall with such a diminished crest? How live a poor indebted man where I was once the wealthy, and honored? My children are provided [for]; thank God for that! I was to have gone there in joy and prosperity to receive my friends. My dogs will wait for me in vain. It is foolish, but the thoughts of parting from these dumb creatures have moved me more than any of the painful reflections I have put down. Poor things, I must get them kind masters; there may be yet those who loving me may love my dog because it has been mine. I must end this, or I shall lose the tone of mind with which men should meet distress. I find my dogs' feet on my knees. I hear them whining and seeking me everywhere—this is nonsense, but it is what they would do could they know how things are. Poor Will! Laidlaw! Poor Tom Purdie! this will be news to wring your heart, and many a poor fellow's besides to whom my prosperity was daily bread.''

After touching on some other matters he comes back to Abbotsford,—''Yet to save Abbotsford I would attempt all that was possible. My heart clings to the place I have created. There is scarce a tree on it that does not owe its being to me, and the pain of leaving it is greater than I can bear.''

A Mr. Skene, in whose gardens Scott while in Edinburgh about a month later took a walk, has left a record of a conversation with Scott. He wrote immediately after the walk so as to record the conversation. This is what Scott said: ''Do you know I experience a sort of determined pleasure in confronting the very worst aspect of this sudden reverse—in standing, as it were, in the breach that has overthrown my fortunes, and saying, Here I stand, at least, an honest man. And God knows if I have enemies, this I may at least with truth say, that I have never wittingly given cause of enmity in the whole course of my life, for even the burnings of political hate seemed to find nothing in my nature to feed the flame. I am not conscious of having borne a grudge towards any man, and at this moment of my overthrow, so help me God, I wish well and feel kindly to every one. And if I thought that any of my works contained a sentence hurtful to any one's feelings, I would burn it.''

Scott worked so assiduously that by January, 1828, he had reduced his debt $200,000. On the 17th of December, 1830, more than the half of his debt had been paid. On that day his creditors had a meeting during which the following resolutions were passed:

''That Sir Walter Scott be requested to accept of his furniture, plate, linen, paintings, library, and curiosities of every description as the best means the creditors have of expressing their very high sense of his most honorable conduct, and in grateful acknowledgment for the unparalleled and most successful exertions he has made, and continues to make, for them.''

That the creditors of Scott would be glad to show their gratitude is easy to believe when one learns that while Scott was paying pound for pound the other members of the firm paid their creditors less than three shillings to the pound. That Scott did his herculean task at great sacrifice is known. How much of pain and worry he endured is not so well known. At one time he writes: ''After all, I have fagged through six pages, and made poor Wurmser lay down his sword on the glacis of Mantua—and my head aches—my eyes ache—my back aches—so does my breast—and I am sure my heart aches—what can duty want more?''

XIX

WALTER SAVAGE LANDOR, whose course of life ran from 1775 to 1864, in his old age confessed, "I never did a single wise thing in the whole course of my existence, although I have written many which have been thought so." This is the exaggeration of an old man who has been impressed by the frailty of human endeavor. Nevertheless, Landor is a striking illustration of the artistic temperament. He was impractical. Landor could not make a good fist. Even when angry, a frame of mind in which he found himself very frequently, he did not clench his fists without leaving his thumbs in relaxation—a sure sign, it is said, of the lack of tenacity of purpose and tact in practical dealings. He would adjust his spectacles on his forehead, and then, forgetting what he had done, would overturn everything in his wild search for them. When he started out on a trip he would take the greatest pains to remember the key of his portmanteau, and then forget to take the portmanteau; and then on discovering the absence of the portmanteau he would launch out into the most vehement denunciation of the carelessness and depravity of the railroad officials, heaping objurgations upon them, their fathers, and their grandfathers. Then after he had exhausted his vocabulary of invective and eased his soul, the humor of the situation would appeal to him and he would begin to laugh, quietly at first, and then in louder and louder strains until his merriment seemed more formidable than his wrath.

When Landor says that he never did a wise thing but has written many, one is led to think of his marriage. No one wrote about marriage more seriously than Landor, no one entered upon marriage more recklessly. "Death itself," he once wrote, "to the reflecting mind is less serious than marriage. The elder plant is cut down that the younger may have room to flourish; a few tears drop into the loosened soil, and buds and blossoms spring over it. Death is not even a blow, it is not even a pulsation; it is a pause. But marriage unrolls the awful lot of numberless generations." The man who could write thus impressively about marriage one spring evening at Bath attended a ball. There he met a beautiful young lady whom he admired. As soon as he set eyes on her he exclaimed, "By heaven! that's the nicest girl in the room, and I'll marry her." He married her and was ever after unhappy. "God forbid," once growled Landor, "that I should do otherwise than declare that she always *was* agreeable—to every one but *me*." Landor was not in the habit of talking about his domestic troubles, but at one time when he was contrasting other and more agreeable marriages he was heard to say that he "unfortunately was taken by a pretty face."

Kenyon related to a friend an incident of the Landor honeymoon that is significant. On one occasion, it seems, the newly married couple were sitting side by side; Landor was reading some of his own verses to his bride—and who could read more exquisitely?—when all at once the lady, releasing herself from his arm, jumped up, saying, "Oh, do stop, Walter, there's that dear delightful Punch performing in the street. I must look out of the window." Exit poetry forever.

It would have been difficult for any woman to live amicably with Landor. In his youth he was suspended from college, and when he was a very old man he was fined $5,000 for writing a libelous article. Between these two periods his life was made up of many fits of passion. His rustication, or suspension from Trinity College, Cambridge, came about in the following manner: One evening Landor invited his friends to wine. His gun, powder, and shot were in the next room, as he had been out hunting in the morning of that day. In a room opposite to Landor's lived a young man whom Landor disliked. The two parties exchanged taunts. Finally in a spirit of bravado Landor took his gun and fired a shot through the closed shutters of the enemy. Quite naturally this bit of pleasantry was not appreciated by the owner of the shutters and complaint was lodged. When the investigation was made the president tried to be as lenient as he possibly could, but his conciliatory manner was stubbornly met by the youthful culprit. When rustication was pronounced it was hoped that Landor would return to the college to honor it and himself by an earnest devotion to his studies. But he never returned.

When Landor was living in Florence the Italians thought him the ideally mad Englishman.

He lived for a time in the Medici palace, but his friendly relations with the landlord, a nobleman bearing the distinguished name of the palace, had an abrupt termination. Landor imagined that the marquis had unfairly coaxed away his coachman, and he wrote a letter of complaint. The next day in comes the strutting marquis with his hat on in the presence of Mrs. Landor and some visitors. One of the visitors describes the scene: ''He had scarcely advanced three steps from the door, when Landor walked up to him quickly and knocked his hat off, then took him by the arm and turned him out. You should have heard Landor's shout of laughter at his own anger when it was all over; inextinguishable laughter, which none of us could resist.'' This reminds one of the story Milnes told to Emerson, that Landor once became so enraged at his Italian cook that he picked him up and threw him out of the window, and then exclaimed, ''Good God, I never thought of those violets!''

Quite in strong contrast to the irascible side of his nature was his tender love for his children, of which he had four, the last born in 1825. In them he took constant delight. In their games *Babbo,* as he was affectionately termed, was the most gleeful and frolicsome of them all. When he was separated from them he was in continual anxiety. On one of his trips he received the first childish letter from his son Arnold. In his reply the concluding lines reveal the intense affection of the father:

I shall never be quite happy until I see you again and put my cheek upon your head. Tell my sweet Julia that if I see twenty little girls I will not romp with any of them before I romp with her, and kiss your two dear brothers for me. You must always love them as much as I love you, and you must teach them how to be good boys, which I cannot do so well as you can. God preserve and bless you, my own Arnold. My heart beats as if it would fly to you, my own fierce creature. We shall very soon meet.   Love your,

BABBO.

In literature Landor will be remembered as the author of *Imaginary Conversations,* composed during his years of retirement at Florence. In these *Conversations* we hear the great men and women of the past who converse as Landor imagined they might have talked. Landor's prose style is admired because of its simplicity and classic purity. After the publication of the first two volumes of this work Landor was visited as a man of genius by Englishmen and Americans. One day Hogg, the friend of Shelley, was announced while Hare, a well-known Englishman, was sitting in the room. Landor said, as he considered the names of his two visitors, that he felt like La Fontaine with all the better company of the beasts about him. Hazlitt was one of his frequent visitors. One of their reported conversations is about Wordsworth. Upon Landor's saying that he had never seen the famous Lake poet, Hazlitt asked, "But you have seen a horse, I suppose?" and on receiving an affirmative answer, continued, "Well, sir, if you have seen a horse, I mean his head, sir, you may say you have seen Wordsworth, sir."

Emerson was desirous of seeing Landor. One of the motives that led him to take his first trip abroad was the desire to see five distinguished men. These men were Coleridge, Wordsworth, Landor, DeQuincey, and Carlyle. "On the 15th May," writes Emerson in his *English Traits,* "I dined with Mr. Landor. I found him noble and courteous, living in a cloud of pictures at his Villa Gherardesca, a fine house commanding a beautiful landscape. I had inferred from his books, or magnified from some anecdotes, an impression of Achillean wrath,—an untamable petulance. I do not know whether the imputation were just or not, but certainly on this May day his courtesy veiled that haughty mind and he was the most patient and gentle of hosts.''

Landor used to say somewhat loftily, ''I do not remember that resentment has ever made me commit an injustice.'' And in this connection he related to a friend an incident of his early married life, when he was living at Como, where he had for his next-door neighbor the Princess of Wales. Landor and his royal neighbor had a quarrel arising from trespassing by the domestics of the Princess. ''The insolence of her domestics,'' said Landor, ''was only equaled by the intolerable discourtesy of her Royal Highness when she was appealed to in the matter.''

Some years later when the Milan Commission was carrying on its ''delicate investigation'' concerning the character of the Queen, about whom there had been rumors detrimental to her character, Landor was asked to give confidential testimony against Queen Caroline. This made Landor indignant and he replied,—''Her Royal Highness is my enemy; she has deeply injured me, therefore I can say nothing against her, and I never will.''

It is significant that shortly before this application for testimony was made, George IV took an opportunity to ask Landor to dinner. ''I declined the honor," said the old lion, "on the plea that I had an attack of quinsy. I always have quinsy when royal people ask me to dinner," he added, laughing immoderately.

Ah, what avails the sceptered race,
  Ah, what the form divine!
What every virtue, every grace!—
  Rose Aylmer, all were thine.

Rose Aylmer, whom these wakeful eyes
  May weep but never see,
A night of memories and of sighs
  I consecrate to thee.

XX

SIR GEORGE MURRAY SMITH, leading member of the famous publishing house of Smith, Elder and Company, was well acquainted with the leading literary men of England during an active career of sixty years. The following account of Leigh Hunt is especially entertaining:

"Business was by no means Leigh Hunt's strong point. In this respect, but not otherwise, he may have suggested Skimpole to Charles Dickens. On one of my visits I found him trying to puzzle out the abstruse question of how he should deduct some such sum as thirteen shillings and ninepence from a sovereign. On another occasion I had to pay him a sum of money, £100 or £200, and I wrote him a check for the amount. 'Well,' he said, 'what am I to do with this little bit of paper?' I told him that if he presented it at the bank they would pay him cash for it, but I added, 'I will save you that trouble.' I sent to the bank and cashed the check for him. He took the notes away carefully inclosed in an envelope. Two days afterward Leigh Hunt came in a state of great agitation to tell me that his wife had burned them. He had thrown the envelope, with the bank notes inside, carelessly down, and his wife had flung it into the fire. Leigh Hunt's agitation while on his way to bring this news had not prevented him from purchasing on the road a little statuette of Psyche which he carried, without any paper round it, in his hand. I told him I thought something might be done in the matter; I sent to the bankers and got the numbers of the notes, and then in company with Leigh Hunt went off to the Bank of England. I explained our business, and we were shown into a room where three old gentlemen were sitting at tables. They kept us waiting some time, and Leigh Hunt, who had meantime been staring all round the room, at last got up, walked up to one of the staid officials, and addressing him said in wondering tones: 'And this is the Bank of England! And do you sit here all day, and never see the green woods and the trees and flowers and the charming country?' Then in tones of remonstrance he demanded, 'Are you contented with such a life?' All this time he was holding the little naked Psyche in one hand, and with his long hair and flashing eyes made a surprising figure. I fancy I can still see the astonished faces of the three officials; they would have made a most delightful picture. I said, 'Come away, Mr. Hunt, these gentlemen are very busy.' I succeeded in carrying Leigh Hunt off, and, after entering into certain formalities, we were told that the value of the notes would be paid in twelve months. I gave Leigh Hunt the money at once, and he went away rejoicing.''

XXI

MY father died when I was about seven years
old, says the author of the *Confessions of
an Opium-Eater,* and left me to the care
of four guardians. I was sent to various
schools, great and small, and was very early distinguished for my classical attainments, especially for my knowledge of Greek. At thirteen I
wrote Greek with ease, and at fifteen my command of that language was so great, that I not
only composed Greek verses in lyric meters, but
would converse in Greek fluently, and without
embarrassment—an accomplishment which I have
not since met with in any scholar of my times,
and which, in my case, was owing to the practice
of daily reading off the newspapers into the best
Greek I could furnish *extempore;* for the necessity of ransacking my memory and invention for
all sorts and combinations of periphrastic expressions, as equivalents for modern ideas, images,
relations of things, etc., gave me a compass of
diction which would never have been called out
by a dull translation of moral essays, etc. "That
boy," said one of my masters, pointing the attention of a stranger to me, "that boy could harangue an Athenian mob better than you or I

102

could address an English one.'' He who honored me with this eulogy was a scholar, ''and a ripe and good one,'' and of all my tutors, was the only one whom I loved or reverenced. Unfortunately for me (and, as I afterwards learned, to this worthy man's great indignation), I was transferred to the care, first of a blockhead, who was in a perpetual panic lest I should expose his ignorance; and, finally, to that of a respectable scholar, at the head of a great school on an ancient foundation. This man had been appointed to his situation by —— College, Oxford, and was a sound, well-built scholar, but (like most men whom I have known from that college) coarse, clumsy, and inelegant. A miserable contrast he presented, in my eyes, to the Etonian brilliancy of my favorite master; and, besides, he could not disguise from my hourly notice the poverty and meagerness of his understanding. It is a bad thing for a boy to be, and know himself, far beyond his tutors, whether in knowledge or power of mind. This was the case, so far as regarded knowledge at least, not with myself only, for the two boys who jointly with myself composed the first form were better Grecians than the head-master, though not more elegant scholars. . . . I who had a small patrimonial property, the income of which was sufficient to support me at college, wished to be sent thither immediately. I made earnest representations on the subject to my guardians, but all to no purpose. One, who was more reasonable, and had more knowledge of the world than the rest, lived at a distance; two of the other three resigned all their authority into the hands of the fourth, and this fourth, with whom I had to negotiate, was a worthy man, in his way, but haughty, obstinate, and intolerant of all opposition to his will. After a certain number of letters and personal interviews, I found that I had nothing to hope for, not even a compromise of the matter, from my guardian: unconditional submission was what he demanded, and I prepared myself, therefore, for other measures. Summer was now coming on with hasty steps, and my seventeenth birthday was fast approaching, after which day I had sworn within myself that I would no longer be numbered among schoolboys. Money being what I chiefly wanted, I wrote to a woman of high rank, who, though young herself, had known me from a child, and had latterly treated me with great distinction, requesting that she would "lend" me five guineas. For upward of a week no answer came, and I was beginning to despond, when at length a servant put into my hands a double letter, with a coronet on the seal. The letter was kind and obliging; the fair writer was on the sea-coast, and in that way the delay had arisen; she inclosed double of what I had asked, and good-naturedly hinted that if I should *never* repay her, it would not absolutely ruin her. Now, then, I was prepared for my scheme: ten guineas, added to about two that I had remaining from my pocket-money, seemed to me sufficient for an indefinite length of time, and at that happy age, if no *definite* boundary can be assigned to one's power, the spirit of hope and pleasure makes it virtually infinite.

It is a just remark of Dr. Johnson's (and, what cannot often be said of his remarks, it is a very feeling one) that we never do anything consciously for the last time (of things, that is, which we have long been in the habit of doing) without sadness of heart. This truth I felt deeply when I came to leave ——, a place which I did not love, and where I had not been happy. On the evening before I left —— forever, I grieved when the ancient and lofty schoolroom resounded with the evening service, performed for the last time in my hearing; and at night, when the muster-roll of names was called over, and mine (as usual) was called first, I stepped forward, and passing the head-master, who was standing by, I bowed to him, and looked earnestly in his face, thinking to myself, "He is old and infirm, and in this world I shall not see him again." I was right; I never *did* see him again, nor never shall. He looked at me complacently, smiled good-naturedly, returned my salutation (or rather my valediction), and we parted (though he knew it not) forever. I could not reverence him intellectually, but he had been uniformly kind to me, and had allowed me many indulgences, and I grieved at the thought of the mortification I should inflict upon him.

The morning came which was to launch me into the world, and from which my whole succeeding life has, in many important points, taken its coloring. I lodged in the head-master's house, and had been allowed, from my first entrance, the indulgence of a private room, which I used both as a sleeping-room and as a study. At half after three I rose, and gazed with deep emotion at the ancient towers of ——, "drest in earliest light," and beginning to crimson with the radiant luster of a cloudless July morning. I was firm and immovable in my purpose, but yet agitated by anticipation of uncertain danger and troubles; and if I could have foreseen the hurricane, and perfect hail-storm of affliction, which soon fell upon me, well might I have been agitated. To this agitation the deep peace of the morning presented an affecting contrast, and in some degree a medicine. The silence was more profound than that of midnight, and to me the silence of a summer morning is more touching than all other silence, because, the light being broad and strong as that of noonday at other seasons of the year, it seems to differ from perfect day chiefly because man is not yet abroad, and thus, the peace of nature, and of the innocent creatures of God, seem to be secure and deep, only so long as the presence of man, and his restless and unquiet spirit, are not there to trouble its sanctity.

I dressed myself, took my hat and gloves, and lingered a little in the room. For the last year and a half this room had been my ''pensive citadel:'' here I had read and studied through all the hours of the night, and, though true it was that, for the latter part of this time, I, who was framed for love and gentle affections, had lost my gayety and happiness, during the strife and fever of contention with my guardian, yet, on the other hand, as a boy so passionately fond of books, and dedicated to intellectual pursuits, I could not fail to have enjoyed many happy hours in the midst of general dejection. I wept as I looked round on the chair, hearth, writing-table, and other familiar objects, knowing too certainly that I looked upon them for the last time. While I write this, it is eighteen years ago, and yet, at this moment, I see distinctly, as if it were yesterday, the lineaments and expressions of the object on which I fixed my parting gaze: it was a picture of the lovely ——, which hung over the mantelpiece, the eyes and mouth of which were so beautiful, and the whole countenance so radiant with benignity and divine tranquillity, that I had a thousand times laid down my pen, or my book, to gather consolation from it, as a devotee from his patron saint. While I was yet gazing upon it, the deep tones of —— clock proclaimed that it was four o'clock. I went up to the picture, kissed it, and then gently walked out and closed the door forever!

XXII

MACAULAY'S CHILDHOOD

MACAULAY is one of the brilliant lights of the first half of the last century. Trevelyan's *Life and Letters* of Macaulay gives us an interesting glimpse of his childhood. When his parents moved from the heart of London into a less crowded district, Macaulay, baby though he was, kept the early impressions of the place.

"He remembered," says his biographer, "standing up at the nursery window by his father's side, looking at a cloud of black smoke pouring out of a tall chimney. He asked if that was hell: an inquiry that was received with great displeasure which at the time he could not understand. The kindly father must have been pained almost against his own will at finding what feature of his stern creed it was that had embodied itself in so very material a shape before his little son's imagination. When in after days, Mrs. Macaulay was questioned as to how soon she began to detect in the child a promise of the future, she used to say that his sensibilities and affections were remarkably developed at an age which to her hearers appeared next to incredible. He would cry for joy on seeing her after a few

hours' absence, and (till her husband put a stop
to it) her power of exciting his feelings was often
made an exhibition to her friends. She did not
regard this precocity as a proof of cleverness,
but, like a foolish young mother, only thought
that so tender a nature was marked for early
death.

"The new residence was in the High Street of
Clapham, a more commodious part of London
than that which they had just left. "It was a
roomy, comfortable dwelling, with a very small
garden behind, and in front a very small one
indeed, which has entirely disappeared beneath
a large shop thrown out toward the roadway by
the present occupier, who bears the name of Heywood. Here the boy passed a quiet and most
happy childhood. From the time that he was
three years old he read incessantly, for the most
part lying on the rug before the fire, with his
book on the floor, and a piece of bread and butter
in his hand. A very clever woman who then lived
in the house as parlor-maid told how he used to
sit in his nankeen frock, perched on the table by
her as she was cleaning the plate, and expounding
to her out of a volume as big as himself. He did
not care for toys, but was very fond of taking
his walk, when he would hold forth to his companion, whether nurse or mother, telling inter-
minable stories, out of his own head, or repeating what he had been reading in language far
above his years. His memory retained without
effort the phraseology of the book which he had
been last engaged on, and he talked, as the maid
said, 'quite printed words,' which produced an
effect that appeared formal, and often, no doubt,

exceedingly droll. Mrs. Hannah More was fond of relating how she called at Mr. Macaulay's, and was met by a fair, pretty, slight child, with abundance of light hair, about four years of age, who came to the front door to receive her, and tell her that his parents were out, but that if she would be good enough to come in he would bring her a glass of old spirits, a proposition which greatly startled the old lady, who had never aspired beyond cowslip-wine. When questioned as to what he knew about old spirits he could only say that Robinson Crusoe often had some. About this period his father took him on a visit to Lady Waldegrave at Strawberry Hill, and was much pleased to exhibit to his old friend the fair, bright boy, dressed in a green coat with red collar and cuffs, a frill at the throat, and white trousers. After some time had been spent among the wonders of the Orford Collection, of which he ever after carried a catalogue in his head, a servant who was waiting on the company in the great gallery spilled some hot coffee over his legs. The hostess was all kindness and compassion, and when, after a while, she asked him how he was feeling, the little fellow looked up in her face, and replied, 'Thank you, madam, the agony is abated.'

"But it must not be supposed his quaint manners proceeded from affectation or conceit, for all testimony declares that a more simple and natural child never lived, or a more lively and merry one. He had at his command the resources of the Common; to this day the most unchanged spot within ten miles of St. Paul's, and which to all appearance will ere long hold that pleasant pre-eminence within ten leagues. That delightful wilderness of gorse bushes, and poplar groves and gravel pits, and ponds great and small, was to little Tom Macaulay a region of inexhaustible romance and mystery. He explored its recesses; he composed, and almost believed, its legends; he invented for its different features a nomenclature which has been faithfully preserved by two generations of children. A slight ridge intersected by deep ditches toward the west of the Common, the very existence of which no one above eight years old would notice, was dignified with the title of the Alps; while the elevated island, covered with shrubs, that gives a name to the Mount pond, was regarded with infinite awe, as being the nearest approach within the circuit of his observation to a conception of the majesty of Sinai. Indeed, at this period his infant fancy was much exercised with the threats and terrors of the Law. He had a little plot of ground at the back of the house, marked out as his own by a row of oyster shells, which a maid one day threw away as rubbish. He went straight to the drawing-room, where his mother was entertaining some visitors, walked into the circle and said, very solemnly, 'Cursed be Sally; for it is written, cursed be he that removeth his neighbor's landmark.'

"When still the merest child, he was sent as a day-scholar to Mr. Greaves, a shrewd Yorkshire-man with a turn for science, who had been brought originally to the neighborhood in order to edu-cate a number of African youths sent over to imbibe Western civilization at the fountain-head. The poor fellows had found as much difficulty in keeping alive at Clapham as Englishmen experience at Sierra Leone; and, in the end, their tutor set up a school for boys of his own color, and one time had charge of almost the entire rising generation of the Common. Mrs. Macaulay explained to Tom that he must learn to study without the solace of bread-and-butter, to which he replied, 'Yes, Mama, industry shall be my bread and attention my butter.' But, as a matter of fact, no one ever crept more unwillingly to school. Each several afternoon he made piteous entreaties to be excused returning after dinner, and was met by the unvarying formula, 'No, Tom, if it rains cats and dogs, you shall go.'

"His reluctance to leave home had more than one side to it. Not only did his heart stay behind, but the regular lessons of the class took him away from occupations which in his eyes were infinitely more delightful and important; for these were probably the years of his greatest literary activity. As an author he never again had more facility, or anything like so wide a range. In September, 1808, his mother writes: 'My dear Tom continues to show marks of uncommon genius. He gets on wonderfully in all branches of his education, and the extent of his reading, and of the knowledge he derived from it, are truly astonishing in a boy not yet eight years old. He is at the same time as playful as a kitten. To give you some idea of the activity of his mind I will mention a few circumstances that may interest you and Colin. You will believe that to him we never appear to regard anything he does as anything more than a schoolboy's amusement. He took it into his head to write a compendium of universal history about a year ago, and he really contrived to give a tolerably connected view of the leading events from the creation to the present time, filling about a quire of paper. He told me one day that he had been writing a paper which Henry Daly was to translate into Malabar, to persuade the people of Travancore to embrace the Christian religion. On reading it, I found it to contain a very clear idea of the leading facts and doctrines of that religion, with some strong arguments for its adoption. He was so fired with reading Scott's *Lay* and *Marmion,* the former of which he got entirely, and the latter almost entirely, by heart, merely from his delight in reading them, that he determined on writing himself a poem in six cantos which he called *The Battle of Cheviot.'* "

XXIII

IN 1848 Macaulay was a famous man. He had served in India and had written the first part of his *History of England*. In this year after a lapse of nine years he again keeps a diary. From this diary we quote extracts showing how he became famous.

"Dec. 4th, 1848.—I have felt to-day somewhat anxious about the fate of my book. The sale has surpassed expectation: but that proves only that people have formed a high idea of what they are to have. The disappointment, if there is disappointment, will be great. All that I hear is laudatory. But who can trust to praise that is poured into his own ear? At all events, I have aimed high; I have tried to do something that may be remembered; I have had the year 2000, or even 3000, often in my mind; I have sacrificed nothing to temporary fashions of thought and style; and if I fail, my failure will be more honorable than nine-tenths of the successes that I have witnessed."

"Dec. 12th, 1848.—Longman called. A new edition of three thousand copies is preparing as fast as they can work. I have reason to be pleased. Of the *Lay of the Last Minstrel* two

114

thousand two hundred and fifty copies were sold in the first year; of *Marmion* two thousand copies in the first month; of my book three thousand copies in ten days. Black says that there has been no such sale since the days of *Waverley*. The success is in every way complete beyond all hope and is the more agreeable to me because expectation had been wound up so high that disappointment was almost inevitable. I think, though with some misgivings, that the book will live."

"January 11th, 1849.—I am glad to find how well my book continues to sell. The second edition of three thousand was out of print almost as soon as it appeared, and one thousand two hundred and fifty of the third edition are already bespoken. I hope all this will not make me a coxcomb. I feel no intoxicating effect; but a man may be drunk without knowing it. If my abilities do not fail me, I shall be a rich man, as rich, that is to say, as I wish to be. But that I am already, if it were not for my dear ones. I am content, and should have been so with less. On the whole, I remember no success so complete, and I remember all Byron's poems and all Scott's novels."

"Saturday, January 27th.—Longman has written to say that only sixteen hundred copies are left of the third edition of five thousand, and that two thousand more copies must be immediately printed, still to be called the third edition. . . . Of such a run I had never dreamed. But I had thought that the book would have a permanent place in our literature, and I see no reason to alter that opinion."

"February 2d.—Mahon sent me a letter from Arbuthnot, saying that the Duke of Wellington was enthusiastic in admiration of my book. Though I am almost callous to praise now, this praise made me happy for two minutes. A fine old fellow!"

The above selections are from Macaulay's diary, as was said. Now come several from letters to a Mr. Ellis, to whom Macaulay sent many.

"March 8th, 1849.

"At last I have attained true glory. As I walked through Fleet Street the day before yesterday, I saw a copy of Hume at a book-seller's window with the following label: 'Only £2 2s. Hume's *History of England,* in eight volumes, highly valuable as an introduction to Macaulay.' I laughed so convulsively that the other people who were staring at the books took me for a poor demented gentleman. Alas for poor David! As for me, only one height of renown remains to be attained. I am not yet in Madam Tussaud's wax-works. I live, however, in hope of seeing one day an advertisement of a new group of figures—Mr. Macaulay, in one of his own coats, conversing with Mr. Silk Buckingham in Oriental costume, and Mr. Robert Montgomery in full canonicals."

"March 9th, 1850.

"I have seen the hippopotamus, both asleep and awake, and I can assure you that, awake or asleep, he is the ugliest of the works of God. But you must hear of my triumphs. Thackeray swears that he was eye-witness and ear-witness of the proudest event of my life. Two damsels were about to pass that doorway which we, on Monday, in vain attempted to enter, when I was pointed out to them. 'Mr. Macaulay,' cried the lovely pair. 'Is that Mr. Macaulay? Never mind the hippopotamus.' And having paid a shilling to see Behemoth, they left him in the very moment at which he was about to display himself to them in order to see—but spare my modesty. I can wish for nothing more on earth, now that Madam Tussaud, in whose Parthenon I once hoped for a place, is dead.''

In his diary of June 30th, 1849, we find: ''To-day my yearly account with Longman is wound up. I may now say that my book has run the gauntlet of criticism pretty thoroughly. The most savage and dishonest assailant has not been able to deny me merit as a writer. All critics who have the least pretense to impartiality have given me praise which I may be glad to think that I at all deserve.... I received a note from Prince Albert. He wants to see me at Buckingham Palace at three to-morrow. I answered like a courtier; yet what am I to say to him? For, of course, he wants to consult me about the Cambridge professorship. How can I be just at once to Stephen and to Kemble?''

''Saturday, July 1st.—To the Palace. The Prince, to my extreme astonishment, offered me the professorship, and very earnestly and with many flattering expressions, pressed me to accept it. I was resolute, and gratefully and respectfully declined. I should have declined, indeed, if only in order to give no ground to anybody to accuse me of foul play, for I have had difficulty enough in steering my course so as to deal properly both by Stephen and Kemble, and if I had marched off with the prize, I could not have been astonished if both had entertained a very unjust suspicion of me. But, in truth, my temper is that of the wolf in the fable, I cannot bear the collar, and I have got rid of much finer and richer collars than this. It would be strange if, having sacrificed for liberty, a seat in the Cabinet and twenty-five hundred pounds a year, I should now sacrifice liberty for a chair at Cambridge and four hundred pounds a year. Besides, I never could do two things at once. If I lectured well, my *History* must be given up, and to give up my *History* would be to give up much more than the emoluments of the professorship—if emolument were my chief object, which it is not now, nor ever was. The prince, when he found me determined, asked me about the other candidates.''

XXIV

DICKENS WRITES THE PICKWICK PAPERS

W E are always interested in the beginnings of a successful career, for humanity with all its selfishness takes a generous pleasure in the advancement of those who have made an honest fight for fame or wealth. The first success of Dickens came with the publication of the *Pickwick Papers,* by the publication of which the publishers, it is said, made $100,000,—much to their astonishment.

We all know the early career of the famous novelist: How he passed a boyhood of poverty; how he became a stenographer, a good one, for said a Mr. Beard, "There never was such a short-hand writer," at the time Dickens entered the gallery as a Parliament reporter; how he later became a reporter for the *Morning Chronicle.* In the December number of the *Old Monthly Magazine* his first published story saw the light. This was in 1833, when Dickens was twenty-one. The story first went under the name of *A Dinner at Poplar Walk,* but it afterwards was changed to *Mr. Mims and his Cousin.* Then came *Sketches by Boz* in 1835, and in 1836 *Pickwick* appeared in serial form, the book coming out a year later.

An amusing and striking illustration of the

widespread interest in the story of *Pickwick,* if we may call so rambling an account as *Pickwick* a story, is related by Carlyle: "An archdeacon with his own venerable lips repeated to me the other night a strange profane story: of a solemn clergyman who had been administering ghostly consolation to a sick person; having finished, satisfactorily as he thought, and got out of the room, he heard the sick person ejaculate, 'Well, thank God, *Pickwick* will be out in ten days any way!'— this is dreadful."

We are always interested in knowing whether the author received adequate remuneration for his work. Literature is not a commercial venture. The man who says, "Go to, now I shall make money by my pen!" is not the one who achieves a masterpiece. Nevertheless we are glad to know that genius is rewarded. It is more comforting to learn that Pope received $45,000 for his translations of Homer than that Milton got $25 for his *Paradise Lost;* that Scott received over $40,000 for *Woodstock,* a novel written in three months, than that the author of the *Canterbury Tales* two years before his death was obliged to petition the king, "for God's sake and as a work of charity," for the grant of a hogshead of wine yearly at the port of London.

Did Dickens receive anything for his *Pickwick?* Mr. Chapman, one of the publishers, told Mr. Forster, the friend and biographer of Dickens, that there was but a verbal agreement. The publishers were to pay 15 guineas for each number and as there were twenty numbers it is not hard to estimate his receipts on such a basis. The publishers, however, were to add to this compensation according to the sale. Mr. Chapman thinks that his firm paid about 3,000 pounds for *Pickwick*, but Mr. Forster thinks the sum was about 2,500 pounds. While this sum bears but a small proportion to what Dickens would have received had he made a good bargain with his publishers, it is yet a large sum to one beginning his literary career, and must have been deeply appreciated by Dickens, who had been so poor that he was paid 30 pounds in advance for the first two numbers, so that he might "go and get married."

Pickwick was soon followed by *Oliver Twist*, and then came *Nicholas Nickleby*, and the long series of successful novels that brought the author both fame and money. For when Dickens died he had a fortune of £93,000. Some of this was made in America, where his "readings" were attended by great crowds. On his second tour to America, after he had given thirty-seven readings, about one-half the entire number, he sent home a check for £10,000. Some evenings he took in $2,000.

One reason why Dickens is a popular novelist is that he understands the common emotions of humanity. He may be "stagey," be lacking in plot, given to exaggeration, indulge in cheap pathos, but in spite of all these defects his abounding vitality, his sympathy with the common lot, his imagination, are of such transcendent power that his world of readers adores the name of Dickens. Dickens was a good man. While not closely following the forms of religion, his life was better than that of many who follow the letter but break the spirit. As an illustration of his Christian belief I quote an extract from his letter to his youngest son, who was about to go to Australia:

September, 1868.

Never take a mean advantage of any one in any transaction, and never be hard upon people who are in your power. Try to do to others as you would have them do to you, and do not be discouraged if they fail sometimes. It is much better for you that they should fail in obeying the greatest rule laid down by our Saviour than that you should. I put a New Testament among your books for the very same reasons, and with the very same hopes, that made me write an easy account of it for you, when you were a little child. Because it is the best book that ever was, or will be, known in the world; and because it teaches you the best lessons by which any human creature, who tries to be truthful and faithful to duty, can possibly be guided. . . . You will remember that you have never at home been harassed about religious observances, or mere formalities—I have always been anxious not to weary my children with such things, before they are old enough to have opinions respecting them. You will therefore understand the better that I now most solemnly impress upon you the truth and beauty of the Christian Religion, as it came from Christ Himself, and the impossibility of your going far wrong if you humbly but heartily respect it. . . . Never abandon the wholesome practice of saying your own private prayers, night and morning. I have never abandoned it myself, and I know the comfort of it.

CHARLES DICKENS

XXV

MY first sight of Dickens, writes Herman Merivale in a gossipy article in an English magazine, was characteristic enough. I was in the second or third row of seats with some friends, at one of his readings of *Oliver Twist*. As Thackeray was a gossip on the platform, so Dickens was an actor. Like all speakers and actors, he longed for sympathy somewhere; an unanswering audience kills us, on whichever side the fault may lie. In the days of my political measles I have harangued a London audience for an hour and twenty minutes when I have meant to speak for a quarter of an hour; and in an out-of-the-way Hampshire district, where I had gone on purpose to address the rurals for a set hour, I have sate down, covered with confusion, in ten minutes, not being able to hit on anything that interested them at all. I saw too plainly, in all their good-natured faces, that they regarded me as the greatest ass they had ever seen, or as an odd kind of cow gone wrong, and of no use to the three acres. Dickens's audience that night was dull, and he became so, too. I was disappointed. His characters were not lifelike, and his acting was not good, and got

123

worse as he went on.   It was the inevitable law of reaction.   His audience bored him, and be began to bore me, amongst the rest.   He was not "in touch" with us, that is all; and his eyes wandered as hopelessly in search of some sympathetic eye to catch them, as the gladiators of old, for mercy in the circus.   Then suddenly, at one point of his reading, he had to introduce the passing character of a nameless individual in a London crowd, a choleric old gentleman who has only one short sentence to fire off.   This he gave so spontaneously, so inimitably, that the puppet became an absolute reality in a second.   I saw him, crowd, street, man, temper, and all.   For I am, I may say, what is called a very good audience.   I like what I like, and I hate what I hate; and on one occasion growled at the theater so audibly at what I thought some very bad acting that I began to hear ominous cries of "Turn him out!"   It was the first night of one of my own plays.   Dickens's electric flash bowled me over so completely and instantly that I broke into a peal of laughter, and as we sometimes do when hard hit, kept on laughing internally, which is half tears, and half hiccough, for some time afterwards.   Upon my word, I am laughing now, as I recall it.   It was so funny.   The audience of course glared at me with the well-known look of rebuke.   "How *dare* you express your feelings out loud, and disturb us!"

But Dickens's eye—I wasn't much more than a boy, and he didn't know me from Adam—went at once straight for mine.   "Here's somebody who likes me, anyhow," it said.   For the next few minutes he read at me, if ever man did.   The sympathetic unit is everything to us.   And on my word the result was that he so warmed to his work that he got the whole audience in his hand, and dispensed with me. Only once again—oh, how like him it was!—he fixed me with his eye just towards the end of the reading, and made a short but perceptible pause. I wondered what was coming—and soon knew. The choleric old party in the street had to appear for one passing instant more, and fire off one more passing sentence. Which he did—with the same results. Good heavens! what an actor Dickens was.

When that reading ended—with the success which it deserved—never did that most expressive of all human features, the eye, thank a boy more expressively. Over all things cultivate sympathy. If antipathy goes with it, so much the better. If the magnet must attract, it likewise must repel. Dickens was a magnet of the magnets; but in his case I must confess, that when a modern specimen tells me he can't laugh at him, he makes me feel rather as Heine felt when somebody told him that he—the somebody—was an atheist; frightened.

. . . Dickens is perhaps best described as to my immense amusement, and by the most delicious misprint I ever saw, I found myself once described in the "Visitors' List" in an English paper abroad—"Human Marvel, and family." It looked like some new kind of acrobat. Of Charles Dickens's great kindnesses to me in after days, and of some personal experiences of his stage passion, at the end of his life, I ventured to gossip with readers of the *Bar,* some months ago, in a paper called "With the Majority." In one sense, yes; but in another—in what a minority, Thackeray and he!

XXVI

ON THE DEATH OF DICKENS

WHEN Charles Dickens died the English papers and magazines were filled with criticisms and appreciations of the great writer. It may be interesting to glance at a few extracts from these:

From *Fraser's Magazine.*—On the eighth of June, 1870, the busiest brain and the busiest hand that ever guided pen over paper finished their appointed work, and that pen was laid aside forever. Words of its inditing were sure of immediately reaching and being welcomed by a larger number of men and women than those of any other living writer—perhaps of any writer who has ever lived.

About six o'clock on that summer evening, having done his day's work with habitual assiduity, Charles Dickens sat down to dinner with some members of his family. He had complained of headache, but neither he nor any one felt the least apprehension. The pain increased, the head drooped forward, and he never spoke again. Breathing went on for four-and-twenty hours, and then there was nothing left but . . . dismay and sorrow. When the sad news was made public it fell with the shock of a personal loss on the hearts of countless millions, to whom the name of the famous author was like that of an intimate and dear friend. . . .

Anthony Trollope in *St. Paul's.*—It seems to have been but the other day that, sitting where I now sit, in the same chair, at the same table, with the same familiar things around me, I wrote for the *Cornhill Magazine* a few lines in remembrance of Thackeray, who had then been taken from us, and when those lines appeared they were preceded by others, very full of feeling, from his much older friend, Charles Dickens. Now I take up my pen again because Charles Dickens has also gone, and because it is not fit that this publication should go forth without a word spoken to his honor.

It is singular that two men in age so nearly equal, in career so nearly allied, friends so old, and rivals so close, should each have left us so suddenly, without any of that notice, first doubting and then assured, which illness gives; so that in the case of the one as of the other, the tidings of death's dealings have struck us a hard and startling blow, inflicting not only sorrow, but for a while that positive, physical pain which comes from evil tidings which are totally unexpected. It was but a week or two since that I was discussing at the club that vexed question of American copyright with Mr. Dickens, and while differing from him somewhat, was wondering at the youthful vitality of the man who seemed to have done his forty years of work without having a trace of it left upon him to lessen his energy, or rob his feelings of their freshness. It was but the other day that he spoke at the Academy dinner, and those who heard him then heard him at his best; and those who did not hear him, but only read his words, felt how fortunate it was that there should be such a man to speak for literature on such an occasion. When he took farewell of the public as a public reader, a few months since, the public wondered that a man in the very prime of his capacity should retire from such a career. But though there was to be an end to his readings, there was not, therefore, to be an end of his labors. He was to resume, and did resume, his old work, and when the first number of *Edwin Drood's Mystery* was bought up with unprecedented avidity by the lovers of Dickens's stories, it was feared, probably, by none but one that he might not live to finish his chronicle. He was a man, as we all thought, to live to be a hundred. He looked to be full of health, he walked vigorously, he stood, and spoke, and, above all, he laughed like a man in the full vigor of his life. . . .

He would attempt nothing—show no interest in anything—which he could not do, and which he did not understand. But he was not on that account forced to confine himself to literature. Every one knows how he read. Most readers of these lines, though they may never have seen him act,—as I never did,—still know that his acting was excellent. As an actor he would have been at the top of his profession. And he had another gift,—had it so wonderfully, that it may almost be said that he has left no equal behind him. He spoke so well, that a public dinner became a blessing instead of a curse, if he was in the chair,—had its compensating twenty minutes of pleasure, even if he were called upon to propose a toast, or to thank the company for drinking his health. For myself, I never could tell how far his speeches were ordinarily prepared:—but I can declare that I have heard him speak admirably when he has had to do so with no moment of preparation.

A great man has gone from us—such a one that we may surely say of him that we shall not look upon his like again. As years roll on, we shall learn to appreciate his loss. He now rests in the spot consecrated to the memory of our greatest and noblest; and Englishmen would certainly not have been contented had he been laid elsewhere.

XXVII

WE are fortunate in having Ruskin's own account of how he passed his childhood days. In *Præterita* we have his autobiography. His description of his early days runs as follows:

"I am and my father was before me a violent Tory of the old school (Walter Scott's school, that is to say, and Homer's); I name these two out of the numberless great Tory writers, because they were my own two masters. I had Walter Scott's novels and the *Iliad* (Pope's translation), for my only reading when I was a child, on weekdays; on Sunday their effect was tempered by *Robinson Crusoe* and the *Pilgrim's Progress,* my mother having it deeply in her heart to make an evangelical clergyman of me. Fortunately, I had an aunt more evangelical than her mother, and my aunt gave me cold mutton for Sunday's dinner, which, as I much preferred it hot, greatly diminished the influence of the *Pilgrim's Progress,* and the end of the matter was, that I got all of the imaginative teachings of De Foe and Bunyan, and yet—am not an evangelical clergyman.

"I had, however, still better teaching than theirs, and that compulsorily, and every day of the week.

"Walter Scott and Pope's Homer were reading of my own election, but my mother forced me, by steady daily toil, to learn long chapters of the Bible by heart, as well as to read it every syllable through, aloud, hard names and all, from Genesis to the Apocalypse, about once a year: and to that discipline—patient, accurate, and resolute—I owe, not only a knowledge of the book, which I find occasionally serviceable, but much of my general power of taking pains, and the best part of my taste in literature. From Walter Scott's novels I might easily, as I grew older, have fallen to other people's novels; and Pope might, perhaps, have led me to take Johnson's English, or Gibbon's, as types of language; but once knowing the 32d of Deuteronomy, or the 119th Psalm, the 15th of 1st Corinthians, the Sermon on the Mount, and most of the Apocalypse, every syllable by heart, and having always a way of thinking with myself what words meant, it was not possible for me, even in the foolishest times of youth, to write entirely superficial or formal English, and the affectation of trying to write like Hooker or George Herbert was the most innocent I could have fallen into."

*   *   *   *   *   *   *   *

"As years went on, and I came to be four or five years old he (the father) could command a post-chaise and pair for two months in the summer, by help of which, with my mother and me, he went the round of his country customers (who liked to see the principal of the house his own traveler); so that, at a jog-trot pace, and through the panoramic opening of the four windows of a post-chaise, made more panoramic still to me because my seat was a little bracket in front (for we used to hire the chaise regularly for the two months out of Long Acre, and so could have it bracketed and pocketed as we liked), I saw all the highroads, and most of the cross ones, of England and Wales, and great part of lowland Scotland, as far as Perth, where every other year we spent the whole summer; and I used to read the *Abbot* at Kinross, and the *Monastery* at Glen Farg, which I used to confuse with 'Glendearg,' and thought that the White Lady had as certainly lived by the streamlet in the glen of the Ochlis, as the Queen of Scots in the island of Loch Leven.

"To my farther benefit, as I grew older, I thus saw nearly all the noblemen's houses in England, in reverent and healthy delight of uncovetous admiration,—perceiving, as soon as I could perceive any political truth at all, that it was probably much happier to live in a small house, and have Warwick castle to be astonished at, than to live in Warwick castle and have nothing to be astonished at; but that, at all events, it would not make Brunswick Square in the least more pleasantly habitable, to pull Warwick castle down."

*   *   *   *   *   *   *   *

"Contented, by reason of these occasional glimpses of the rivers of Paradise, I lived until I was more than four years old in Hunter Street, Brunswick Square, the greater part of the year; for a few weeks in the summer breathing country air, by taking lodgings in small cottages (real cottages, not villas, so-called) either about Hampstead, or at Dulwich, at 'Mrs. Ridley's,' the last of a row in a lane which led out into the Dulwich fields on one side, and was itself full of buttercups in spring, and blackberries in autumn. But my chief remaining impressions of those days are attached to Hunter Street. My mother's general principles of first treatment were, to guard me with steady watchfulness from all avoidable pain or danger, and, for the rest, to let me amuse myself as I liked, provided I was neither fretful or troublesome. But the law was, that I should find my own amusement. No toys of any kind were at first allowed, and the pity of my Croydon aunt for my monastic poverty in this respect was boundless. On one of my birthdays, thinking to overcome my mother's resolution by splendor of temptation, she bought the most radiant Punch and Judy she could find in the Soho bazaar, as big as a real Punch and Judy, all dressed in scarlet and gold, and that would dance, tied to the leg of a chair. I must have been greatly impressed, for I remember well the look of the two figures, as my aunt herself exhibited their virtues. My mother was obliged to accept them, but afterward quietly told me it was not right that I should have them, and I never saw them again.

"Nor did I painfully wish, what I was never permitted for an instant to hope, or even imagine, the possession of such things as one saw in toy-shops. I had a bunch of keys to play with, as long as I was capable only of pleasure in what glittered and jingled, as I grew older I had a cart and a ball, and when I was five or six years old, two boxes of well-cut wooden bricks. With these modest, but I still think, entirely sufficient possessions, and being always summarily whipped if I cried, did not do as I was bid, or tumbled on the stairs, I soon attained serene and secure methods of life and motion, and could pass my days contentedly in tracing the squares and comparing the colors of my carpet; examining the knots in the wood of the floor or counting the bricks in the opposite houses; with rapturous intervals of excitement during the filling of the water-cart, through its leathern pipe, from the dripping iron post at the pavement edge; or the still more admirable proceedings of the turncock, when he turned and turned till a fountain sprang up in the middle of the street. But the carpet, and what patterns I could find in bed-covers, dresses, or wall papers to be examined, were my chief resources, and my attention to the particulars in these was soon so accurate, that when at three and a half I was taken to have my portrait painted by Mr. Northcote, I had not been ten minutes alone with him before I asked him why there were holes in his carpet.''

ROBERT BROWNING

From the portrait by Field Talfourd

XXVIII

WHEN Wordsworth heard of the marriage of Robert Browning to Elizabeth Barrett, he is reported to have said, "So Robert Browning and Miss Barrett have gone off together. I hope they understand each other—nobody else would." When Wordsworth said this he was an old man and like most old men unable to appreciate the new. Compared with the simplicity of much of Wordsworth's poetry a poem like *A Death in the Desert* might seem unintelligible; but surely the same objection cannot be urged against the poetry of Mrs. Browning.

The marriage of Robert Browning to Miss Barrett is the one dramatic event in his quiet life. To one who has read his passionate and at times fiery, unconventional poetry, the runaway, unconventional marriage is not unaccountable, but altogether consistent. The manner of it was thus:

In her youth Miss Barrett became an invalid through an injury to her spine, an accident occurring while she was fixing the saddle of her riding horse. As she grew older she was confined to her room. To move from a bed to a sofa seemed a perilous adventure requiring a family discussion. Her father was a strange, unaccountable man, selfish and obstinate, and passionately jealous of the affection of his children. In the meantime Miss Barrett had written poetry that attracted the attention of a kindred spirit. Robert Browning in 1845 wrote to her saying that he had once nearly met her and that his sensations then were those of one who had come to the outside of a chapel of marvelous illumination and found the door barred against him. A little later he suggested that he would like to call on her. This commonplace and altogether natural suggestion threw the invalid into a state of tremulous disapproval. With robust insistence Robert replied, "If my truest heart's wishes avail, you shall laugh at east winds yet as I do." Miss Barrett replied, "There is nothing to see in me nor to hear in me. I never learned to talk as you do in London, although I can admire that brightness of carved speech in Mr. Kenyon and others. If my poetry is worth anything to any eye, it is the flower of me. I have lived most and been most happy in it, and so it has all my colors. The rest of me is nothing but a root fit for the ground and dark." A reply such as this would be construed by any gentleman as a challenge. The substance of Browning's reply was, "I will call at two on Tuesday."

On May 20, 1845, they met. In September, 1846, Miss Barrett walked quietly out of her father's house, was married in a church, and afterwards returned to her father's house as though nothing had happened. Between the marriage and the elopement Robert Browning did not call at the Barrett house on Wimpole Street. One of his biographers says that this absence was due to an inability of Browning to ask the maid at the door for Miss Barrett when there no longer was a Miss Barrett whom he wished to see.

In passing judgment upon the elopement of this remarkable couple one must remember that they were no longer giddy and rash youth. Browning was thirty-four and the romantic Juliet was three years older. Again it must be remembered that the objecting father was a most unreasonable and selfish man. The climax of his selfishness was reached when in opposition to the advice of the physicians Mr. Barrett refused to allow his daughter to go to Italy. "In the summer of 1846," writes Mr. Chesterton, "Elizabeth Barrett was still living under the great family convention which provided her with nothing but an elegant deathbed, forbidden to move, forbidden to see proper daylight, forbidden to see a friend lest the shock should destroy her suddenly. A year or two later, in Italy, as Mrs. Browning, she was being dragged up hill in a wine hamper, toiling up the crests of mountains at four o'clock in the morning, riding for five miles on to what she calls 'an inaccessible volcanic ground not far from the stars.'"

Miss Mitford, the literary gossip of the period, writes a letter to Charles Bonar, in which she gives expression to an opinion concerning Browning's poetry which is not dissimilar to the one we quoted from Wordsworth. Miss Mitford was an intimate friend of Elizabeth Barrett:

"The great news of the season is the marriage of my beloved friend Elizabeth Barrett to Robert Browning. I have seen him once only, many years ago. He is, I hear from all quarters, a man of immense attainment and great conversational power. As a poet I think him overrated. . . . Those things on which his reputation rests, *Paracelsus* and *Bells and Pomegranates,* are to me as so many riddles."

In a later letter she writes to the same correspondent: "I at Miss Barrett's wedding! Ah, dearest Mr. Bonar, it was a runaway match. Never was I so much astonished. He prevailed on her to meet him at church with only the two necessary witnesses. They went to Paris. There they stayed a week. Happening to meet with Mrs. Jameson, she joined them in their journey to Pisa; and accordingly they traveled by diligence, by Rhone boat,—anyhow,—to Marseilles, thence took shipping to Leghorn, and then settled themselves at Pisa for six months. She says she is very happy. God grant it continue! I felt just exactly as if I had heard that Dr. Chambers had given her over when I got the letter announcing her marriage, and found that she was about to cross to France. I never had an idea of her reaching Pisa alive. She took her own maid and her (dog) Flush. I saw Mr. Browning once. Many of his friends and mine, William Harness, John Kenyon, and Henry Chorley, speak very highly of him. I suppose he is an accomplished man, and if he makes his angelic wife happy, I shall of course learn to like him."

The runaway match proved to be a most happy one. This is in disproof of the common thought that a poet is of so sensitive and irritable a disposition that no woman should expect a calm life with a poet. But in this case we have two distinguished poets joining hands. They lived in great happiness, nor was this peace and harmony purchased at the price of servitude and humility of the one. Each respected the other. Their romantic passion was based on a spiritual affinity. The love letters of the Brownings may have some degree of obscurity, but it should be said that the obscurity is one of expression, not the obscurity of misunderstanding in the sense in which some of the Carlyle letters are obscure. The list of literary men whose marriages have proved unhappy is not so long and distinguished as is commonly supposed. Milton, Landor, Coleridge, Shelley, Byron, and Ruskin are conspicuous examples of men who made shipwreck of marriage, but in contrast shine forth the names of Browning, Tennyson, Wordsworth, and Shakspere, for there is no evidence against the belief that Shakspere's marriage was a happy one; then add to these the American names, Longfellow, Lowell, Emerson, Hawthorne, and Holmes, and the list is still incomplete.

In verse Mrs. Browning has most exquisitely expressed the power of love to transform the gloom of her sick-room into the wholesome sunshine of life,—

I saw in gradual vision through my tears,
The sweet, sad years, the melancholy years,
Those of my own life, who by turn had flung
A shadow across me. Straightway I was 'ware,
So weeping, how a mystic shape did move
Behind me, and drew me backward by the hair;
And a voice said in mastery, while I strove,
''Guess now who holds thee?''—''Death!'' I said.
    But, there,
The silver answer rang. ''Not Death, but Love.''

XXIX

S HORTLY after Browning's death a young man published his recollections of the poet in an English magazine. The extracts from that article will help one to appreciate the kindliness of the great poet.

"My first meeting with Browning came about in this wise. I was sitting in the studio of a famous sculptor, who, kindly forgetful of my provincial rawness, was entertaining me with anecdotes of his great contemporaries; amongst them, Browning. To name him was to undo the floodgates of my young enthusiasm. Would my sculptor friend help me to meet the poet, whose teaching had been my only dogma? 'Oh,' said my friend, 'that's easy. Write to him—he is the most amiable fellow in the world—and tell him about yourself, and tell him how much you want to know him. Say, if you like, that you are a friend of mine.' The advice seemed simple but useless. I felt that not even the portfolio of unpublished poems which the imaginative eye might have beheld palpable under my arm could so fortify my modesty. But my friend assured me that Browning would not be offended, so, after waiting some weeks for my crescent courage, I wrote....

140

"I was taken up to his study and shown in. The first thing that struck me was that he had built up a barrier of books around his table, perhaps because he feared a too practical enthusiasm. Huge heaps of books lay on the floor, the chairs, the table, and at first I thought the room otherwise unoccupied. But suddenly a dapper little figure emerged from a huge armchair by the fire, and stepped briskly across the room. For a moment I was bewildered. The poet's face was familiar in photographs, but I had somehow imagined him a tall, gaunt man. I recovered myself to find him standing before me, holding both my hands and saying, 'Now this is really very kind of you, to come so far just to see an old man like me.' Then he dragged up a companion chair and forced me into it, standing for some moments by my side, with his hand on my shoulder. Then he sat down and said, 'Well, tell me all about yourself. Have you not brought some of your poems to show me?' Of course I had not. I wanted to see him and talk of his work. But for a while he would not let me do so. 'We'll talk about me later, if you like, though I'm rather tired of the subject,' he said, and proceeded to question me pretty closely about my aim and work. Then he sat and thought awhile, then came across to me and said, 'Do you know that I was nearly fifty before I made any money out of my writings? That's the truth, and you will understand my reluctance to advise any one to embark on such a cruel career. But—if you really mean to go in for it—I would do anything I could to shorten your time of waiting. So you must just send me some of your work, that I may give you my candid opinion, if you think it's worth having. And now come and see my books.'

. . . "We went down to lunch, and I was introduced to the poet's sister, who is, I was instantly ready to aver, the most charming little lady in the world. I don't remember much of the talk at lunch—except that it turned on Ruskin and his art views, with which latter, it seemed to me, Browning had not much sympathy. He told me two anecdotes designed to prove Ruskin's technical inaccuracy; one relating to Michael Angelo, the other to Browning's own exquisite poem, *Andrea del Sarto*. 'But never mind,' said Browning, 'he writes like an angel.'

"Lunch was finished, and my host apologized for having to turn me out, as he was obliged to attend some 'preposterous meeting,' he said. I was standing in the hall, saying good-by, when suddenly he turned and ran up-stairs. Presently he returned, bringing with him a copy of his wife's poems. 'Will you take this as a record of what I hope is only the first of many meetings?' he said. 'I can't find any of my own in that muddle upstairs, but I would rather you would have this than any of mine.' Yes, I took it, as proud as a boy could be who receives such an honor from his chief idol; prouder than I shall ever be again as I read the inscription: 'With the best wishes and regards of Robert Browning.' And I went away after he had made me promise —as though it were a thing I might be unwilling to do—to let him know when I should be next in town.

. . . "I called again at the beautiful house in De Vere Gardens. The poet had just come in, he told me, from a meeting of the committee for the memorial to Matthew Arnold, and he was evidently very depressed by the sad thoughts which had come upon him of his 'dear old friend, Mat.' 'I have been thinking all the way home,' he said, 'of his hardships. He told me once, when I asked him why he had written no poetry lately, that he could not afford to do it; but that, when he had saved enough, he intended to give up all other work, and go back to poetry. I wonder if he has gone back to it *now*.' Here Browning's voice shook, and he was altogether more deeply moved than I had ever seen him. 'It's very hard, isn't it?' he went on, 'that a useless fellow like me should have been able to give up all his life to it—for, as I think I told you, my father helped me to publish my early books—while a splendid poet like Arnold actually could not afford to write the poetry we wanted of him.'

. . . "The last visit I paid to Browning was short enough, but since it *was* the last, and was marked by one of the most graceful acts ever done to me, I may record it as the conclusion of these memories. He had written inviting me to call soon, but without naming a day or hour. 'If I should happen to be engaged,' he had said, 'I know that your kindness will understand and forgive me.' So I called on the first morning when I was free for an hour. He came across the room with his accustomed heartiness of voice and hand. 'But, my dear boy, why did you come today? In ten minutes I have an important business appointment which I *must* keep.' The ten minutes went all too soon, and I took my hat to go. He was profuse, but plainly sincere, in his apologies for turning me out, and made me promise to come again at a specified hour. I had hardly left the door, when I heard the scurry of footsteps and his voice calling me. I turned and saw him, hatless, at the foot of the steps. 'One moment,' he cried; 'I can't let you go till you tell me again that you are not offended, and I shan't believe *that* till you promise once again to come. Now, promise'—holding both my hands. Of course I promised, wondering how many smaller men would have shown the same courtesy. For some reason on my part, which I now forget, that appointment was never kept, and I saw him no more.

"As I stood in Poet's Corner that bitter day of last January, and saw him put to rest, I could not but think of him as I had seen him last, with the sunlight on his white hair, and I felt his warm hands, and heard his kindly voice saying, 'Now, promise!' and I could but think of that meeting as a tryst not broken, but deferred. And as I thought again of that life, so rich, so vivid, so complete; of that strong soul which looked ever forth, and saw promise of clear awaking to something nobler than the sweetest dream, I knew that here, at least, was one to whom death could do no wrong."

—Adapted from *Littell's Living Age.*

ALFRED TENNYSON

From a photograph from life

XXX

WILLIAM KNIGHT, a celebrated Scotch professor and the great expounder of the life and poetry of Wordsworth, in 1890 spent two days with Tennyson at Farringford. In an English magazine he has published his reminiscence of that visit. After relating the feelings of respect and the reverential sentiment with which he approached the place he says: "In the avenue leading to the house, the spreading trees just opening into leaf, with spring flowers around and beneath—yellow cowslips and blue forget-me-nots—and the song of birds in the branches overhead, seemed a fitting prelude to all that followed. Shortly after I was seated in the ante-room, the poet's son appeared, and, as his father was engaged, he said, 'Come and see my mother.' We went into the drawing-room, where the old lady was reclining on a couch. Immediately the lines beginning 'Such age, how beautiful' came into mind. No one could ever forget his first sight of Lady Tennyson, her graciousness, and the radiant though fragile beauty of old age. Both her eye and her voice had an inexpressible charm. She inquired with much interest for the widow of one of my colleagues at the University, who used formerly to live in the island, close to Farringford, and whose family were friends as well as near neighbors. Soon afterwards Tennyson entered, and almost at once proposed that we should go out of doors. After a short stroll on the lawn under the cedars, we went into the 'careless ordered garden,' walked round it, and then sat down in the small summer-house. It is a quaint rectangular garden, sloping to the west, where nature and art blend happily, —orchard trees, and old-fashioned flower-beds, with stately pines around, giving to it a sense of perfect rest. This garden is truly a 'haunt of ancient peace.' Left there alone with the bard for some time, I felt that I sat in the presence of one of the Kings of Men. His aged look impressed me. There was the keen eagle eye, and, although the glow of youth was gone, the strength of age was in its place. The lines in his face were like the furrows in the stem of a wrinkled oak-tree, but his whole bearing disclosed a latent strength and nobility, a reserve of power, combined with a most courteous grace of manner. I was also struck by the negligé air of the man, so different from that of Browning or Arnold or Lowell. . . .

"We talked much of the sonnet. He thought the best in the language were Milton's, Shakspere's, and Wordsworth's; after these three those by his own brother Charles. He said, 'I at least like my brother's next to those by the "three immortals." ' . . .

"He had no great liking, he said, for arranging the poets in a hierarchy. He found so much that surpassed him in different ways in all the great ones; but he thought that Homer, Æschylus, Sophocles, Virgil, Dante, Shakspere, and Goethe,

—these seven,—were the greatest of the great, up to the year 1800. They are not all equal in rank, and even in the work of that heptarchy of genius, there were trivial things to be found. . . .

"Just at this stage of our talk Mrs. Hallam Tennyson, Mrs. Douglas Freshfield, and her daughter came up the garden-walk to the summer-house. Miss Freshfield wore a hat on which was an artificial flower, a lilac-branch. It at once caught Tennyson's eye. There was a lilac-tree in bloom close at hand, and he said, 'What is that you are wearing? It's a flowery lie, it's a speaking mendacity.' He asked how she could wear such a thing in the month of May! We rose from the bower, and all went down the garden-walk to see the fig-tree at the foot of it, and sundry other things at the western entrance-door, where Miss Kate Greenaway was painting. We returned along a twisting alley under the rich green foliage of elms and ilexes. . . .

"Listening to the wind in the trees and the sound of running water—although it was the very tiniest of rillets—led us away from philosophy, and he talked of Sir Walter Scott, characterizing him as the greatest novelist of all time. He said, 'What a gift it was that Scotland gave to the world in him. And your Burns! He is supreme amongst your poets.' He praised Lockhart's *Life of Scott*, as one of the finest of biographies; and my happening to mention an anecdote of Scott from that book led to our spending the greater part of the rest of our walk in the telling of stories. Tennyson was an admirable storyteller. He asked me for some good Scotch anecdotes, and I gave him some, but he was able to cap each of them with a better one of his own—all of which he told with arch humor and simplicity.

"He then told some anecdotes of a visit to Scotland. After he had left an inn in the island of Skye, the landlord was asked, 'Did he know who had been staying in his house? It was the poet Tennyson.' He replied, 'Lor', to think o' that! and sure I thoucht he was a shentleman!' Near Stirling the same remark was made to the keeper of the hotel where he had stayed. 'Do you ken who you had wi' you t' other night?' 'Naa, but he was a pleesant shentleman.' 'It was Tennyson, the poet.' 'An' what may *he* be?' 'Oh, he is the writer o' verses such as you see i' the papers.' 'Noo, to think o' that, jest a pooblic writer, an' I gied him ma best bedroom!' Of Mrs. Tennyson, however, the landlord remarked, 'Oh, but *she* was an angel!'

"I have said that the conversational power of Tennyson struck me quite as much as his poetry had done for forty years. To explain this I must compare it with that of some of his contemporaries. It was not like the meteoric flashes and fireworks of Carlyle's talk, which sometimes dazzled as much as it instructed, and it had not that torrent-rush in which Carlyle so often indulged. It was far more restrained. It had neither the continuousness nor the range of Browning's many-sided conversation, nor did it possess the charm of the ethereal visionariness of Newman's. It lacked the fullness and consummate sweep of Mr. Ruskin's talk, and it had neither the historic range and brilliance of Dean Stanley's, nor the fascinating subtlety—the elevation and the depth combined—of that of the late F. D. Maurice. *But* it was clear as crystal, and calm as well as clear. It was terse and exact, precise and luminous. Not a word was wasted and every phrase was suggestive. Tennyson did not monopolize conversation. He wished to know what other people thought, and therefore to hear them state it, that he might understand their position and ideas. But in all his talk on great problems, he at once got to their essence, sounding their depths with ease, or, to change the illustration, he seized the kernel, and let the shell and fragments alone. There was a wonderful simplicity allied to his clear vision and his strength. He was more child-like than the majority of his contemporaries, and along with this there was— what I have already mentioned—*a great reserve of power*. His appreciation of other workers belonging to his time was remarkable. Neither he nor Browning disparaged their contemporaries, as Carlyle so often did, when he spotted their weaknesses, and put them in the pillory. From first to last, Tennyson seemed to look sympathetically on all good works, and he had a special veneration for the strong silent thinkers and workers.

"Tennyson appreciated the work of Darwin and Spencer far more than Carlyle did, and many of the ideas and conclusions of modern science are to be found in his poetry. Nevertheless he knew the limitation of science, and he held that it was the noble office of poetry, philosophy, and religion combined to supplement and finally to transcend it."

XXXI

ON Christmas day, 1832, Emerson sailed out of Boston harbor to pay a visit to Europe. His health needed a change of work and scene. His wife had died, he had separated from his congregation, he manifestly was in need of some recreation, and so his friends had advised him to take a trip abroad. On the 2d of February he landed at Malta. From there he traveled through Italy and finally entered England, ready to make the acquaintance of English celebrities whom he had long admired.

He writes in his journal: "Carlisle in Cumberland, Aug. 26. I am just arrived in merry Carlisle from Dumfries. A white day in my years. I found the youth I sought in Scotland, and good and wise and pleasant he seems to me, and his wife a most accomplished, agreeable woman. Truth and peace and faith dwell with them and beautify them. I never saw more amiableness than is in his countenance."

This passage, of course, refers to his visit to Carlyle, to visit whom Emerson had driven over from Dumfries to Craigenputtock, where Carlyle had been living for the last five years. In this connection it is interesting to read what the man

RALPH WALDO EMERSON
From a wood engraving of a life photograph

visited had to say about his visitor: "That man," Carlyle said to Lord Houghton, "came to see me. I don't know what brought him, and we kept him one night, and then he left us. I saw him go up the hill; I didn't go with him to see him descend. I preferred to watch him mount and vanish like an angel."

In writing of this interview, Mr. Cabot, one of the biographers of Emerson, says: "To Emerson the interview was a happy one, and gratified the chief wish he had in coming to England, though he did not find all that he had sought. He had been looking for a master, but in the deepest matters Carlyle, he found, had nothing to teach him. 'My own feeling,' he says in a letter to Mr. Ireland a few days afterwards, 'was that I had met with men of far less power who had got greater insight into religious truth.' But he had come close to the affectionate nature and the nobility of soul that lay behind the cloud of whim and dyspepsia, and he kept to that, and for the rest, confined his expectations thenceforth to what Carlyle had to give. 'The greatest power of Carlyle,' he afterwards wrote, 'like that of Burke, seems to me to reside in the form. Neither of them is a poet, born to announce the will of the god, but each has a splendid rhetoric to clothe the truth.' "

During this first visit Emerson dined with Lafayette and a hundred Americans. By the time he made his second visit Emerson was a far more distinguished man than during his first trip. His second visit was made in 1847. This time he was a lion among men. He again calls on the Carlyles. This time the door is opened by Jane.

"They were very little changed (he writes)

from their old selves of fourteen years ago, when I left them at Craigenputtock. 'Well,' said Carlyle, 'here we are, shoveled together again.' The flood-gates of his talk are quickly opened and the river is a great and constant stream. We had large communication that night until nearly one o'clock, and at breakfast next morning it began again. At noon or later we went together, Carlyle and I, to Hyde Park and the palaces, about two miles from here, to the National Gallery, and to the Strand—Carlyle melting all Westminster and London down into his talk and laughter as he walked. We came back to dinner at five or later, then Dr. Carlyle came in and spent the evening, which again was long by the clock, but had no other measure. Here in this house we breakfast about nine; Carlyle is very apt, his wife says, to sleep till ten or eleven, if he has no company. An immense talker he is, and altogether as extraordinary in his conversation as in his writing—I think even more so. You will never discover his real vigor and range, or how much more he might do than he has ever done, without seeing him. I find my few hours' discourse with him in Scotland, long since, gave me not enough knowledge of him, and I have now at last been taken by surprise. . . . Carlyle and his wife live on beautiful terms. Nothing could be more engaging than their ways, and in her book-case all his books are inscribed to her, as they came, from year to year, each with some significant lines."

In another place he writes:

"I had good talk with Carlyle last night. He says over and over for years, the same thing. Yet his guiding genius is his moral sense, his perception of the sole importance of truth and justice, and he too says that there is properly no religion in England. He is quite contemptuous about *Kunst* (art) also, in Germans, or English, or Americans. . . . His sneers and scoffs are thrown in every direction. He breaks every sentence with a scoffing laugh—'windbag,' 'monkey,' 'donkey,' 'bladder;' and let him describe whom he will, it is always 'poor fellow.' I said 'What a fine fellow you are to bespatter the whole world with this oil of vitriol!' 'No man,' he replied, 'speaks truth to me.' I said, 'See what a crowd of friends listen to and admire you.' 'Yes, they come to hear me, and they read what I write; but not one of them has the smallest intention of doing these things.' "

While Emerson was in London he was elected to membership in the Athenæum Club, during his stay in England. Here he had the opportunity of meeting many famous men. He writes:

"Milnes and other good men are always to be found there. Milnes is the most good-natured man in England, made of sugar; he is everywhere and knows everything. He told of Landor that one day, in a towering passion, he threw his cook out of the window, and then presently exclaimed, 'Good God, I never thought of those violets!' The last time he saw Landor he found him expatiating on our custom of eating in company, which he esteems very barbarous. He eats alone, with half-closed windows, because the light interferes with the taste. He has lately heard of some tribe in Crim Tartary who have the practice of eating alone, and these he extols as much superior to the English. . . . Macaulay is the king of diners-out.

I do not know when I have seen such wonderful vivacity. He has the strength of ten men, immense memory, fun, fire, learning, politics, manners, and pride, and talks all the time in a steady torrent. You would say he was the best type of England.''

Of Tennyson he writes: ''I saw Tennyson, first at the house of Coventry Patmore, where we dined together. I was contented with him at once. He is tall and scholastic looking, no dandy, but a great deal of plain strength about him, and though cultivated, quite unaffected. Quiet, sluggish sense and thought; refined, as all English are, and good-humored. There is in him an air of great superiority that is very satisfactory. He lives with his college set, . . . and has the air of one who is accustomed to be petted and indulged by those he lives with. Take away Hawthorne's bashfulness, and let him talk easily and fast, and you would have a pretty good Tennyson. I told him that his friends and I were persuaded that it was important to his health to make an instant visit to Paris, and that I was to go on Monday if he was ready. He was very good-humored, and affected to think that I should never come back alive from France; it was death to go. But he had been looking for two years for somebody to go to Italy with, and was ready to set out at once, if I would go there. . . . He gave me a cordial invitation to his lodgings (in Buckingham Palace), where I promised to visit him before I went away. . . . I found him at home in his lodgings, but with him was a clergyman whose name I did not know, and there was no conversation. He was sure again that he was taking a final farewell

of me, as I was going among the French bullets,
but promised to be in the same lodgings if I should
escape alive. . . . Carlyle thinks him the best
man in England to smoke a pipe with, and used
to see him much; had a place in his little garden,
on the wall, where Tennyson's pipe was laid up.''

XXXII

ANOTHER poet whom I knew at Oxford as an undergraduate, and whom I watched and admired to the end of his life, was Matthew Arnold. He was beautiful as a young man, strong and manly, yet full of dreams and schemes. His Olympian manners began even at Oxford; there was no harm in them, they were natural, not put on. The very sound of his voice and the wave of his hand were Jovelike. . . . Sometimes at public dinners, when he saw himself surrounded by his contemporaries, most of them judges, bishops, and ministers, he would groan over the drudgery he had to go through every day of his life in examining dirty school-boys and school-girls. But he saw the fun of it, and laughed. What a pity it was that his friends —and he had many—could find no better place for him. Most of his contemporaries rose to high position in Church and State, he remained to the end an examiner of elementary schools. Of course it may be said that like so many of his literary friends, he might have written novels and thus eked out a living by potboilers of various kinds. But there was something nobler and refined in him which restrained his pen from such

work. Whatever he gave to the world was to be
perfect, as perfect as he could make it, and he
did not think that he possessed the talent for
novels. His saying that "no Arnold can ever
write a novel" is well known, but it has been
splendidly falsified of late by his own niece.
Arnold was a delightful man to argue with, not
that he could easily be convinced that he was
wrong, but he never lost his temper, and in the
most patronizing way he would generally end by,
"Yes, yes! my good fellow, you are quite right,
but, you see, my view of the matter is different,
and I have little doubt it is the true one!" This
went so far that even the simplest facts failed to
produce any impression on him. . . .

Ruskin often came to spend a few days with his
old friends, and as uncompromising and severe
as he could be when he wielded his pen, he was
always most charming in conversation. He never,
when he was with his friends, claimed the right
of speaking with authority, even on his own
special subjects, as he might well have done. It
seemed to be his pen that made him say bitter
things. . . . He was really the most tolerant and
agreeable man in society. He could discover
beauty where no one else saw it, and make allowance where others saw no excuse. I remember
him as diffident as a young girl, full of questions,
and grateful for any information. Even on art
topics I have watched him listening almost defer-
entially to others who laid down the law in his
presence. His voice was always most winning,
and his language simply perfect. He was one of
the few Englishmen I knew who, instead of tum-
bling out their sentences like so many portman-

teaus, bags, tugs, and hat-boxes from an open railway van, seemed to take a real delight in building up his sentences, even in familiar conversation, so as to make each deliverance a work of art. . . .

And what a beautiful mind his was, and what lessons of beauty he has taught us all. At the same time, he could not bear anything unbeautiful, and anything low or ignoble in men revolted him and made him thoroughly unhappy. I remember once taking Emerson to lunch with him, in his rooms in Corpus Christi College. Emerson was an old friend of his, and in many respects a cognate soul. But some quite indifferent subject turned up, a heated discussion ensued, and Ruskin was so upset that he had to quit the room and leave us alone. Emerson was most unhappy, and did all he could to make peace, but he had to leave without a reconciliation. . . .

Another though less frequent visitor to Oxford was Tennyson. His first visit to our house was rather alarming. We lived in a small house in High Street, nearly opposite Magdalen College, and our establishment was not calculated to receive sudden guests, particularly a poet laureate. He stepped in one day during the long vacation, when Oxford was almost empty. Wishing to show the great man all civility, we asked him to dinner that night and breakfast the next morning. At that time almost all the shops were in the market, which closed at one o'clock. My wife, a young housekeeper, did her best for our unexpected guest. He was known to be a gourmand, and at dinner he was evidently put out by finding the sauce with the salmon was not the one he preferred. He was pleased, however, with the wing of a chicken, and said it was the only advantage he got from being a poet laureate, that he generally received the liver-wing of a chicken. The next morning at breakfast, we had rather plumed ourselves on having been able to get a dish of cutlets, and were not a little surprised when our guest arrived, to see him whip off the cover of a hot dish, and to hear the exclamation, "Mutton chops! the staple of every bad inn in England." However, these were but minor matters, though not without importance in the eyes of a young wife to whom Tennyson had been like one of the immortals. He was full of interest and inquiries about the East, more particularly about Indian poetry, and I believe it was then that I told him that there was no rhyme in Sanskrit poetry, and ventured to ask him why there should be in English. He was not so offended as Samuel Johnson seems to have been, who would probably have answered my question by "You are a fool, sir; use your own judgment," while Tennyson made the very sensible answer that rhyme assisted the memory. . . .

It was generally after dinner . . . that Tennyson began to thaw, and to take a more active part in conversation. People who have not known him then, have hardly known him at all. During the day he was often very silent and absorbed in his own thoughts, but in the evening he took an active part in the conversation of his friends. His pipe was almost indispensable to him, and I remember one time when I and several friends were staying at his house, the question of tobacco turned up. I confessed that for years I had been a perfect slave to tobacco, so that I could neither read nor write a line without smoking, but that at last I had rebelled against the slavery, and had entirely given up tobacco. Some of his friends taunted Tennyson that he could never give up tobacco. "Anybody can do that," he said, "if he chooses to do it." When his friends still continued to doubt and to tease him, "Well," he said, "I shall give up smoking from to-night." The very same evening I was told that he threw his tobacco and his pipes out of the window of his bedroom. The next day he was most charming, though somewhat self-righteous. The second day he became very moody and captious, the third day no one knew what to do with him. But after a disturbed night I was told that he got out of bed in the morning, went quietly into the garden, picked up one of his broken pipes, stuffed it with the remains of the tobacco scattered about, and then having had a few puffs, came to breakfast, all right again.

He once very kindly offered to lend me his house in the Isle of Wight. "But mind," he said, "you will be watched from morning till evening." This was, in fact, his great grievance, that he could not go out without being stared at. Once taking a walk with me and my wife on the downs behind his house, he suddenly started, left us, and ran home, simply because he had descried two strangers coming towards us.

I was told that he once complained to the queen, and said that he could no longer stay in the Isle of Wight, on account of the tourists who came to stare at him. The queen, with a kindly irony, remarked that she did not suffer much from that grievance, but Tennyson not seeing what she meant, replied, "No, madam, and if I could clap a sentinel wherever I liked, I should not be troubled either."

It must be confessed that people were very inconsiderate. Rows of tourists sat like sparrows on the paling of his garden, waiting for his appearance. The guides were actually paid by sight-seers, particularly by those from America, for showing them the great poet. Nay, they went so far as to dress up a sailor to look like Tennyson, and the result was that, after their trick had been found out, the tourists would walk up to Tennyson and ask him, "Now, are you the real Tennyson?" This, no doubt, was very annoying, and later on Lord Tennyson was driven to pay a large sum for some useless downs near his house, simply in order to escape from the attentions of admiring travelers.

XXXIII

THE EARLY EDUCATION OF JOHN STUART MILL

AT an age when most children are playing with a Noah's Ark or a doll, John Stuart Mill was initiated into the mysteries of the Greek language. "I have no remembrance of the time when I began to learn Greek," writes Mill, "I have been told that it was when I was three years old." Latin was not begun until his eighth year. By that time he had read in Greek,— Æsop, the Anabasis, the whole of Herodotus, the Cyropædia, the Memorabilia, parts of Diogenes Laertius, and of Lucian, Isocrates; also six dialogues of Plato. An equipment like this suggests the satiric lines of Hudibras:

> Besides, 'tis known he could speak Greek
> As naturally as pigs squeak.

In considering the difficulties that this child— shall we say babe?—had to overcome one must remember that the aids to learning Greek were not then what they are now. In 1820 the Greek lexicon was a ponderous thing, almost as big and heavy as the infant student himself. Worse than this, the definitions were not in English, but in Greek and Latin, and as the boy had not yet learned Latin he had to ask his father for the meaning of every new word. The immense task placed thus upon the child makes one feel indignant and wish that some organization for the prevention of cruelty to infants had interfered with the ambition of the learned father. But we must admire the patience of the father, however we may question his good sense. "What he himself was willing to undergo for the sake of my instruction," says the son in describing his father's teaching, "may be judged from the fact, that I went through the whole process of preparing my Greek lessons in the same room and at the same table at which he was writing. . . . I was forced to have recourse to him for the meaning of every word which I did not know. This incessant interruption, he, one of the most impatient of men, submitted to, and wrote under that interruption several volumes of his History and all else that he had to write during those years."

But this does not tell the whole story. Fearing that the Greek might be too heavy and concentrated a food for the tender intellect of his child, the considerate father added a diet of English history and biography. The boy carefully studied and made notes upon Robertson, Hume, Gibbon, Watson, Hooke, Langhorne's *Plutarch,* Burnet's *History of His Own Time,* Millar's *Historical View of the English Government,* Mosheim's *Ecclesiastical History.* In biography and travel he read the life of Knox, the histories of the Quakers, Beaver's *Africa,* Collin's *New South Wales,* Anson's *Voyages,* and Hawkesworth's *Voyages Round the World.* "Of children's books, any more than of playthings, I had scarcely any, except an occasional gift from a relation or acquaintance. . . . It was no part, however, of my father's system to exclude books of amusement, though he allowed them very sparingly. Of such books he possessed at that time next to none, but he borrowed several for me; those which I remember are the *Arabian Nights*, Cazotte's *Arabian Tales, Don Quixote,* Miss Edgeworth's *Popular Tales,* and a book of some reputation in its day, Brooke's *Fool of Quality."*

All this, it is to be remembered, was done by a boy who was not beyond his eighth year. In his eighth year he began Latin, not only as a learner but as a teacher. It was his duty to teach the younger children of the family what he had learned. This practice he does not recommend. "The teaching, I am sure, is very inefficient as teaching, and I well know that the relation between teacher and taught is not a good moral discipline to either." By the time this prodigy of intellect and industry reached the age of fourteen he had studied the following formidable list: Virgil, Horace, Phaedrus, Livy, Sallust, the Metamorphoses, Terence, Cicero, Homer, Thucydides, the Hellenica, Demosthenes, Æschines, Lysias, Theocritus, Anacreon, Aristotle's Rhetoric; Euclid, Algebra, the higher mathematics, Joyce's Scientific Dialogues, and various treatises on Chemistry; and in addition to all this he had read parts of other Greek and Latin authors, and much of English poetry and history.

A boy with so heavy a burden of learning is very prone to an equal amount of self-conceit. But the father tried to overcome this danger by

holding up a very high standard of comparison,—
"not what other people did, but what a man could
and ought to do." He succeeded so well that the
boy was not aware that his attainments were
extraordinary. "I neither estimated myself
highly nor lowly; I did not estimate myself at
all. If I thought anything about myself, it was
that I was rather backward in my studies, since I
always found myself so, in comparison of what
my father expected of me." To this assertion
Mr. Mill very candidly adds: "I assert this with
confidence, though it was not the impression of
various persons who saw me in my childhood.
They, as I have since found, thought me greatly
and disagreeably self-conceited; probably because
I was disputatious, and did not scruple to give
direct contradictions to things which I heard
said."

A boy who is kept at his studies as assiduously as was young Mill has little time for play or
association with other boys. This lack of contact with companions is a grave defect in the
education of Mill. "I constantly remained
long," writes Mill, "and in a less degree have
always remained, inexpert in anything requiring
manual dexterity; my mind, as well as my hands,
did its work very lamely when it was applied, or
ought to have been applied, to the practical details which, as they are the chief interest of life
to the majority of men, are also the things in
which whatever mental capacity they have,
chiefly shows itself."

On the whole we feel that the childhood of Mill
could hardly have been a happy one. The joy
of physical achievement, the free-hearted aban-

donment of the young barbarian at his play, the power to do as well as to know—these are the birthright of every child.   But while we may pity him for his lack of these joys, we dare not forget that to have lived the life or done the work of John Stuart Mill is no small thing.   And perhaps this life could not have been lived had his education been other than it was.

XXXIV

CARLYLE GOES TO THE UNIVERSITY

ONE of the most tender pictures in the history of English literature is that of Carlyle as he starts for his University career. Just a boy, a child not yet fourteen! It is early morning in November at Ecclefechan—and Edinburgh with its famous University is a hundred miles away. The father and mother have risen early to get Thomas ready—not for the cab to take him to the "purple luxury and plush repose" of the Pullman on the Limited Express. No, Tom is going to walk,—his only companion a boy two or three years older. These rugged, poor, and godly parents had long discussed the sending of Tommy to the great University. James Bell, one of the wise men of the community, had said: "Educate a boy, and he grows up to despise his ignorant parents," but they knew that depended on the boy. "Thou hast not done so; God be thanked," said James Carlyle to his son in after years.

But let us come back to our picture. In our mind's eye we see the Scotch lad starting out on his hundred-mile trip in the mist of a foggy November morning. Almost three-score years after, Carlyle himself beautifully describes the event: "How strangely vivid, how remote and wonderful, tinged with the views of far-off love and sadness, is that journey to me now after fifty-seven years of time! My mother and father walking with me in the dark frosty November morning through the village to set us on our way; my dear and loving mother, her tremulous affection, etc."

That's the picture of an unknown boy going to the University to become what every pious Scotch mother wants her boy to be—a minister of the gospel.

Here is another picture, taken about sixty years later. In a somewhat plainly furnished room in a house on a quiet street in Chelsea, a part of London, an old man "worn, and tired, and bent, with deep-lined features, a firm under-jaw, tufted gray hair, and tufted gray and white beard, and sunken and unutterably sad eyes, is returning from the fireplace, where with trembling fingers he had been lighting his long clay pipe, and now he resumes his place at a reading desk." Let us enter this room with Theodore L. Cuyler, who in his *Recollections of a Long Life* tells us: "Thirty years afterwards, in June, 1872, I felt an irrepressible desire to see the grand old man once more, and I accordingly addressed him a note, requesting him the favor of a few minutes' interview. . . . After we had waited some time, a feeble, stooping figure, attired in a long blue flannel gown, moved slowly into the room. His gray hair was unkempt, his blue eyes were still keen and piercing, and a bright hectic spot of red appeared on each of his hollow cheeks. His hands were tremulous and his voice deep and husky. After a few personal inquiries the old man broke out into a most extraordinary and characteristic harangue on the wretched degeneracy of these evil days. The prophet Jeremiah was cheerfulness itself in comparison with him. . . . Most of his extraordinary harangue was like an eruption of Vesuvius, but the laugh he occasionally gave showed that he was talking about as much for his own amusement as for ours.''

Between these two pictures,—the one showing us the boy trudging away in the mist of the November morning, the other revealing an old man whose home in Chelsea had become the Mecca of the lovers of English literature,—what has occurred?

The young boy has finished his studies at the University; has concluded not to enter the ministry; has studied law; served as tutor; translated a masterpiece of German into English, and finally dedicated his powers to becoming a notability in English literature: wrote *Sartor Resartus,* the *History of the French Revolution,* a *Life of Cromwell,* a *Life of Frederick the Great,* and has become world-renowned as one of the great figures of the Nineteenth Century.

XXXV

CARLYLE AND HIS WIFE

IN 1826 occurred what Saintsbury calls the most important event in the life of Carlyle, —his marriage with Jane Welsh, a young woman who traced her ancestry back to John Knox, the rugged Scotch reformer. Jane was a keen, active, high-strung, sensitive soul. There has arisen a formidable mass of literature discussing the relationship between Thomas and Jane. Were they happy or were they miserable?

Jane Welsh was a Scotch lady whose family was socially superior to that of Carlyle's. Her father had been a physician, while Carlyle's was but a rude stone-mason,—and yet a great man. It is said she married Thomas because she was ambitious and wanted to be the wife of a famous man, and she had discovered in the unknown Thomas the marks of genius. In after years she is reported to have said: "I married for ambition. Carlyle had exceeded all that my wildest hopes ever imagined for him; *and I am miserable.*"

Jeannie had what she had bargained for and yet she was unhappy,—why?

Carlyle was a big-hearted, hard-working, gruff, but kind-hearted individual. I have not a doubt that he loved his Jeannie. But he took no pains to show his love in those tender though trivial devotions that mean so much to the sensitive wife.

During the first few years of their married life, they lived in a lonely place and had but a scant income. We have a very interesting picture of their life at Craigenputtock. Thomas could not eat bakers' bread, so Jeannie baked. The one servant they had was not competent. It may have been this same servant that was responsible for Thomas' finding, altogether unexpectedly, of course, a dead mouse at the bottom of his dish of oatmeal. As to the bread-baking Jean has given us a very graphic account:

"Further we were very poor, and further and worst, being an only child, and brought up to 'great prospects,' I was sublimely ignorant of every branch of useful knowledge, though a capital Latin scholar, and very fair mathematician! It behooved me in these astonishing circumstances to learn to sew! Husbands, I was shocked to find, wore their stockings into holes, and were always losing buttons, and I was expected 'to look to all that;' also it behooved me to learn to *cook!* no capable servant choosing to live at such an out-of-the-way place, and my husband having bad digestion, which complicated my difficulties dreadfully. The bread, above all, bought at Dumfries, 'soured on his stomach' (Oh heaven!), and it was plainly my duty as a Christian wife to bake at home. So I sent for Cobbett's *Cottage Economy,* and fell to work at a loaf of bread. But knowing nothing about the process of fermentation or the heat of ovens, it came to pass that my loaf got put into the oven at the time that

myself ought to have been put into bed; and I
remained the only person not asleep in a house
in the middle of a desert.   One o'clock struck,
and then two, and then three, and still I was sitting there in an immense solitude, my whole body
aching with weariness, my heart aching with a
sense of forlornness and *degradation*.   That I
who had been so petted at home, whose comfort
had been studied by everybody in the house, and
who had never been required to *do* anything, but
cultivate my mind, should have to pass all those
hours of the night in watching *a loaf of bread*,
which mightn't turn out bread after all!   Such
thoughts maddened me, till I laid down my head
on the table and sobbed aloud.   It was then that
somehow the idea of Benvenuto Cellini sitting up
all night watching his Perseus in the furnace
came into my head, and suddenly I asked myself:
'After all, in the sight of the Upper Powers,
what is the mighty difference between a statue
of Perseus and a loaf of bread, so that each be the
thing that one's hand has found to do?' . . . If
he had been a woman living at Craigenputtock,
with a dyspeptic husband, sixteen miles from a
baker, and he a bad one, all these same qualities
would have come out more fitly in a *good* loaf of
bread.

"I cannot express what consolation this germ
of an idea spread over my uncongenial life during
the years we lived at that savage place, where
my two immediate predecessors had gone *mad*,
and the third had taken to drink."

While enjoying the description which Mrs.
Carlyle has painted in such an entertaining manner, it is well to observe that she does not blame

her husband. She seems to be writing the account while she is silently laughing at the absurd preparation her life had had for the duties of the wife of a poor man. But Mr. T. P. O'Connor, who writes in 1895, is outspoken:

"I do not want to speak disrespectfully of poor Carlyle, but in spirit it is somewhat hard to keep one's hand off him, as we reconstruct those scenes in the gaunt house at Craigenputtock. There is a little detail in one scene which adds a deeper horror. I have said that Mrs. Carlyle had to scrub the floors, and as she scrubbed them Carlyle would look on smoking—drawing in from tobacco pleasant comfortableness and easy dreams—while his poor drudge panted and sighed over the hard work, which she had never done before. Do you not feel that you would like to break the pipe in his mouth, and shake him off the chair, and pitch him on to the floor, to take a share of the physical burden which his shoulders were so much more able to bear?"

Another anecdote is that at a dinner while Carlyle was monopolizing the conversation, talking as only he could talk, he, the irritable, turned upon his wife with "Jeanie, don't breathe so hard!" And still again, we hear it said that Tennyson once remarked it was well the Carlyles had married each other for if each had married another there would have been *four* instead of *two* unhappy people. But I think the truer remark was made when Tennyson said to his son, Hallam: "Mr. and Mrs. Carlyle on the whole enjoy life together, or else they would not have chaffed one another so heartily."

The *Century* of some years ago contained this witty skit from the pen of Bessie Chandler:

> And I sit here, thinking, thinking,
> How your life was one long winking
> At Thomas' faults and failings, and his undue share of bile!
> Won't you own, dear, just between us,
> That this living with a genius
> Isn't, after all, so pleasant,—is it, Jeannie Welsh Carlyle?

However, with all that may be said to the contrary, I do not think we dare say that the marriage of Thomas and Jeannie was an unhappy one. After reading fifteen hundred pages of biography and hundreds of letters passing to and fro, I am of the belief of Mr. Tennyson, that on the whole their union was a happy one.

Shortly after Carlyle had been elected Rector of the University of Edinburgh, Jean died suddenly. While out driving one afternoon by Hyde Park, she jumped out to pick up her little dog, over whose foot a carriage had passed. She was never again seen alive. In her carriage she was found dead with her hands folded on her lap. When Carlyle heard of it he was away at Scotsbrig. Later in describing his feelings he wrote: "It had a kind of *stunning* effect on me. Not for above two days could I estimate the immeasurable depth of it, or the infinite sorrow which had peeled my life all bare, and a moment shattered my poor world to universal ruin." And Froude tells us that in Carlyle's old age—he lived to be eighty-five—he often broke forth in these passionate words of Burns:

> Had we never loved sae kindly,
> Had we never loved sae blindly,
> Never met and never parted,
> We had ne'er been broken-hearted.

THOMAS CARLYLE

From a photograph from life

XXXVI

CARLYLE AS LECTURER

IN 1834, the year of the death of Coleridge, we find Carlyle, like many another Scotchman, leaving Scotland to enter the great Babylon, London. The previous six years he had passed with his wife at Craigenputtock. He was almost forty years of age. His wife had great confidence in his ability, which up to this time the world had not recognized. So she urged him to struggle for influence and power in the great heart of the modern world. Number 5, Cheyne Row, Chelsea, is the house they selected. There for the remaining forty-seven years of his life he worked and loved and stormed. Their neighborhood was one famous in association with the names of many *literati*. Near by Smollett wrote *Count Fathom;* in the same locality More had entertained the great scholar, Erasmus; there too had once lived Bolingbroke, and earlier, the Count de Grammont; and last but not least the author of Abou Ben Adhem, Leigh Hunt.

When Emerson once suggested to Carlyle that he come over to America to lecture, Carlyle took kindly to the idea. He kept it in mind as a possibility for years, but he never carried it into effect. But he did lecture in London. His literary work was not bringing him the money he needed. His friends were struck with his ability. Why should he not lecture? This, if well managed, would bring him immediate remuneration. His friends set diligently to work, issued a prospectus, tickets at a guinea a course, and invited persons of influence to attend. Spedding wrote this letter to Monckton Milnes:

"I take the opportunity of writing to make you know, if you do not know already, that Carlyle lectures on German literature next month; the particulars you will find in the inclosed syllabus, which, if it should convey as much knowledge to you as it does ignorance to me, will be edifying. Of course, you will be here to attend the said lectures, but I want you to come up a little before they begin, that you may assist in procuring the attendance of others. The list of subscribers is at present not large, and you are just the man to make it grow. As it is Carlyle's first essay in this kind, it is important that there should be a respectable number of hearers. Some name of decided piety is, I believe, rather wanted. Learning, taste, and nobility are represented by Hallam, Rogers, and Lord Lansdowne. H. Taylor has provided a large proportion of family, wit, and beauty, and I have assisted them to a little Apostlehood. We want your name to represent the great body of Tories, Roman Catholics, High Churchmen, metaphysicians, poets, and Savage Landor. Come!"

Carlyle was busy with his *French Revolution* and so did not make as careful preparation as he might have made. Yet he was so full of his subject that if he could overcome the difficulties of public speaking, he was bound to be interesting. As the day approached both he and his wife grew nervous. For diversion he drew up a humorous ending: "Good Christians, it has become entirely impossible for me to talk to you about German or any literature or terrestrial thing; one request only I have to make, that you would be kind enough to cover me under a tub for the next six weeks and to go your ways with all my blessing." This fortunately he did not need to use. Mrs. Carlyle worried lest he would be late, but by dint of close attention she felt she could have him "at the place of execution" at the appointed hour. How to get him to stop at "four precisely" was another problem. One humorous suggestion was that a lighted cigar might be laid on the table before him when the clock struck the hour.

"May the First, 1837," says Professor Mac-Mechan, "was a notable day. In the afternoon, Carlyle lectured at Almack's, and in the evening Macready produced young Mr. Browning's *Strafford,* for the first time, at Covent Garden. Hallam, of the *Middle Ages,*—'a broad, old, positive man, with laughing eyes,'—was chairman and brought the lecturer face to face with his first audience, the two hundred holders of guinea tickets. It was made up of the elements referred to in Spedding's letter. Learning, taste, nobility, family, wit, and beauty were all represented in that assembly; 'composed of mere quality and notabilities,' says Carlyle. It is easy to figure the scene; the men all clean-shaven, in the clumsy coats, high collars, and enormous neck-cloths of the period, the ladies, and there were naturally more ladies than men, following the vagaries of fashion in 'bishop' sleeves and the 'pretty church-and-state bonnets,' that seemed to Hunt at times, 'to think through all their ribbons.' We call that kind of bonnet 'coal-scuttle' now, but Maclise's portrait of Lady Morgan trying hers on before a glass justifies Hunt's epithet. The lecturer was the lean, wiry type of Scot, within an inch of six feet. In face, he was not the bearded, broken-down Carlyle of the Fry photograph, but the younger Carlyle of the Emerson portrait. Clean-shaven, as was then the fashion, the determination of the lower jaw lying bare, the thick black hair brushed carelessly and coming down on the bony, jutting forehead, violet-blue eyes, deep-set, and alert, the whole face shows the Scot and the peasant in every line. It was a striking face, the union of black hair, blue eyes, and, usually, ruddy color on the high cheek bones, 'as if painted . . . at the plow's tail,' Lady Eastlake remarked, and she was an artist. Harriet Martineau remarks that he was as 'yellow as a guinea,' but this would be due to some temporary gastric disturbance. He was very nervous, as was most natural, and stood with downcast eyes, his fingers picking at the desk before him.

At the beginning his speech was broken, and his throat was dry, drink as he would; but his desperate determination not to break down carried him through. The society people were 'very humane' to him, and the lecturer had a message for them; his matter was new, his manner was interesting; he knew his subject. The rugged Scottish accent came like a welcome draught of caller air from the moorlands of Galloway, to the dwellers in London drawing-rooms, and 'they were not a little astonished when the wild Annandale voice grew high and earnest.' ''

From this first venture which was so successful—he cleared one hundred and thirty-five guineas after all the expenses had been paid—Carlyle was induced to give other series in the next few years. One of the most popular books by Carlyle is *Heroes and Hero Worship;* this first was given in a course of lectures. When ''The Hero as Man of Letters'' was given, Caroline Fox, an ardent admirer of the Scot, was in attendance. She has left a vivid description of the man: ''Carlyle soon appeared, and looked as if he felt a well-dressed London audience scarcely the arena for him to figure in as a popular lecturer. He is a tall, robust-looking man; rugged simplicity and indomitable strength are in his face, and such a glow of genius in it—not always smoldering there, but flashing from his beautiful gray eyes, from the remoteness of their deep setting under that massive brow. His manner is very quiet, but he speaks as one tremendously convinced of what he utters, and who had much, very much, in him that was quite unutterable, quite unfit to be uttered to the uninitiated ear; and when the Englishman's sense of beauty or truth exhibited itself in vociferous cheers, he would impatiently, almost contemptuously, wave his hand, as if that were not the kind of homage which truth demanded. He began in a rather low and nervous voice, with a broad Scotch accent, but it soon grew firm, and shrank not abashed from its great task.''

XXXVII

ON our first day's journey, wrote Mr. Duffy in the *Contemporary Review,* the casual mention of Edmund Burke induced me to ask Carlyle who was the best talker he had met among notable people in London.

He said that when he met Wordsworth first he had been assured that he talked better than any man in England. It was his habit to talk whatever was in his mind at the time, with total indifference to the impression it produced on his hearers. On this occasion he kept discoursing how far you could get carried out of London on this side and on that for sixpence. One was disappointed,—perhaps,—but, after all, this was the only healthy way of talking, to say what is actually in your mind, and let sane creatures who listen to make what they can of it. Whether they understood or not, Wordsworth maintained a stern composure, and went his way, content that the world went quite another road. When he knew him better, he found that no man gave you so faithful and vivid a picture of any person or thing which he had seen with his own eyes.

I inquired if Wordsworth came up to this description he had heard of him as the best talker in England.

"Well," he replied, "it was true you could get more meaning out of what Wordsworth had to say than from anybody else. Leigh Hunt would emit more pretty, pleasant, ingenious flashes in an hour than Wordsworth in a day. But in the end you would find, if well considered, that you had been drinking perfumed water in one case, and in the other you got the sense of a deep, earnest man, who had thought silently and painfully on many things. There was one exception to your satisfaction with the man. When he spoke of poetry he harangued about meters, cadences, rhythms, and so forth, and one could not be at the pains of listening to him. But on all other subjects he had more sense in him of a sound and instructive sort than any other literary man in England."

I suggested that Wordsworth might naturally like to speak of the instrumental part of his art, and consider what he had to say very instructive, as by modifying the instrument, he had wrought a revolution in English poetry. He taught it to speak in unsophisticated language and of the humbler and more familiar interests of life.

Carlyle said, "No, not so; all he had got to say in that way was like a few driblets from the great ocean of German speculation on kindred subjects by Goethe and others. Coleridge, who had been in Germany, brought it over with him, and they translated Teutonic thought into a poor, disjointed, whitey-brown sort of English, and that was nearly all. But Wordsworth, after all, was the man of most practical mind of any of the persons connected with literature whom he had encountered; though his pastoral pipings were far from being of the importance his admirers imagined. He was essentially a cold, hard, silent, practical man, who, if he had not fallen into poetry, would have done effectual work of some sort in the world. This was the impression one got of him as he looked out of his stern blue eyes, superior to men and circumstances.''

I said I had expected to hear of a man of softer mood, more sympathetic and less taciturn.

Carlyle said, ''No, not at all; he was a man quite other than that; a man of an immense head and great jaws like a crocodile's, cast in a mold designed for prodigious work.''

''I begged him,'' continued Mr. Duffy, in writing of conversations with Carlyle, ''to tell me something of the author of a serial I had come across lately, called *Bells and Pomegranates,* printed in painfully small type, on inferior paper, but in which I took great delight. There were ballads to make the heart beat fast, and one little tragedy, *The Blot in the 'Scutcheon,* which, though not over-disposed to what he called sentimentality, I could not read without tears. The heroine's excuse for the sin which left a blot in a 'scutcheon stainless for a thousand years, was, in the circumstances of the case, as touching a line as I could recall in English poetry:

I had no mother, and we were so young.''

He said Robert Browning had a powerful intellect, and among the men engaged in literature in England just now was one of the few from whom it was possible to expect something. He was somewhat uncertain about his career, and he himself (Carlyle) had perhaps contributed to the trouble by assuring him that poetry was no longer a field where any true or worthy success could be won or deserved. If a man had anything to say entitled to the attention of rational creatures, all mortals would come to recognize after a little that there was a more effectual way of saying it than in metrical numbers. Poetry used to be regarded as the natural, and even the essential language of feeling, but it was not at all so; there was not a sentiment in the gamut of human passion which could not be adequately expressed in prose.

Browning's earliest works had been loudly applauded by undiscerning people, but he was now heartily ashamed of them, and hoped in the end to do something altogether different from *Sordello* and *Paracelsus*. He had strong ambition and great confidence in himself, and was considering his future course just now. When he first met young Browning, he was a youth living with his parents, people of respectable position among the Dissenters, but not wealthy neither, and the little room in which he kept his books was in that sort of trim that showed that he was the apple of their eyes. He was about six and thirty at present, and a little time before had married Miss Barrett. She had long been confined to a sofa by a spinal disease, and seemed destined to end there very speedily, but the ending was to be quite otherwise, as it proved. Browning made his way to her in a strange manner, and they fell mutually in love. She rose up from her sick-bed with recovered strength and agility, and was now, it was understood, tolerably well. They married and were living together in Italy, like the hero and heroine of a mediæval romance.

XXXVIII

THE AUTHOR OF "JANE EYRE"

CHARLOTTE BRONTË was born in Yorkshire in 1816. A generation ago everybody was reading and talking about *Jane Eyre,* her most popular novel. The life of the author was not a happy one. She was compelled to teach for a living, and her position as governess was at times humiliating to her proud spirit. Her two sisters, whom she tenderly loved, died young; her brother was no credit to the family, and the life surrounding the parsonage—she was the daughter of a clergyman—was not particularly cheery, yet her many trials but enriched a rare and beautiful character.

While living at the parsonage she would occasionally receive a box of books from her publisher. The following letter is self-explanatory:

"Do not ask me to mention what books I should like to read. Half the pleasure of receiving a parcel from Cornhill consists in having its contents chosen for us. We like to discover, too, by the leaves cut here and there that the ground has been traveled before us. I took up Leigh Hunt's book, *The Town,* with the impression that it would be interesting only to Londoners, and I was surprised, ere I had read many pages, to find myself enchained by his pleasant, graceful, easy style, varied knowledge, just views, and kindly spirit. There is something peculiarly anti-melancholic in Leigh Hunt's writings, and yet they are never boisterous—they resemble sunshine, being at once bright and tranquil.

I like Carlyle better and better. His style I do *not* like, nor do I always concur in his opinions, nor quite fall in with his hero-worship; but there is a manly love of truth, an honest recognition and fearless vindication of intrinsic greatness, of intellectual and moral worth considered apart from birth, rank, or wealth, which commands my sincere admiration. Carlyle would never do for a contributor to the *Quarterly*. I have not read his *French Revolution*. Carlyle is a great man, but I always wish he would write plain English. Emerson's *Essays* I read with much interest and often with admiration, but they are of mixed gold and clay,—deep, invigorating truth, dreary and depressing fallacy, seem to me combined therein.

Scott's *Suggestions on Female Education* I read with unalloyed pleasure; it is justly, clearly, and felicitously expressed. The girls of this generation have great advantages—it seems to me that they receive much encouragement in the acquisition of knowledge and the cultivation of their minds. In these days women may be thoughtful and well read, without being stigmatized as "blues" or pedants.

I have lately been reading *Modern Painters*, and have derived from the work much genuine pleasure, and I hope, some edification; at any rate it has made me feel how ignorant I had previously been on the subjects which it treats. Hitherto I have only had instinct to guide me in judging of art; I feel now as if I had been walking blindfold —this book seems to give me eyes. I *do* wish I had pictures within reach by which to test the new sense. Who can read these glowing descriptions of Turner's works without longing to see them? However eloquent and convincing the language in which another's opinion is placed before you, you still wish to judge for yourself. I like this author's style much; there is both energy and beauty in it. I like himself too, because he is such a hearty admirer. He does not give half measure of praise or veneration. He eulogizes, he reverences with his whole soul. One can sympathize with that sort of devout, serious admiration (for he is no rhapsodist), one can respect it. Yet, possibly, many people would laugh at it. I am truly obliged to Mr. Smith for giving me this book, not often having met with one that has pleased me more.

I congratulate you on the approaching publication of Mr. Ruskin's new work. If the *Seven Lamps of Architecture* resemble their predecessor, *Modern Painters*, they will be no lamps at all, but a new constellation—seven bright stars, for whose rising the reading world ought to be anxiously agaze.

I am beginning to read Eckermann's *Goethe*— it promised to be a most interesting work. Honest, simple, single-minded Eckermann! Great, powerful, giant-souled, but also profoundly egotistical old Johann Wolfgang von Goethe! He *was* a mighty egotist. He thought no more of swallowing up poor Eckermann's existence in his own, than the whale thought of swallowing Jonah

The worst of reading graphic accounts of such men, of seeing graphic pictures of the scenes, the society in which they moved, is that it excites a too tormenting longing to look on the reality; but does such reality now exist? Amidst all the troubled waters of European society, does such a vast, strong, selfish old leviathan now roll ponderous? I suppose not.

*   *   *   *   *   *   *   *

I often wish to say something on the "condition-of-women" question, but it is one on which so much cant has been talked, that one feels a sort of reluctance to approach it. I have always been accustomed to think that the necessity of earning one's living is not, in itself, an evil; though I feel it may become a heavy evil if health fails, if employment lacks, if the demand upon our efforts, made by the weakness of others dependent upon us becomes greater than our strength. Both sons and daughters should early be inured to habits of independence and industry.

A governess' lot is frequently, indeed, bitter, but its results are precious. The mind, feelings, and temper are subjected to a discipline equally painful and priceless. I have known many who were unhappy as governesses, but scarcely one who, having undergone the ordeal, was not ultimately strengthened and improved—made more enduring for her own afflictions, more considerate for the afflictions of others. The great curse of a single female life is its dependency; daughters, as well as sons, should aim at making their way through life. Teachers may be hard-worked, ill-paid, and despised; but the girl who stays at home *doing nothing* is worse off than the worse-paid drudge of a school; the listlessness of idleness will infallibly degrade her nature.

Lonely as I am, how should I be if Providence had never given me courage to adopt a career, perseverance to plead through two long weary years with publishers till they admitted me? How should I be, with youth passed, sisters lost, a resident in a moorland parish where there is not a single resident family? In that case I should have no world at all. The raven weary of surveying the deluge, and with no ark to return to, would be my type.

As it is, something like a hope and motive sustain me still. I wish every woman in England had also a hope and a motive. Alas! I fear there are many old maids who have neither.

—Adapted from *Littell's Living Age.*

XXXIX

THACKERAY, like many other Englishmen of note, came to America to lecture in order to make money. He had delivered lectures in London and in other towns in England on the *English Humorists*. Why not use his popularity in America as a means of acquiring a little fortune for the sake of his wife and two girls. "I must and will go," he wrote to his eldest daughter, "not because I like it, but because it is right I should secure some money against my death for your mother and you two girls. And I think, if I have luck, I may secure nearly a third of the sum that I think I ought to leave behind me by a six months' tour in the States."

Let us, in order to get a first-hand impression, read from letters that he wrote from America:

"The passage is nothing, now it is over; I am rather ashamed of gloom and disquietude about such a trifling journey. I have made scores of new acquaintances and lighted on my feet as usual. I didn't expect to like people as I do, but am agreeably disappointed and find many most pleasant companions, natural and good; natural and well read and well bred too, and I suppose am none the worse pleased because everybody has read all my books and praises my lectures (I preach in a Unitarian Church, and the parson comes to hear me. His name is Mr. Bellows, it isn't a pretty name), and there are 2,000 people nearly who come, and the lectures are so well liked that it is probable I shall do them over again. So really there is a chance of making a pretty little sum of money for old age, imbecility, and those young ladies afterwards. . . . Broadway is miles upon miles long, a rush of life such as I have never seen; not so full as the Strand, but so rapid. The houses are always being torn down and built up again, the railroad cars drive slap into the midst of the city. There are barricades and scaffoldings banging everywhere. I have not been into a house, except the fat country one, but something new is being done to it, and the hammerings are clattering in the passage, or a wall or steps are down, or the family is going to move. Nobody is quiet here, nor am I. The rush and restlessness please me, and I like, for a little, the dash of the stream. I am not received as a god, which I like too. There is one paper which goes on every morning saying I am a snob, and I don't say no. Six people were reading it at breakfast this morning, and the man opposite me this morning popped it under the table-cloth. But the other papers roar with approbation.''

In this letter, of which we have read a fragment, Mr. Thackeray inclosed a clipping from the New York *Evening Post*. This is what the newspaper had to say: ''The building was crowded. . . . Every one who saw Mr. Thackeray last evening for the first time seemed to have had their impressions of his appearance and manner of speech corrected. Few expected to see so large a man; he is gigantic; six feet four at least; few expected to see so old a person; his hair appears to have kept silvery record over fifty years; and then there was a notion in the minds of many that there must be something dashing and 'fast' in his appearance, whereas his costume was perfectly plain; the expression of his face grave and earnest; his address perfectly unaffected, and such as we might expect to meet with, in a well-bred man somewhat advanced in years. His elocution also surprised those who had derived their impressions from the English journals. His voice is a superb tenor, and possesses that pathetic tremble which is so effective in what is called emotive eloquence, while his delivery was as well suited to the communication he had to make as could well have been imagined.

"His enunciation is perfect. Every word he uttered might have been heard in the remotest quarters of the room, yet he scarcely lifted his voice above a colloquial tone. The most striking feature in his whole manner was the utter absence of affectation of any kind. He did not permit himself to appear conscious that he was an object of peculiar interest in the audience, neither was he guilty of the greater error of not appearing to care whether they were interested in him or not. In other words, he inspired his audience with a respect for him, as a man proportioned to the admiration, which his books have inspired for him as an author."

From Philadelphia Thackeray writes: "Oh, I am tired of shaking hands with people, and acting

the lion business night after night.   Everybody
is introduced and shakes hands.   I know thousands of colonels, professors, editors, and what
not, and walk the streets guiltily, knowing that I
don't know 'em, and trembling lest the man opposite to me is one of my friends of the day before.
I believe I am popular, except at Boston among
the newspaper men who fired into me, but a great
favorite with the *monde* there and elsewhere.
Here in Philadelphia it is all praise and kindness.
Do you know there are 500,000 people in Philadelphia?   I daresay you had no idea thereof, and
smile at the idea of there being a *monde* here and
at Boston and New York. . . . I am writing this
with a new gold pen, in such a fine gold case.   An
old gentleman gave it to me yesterday, a white-
headed old philosopher and political economist.
There's something simple in the way these kind
folks regard a man; they read our books as if we
were Fielding, and so forth.   The other night
men were talking of Dickens and Bulwer as if
they were equal to Shakespeare, and I was pleased
to find myself pleased at hearing them praised.
The prettiest girl in Philadelphia, poor soul, has
read *Vanity Fair* twelve times.   I paid her a
great big compliment yesterday, about her good
looks of course, and she turned round delighted
to her friend and said, '*Ai most tallut,*' that is
something like the pronunciation."

In another letter: "Now I have seen three
great cities, Boston, New York, Philadelphia, I
think I like them all mighty well.   They seem to
me not so civilized as our London, but more so
than Manchester and Liverpool.   At Boston is
very good literate company indeed; it is like

Edinburgh for that,—a vast amount of toryism and donnishness everywhere. That of New York the simplest and least pretentious; it suffices that a man should keep fine house, give parties, and have a daughter, to get all the world to him.''

XL

GEORGE ELIOT BECOMES A WRITER OF FICTION

AS one is ready to call Elizabeth Barrett the
greatest poetess of the nineteenth century,
so there is little hesitation in pronouncing
George Eliot the foremost of the many women
who have written fiction. The literary critics
sometimes dispute her supremacy by urging the
claims of Jane Austen, who is said to have Shak-
sperean power in the delineation of character.
But the name of Jane Austen is unknown to the
general public. For every reader of *Pride and
Prejudice* there are a score of readers of *Adam
Bede*.

George Eliot is the pseudonym of Mary Ann
Evans. She took the name of *George* because it
was the first name of Mr. Lewes, and *Eliot* "was
a good, mouth-filling, easily pronounced word."

George Eliot was almost thirty-seven years old
before she began to write fiction; in this respect
reminding us of Scott, who had first achieved fame
as a poet before he began in his maturity to write
fiction. We are happy in having from the pen of
George Eliot herself the account of how she began to write fiction:

"September, 1856, made a new era in my life,
for it was then I began to write fiction. It had

always been a vague dream of mine that some time or other I might write a novel; and my shadowy conception of what the novel was to be, varied, of course, from one epoch of my life to another. But I never went further toward the actual writing of the novel than an introductory chapter describing a Staffordshire village and the life of the neighboring farm-houses; and as the years passed on I lost any hope that I should ever be able to write a novel."

Mr. Lewes encouraged George Eliot by admiring her introductory chapter. He first read it when they were together in Germany. When they had returned to England and she was more successful in her essay writing than he had expected, he continued to urge her to try to write a story. "He began to say very positively, 'You must try and write a story,' and when we were at Tenby he urged me to begin at once. I deferred it, however, after my usual fashion with work that does not present itself as an absolute duty. But one morning, as I was thinking what should be the subject of my first story, my thoughts merged themselves into a dreamy doze, and I imagined myself writing a story, of which the title was *The Sad Fortunes of the Reverend Amos Barton.* I was soon wide awake again and told G. (Mr. Lewes). He said 'Oh, what a capital title!' and from that time I had settled in my mind that this should be my first story. George used to say, 'It may be a failure—it may be that you are unable to write fiction. Or, perhaps, it may be just good enough to warrant your trying again.' Again, 'You may write a *chef-d'œuvre* at once—there's no telling.' But his prevalent impression was, that though I could hardly write a *poor* novel, my effort would want the highest quality of fiction—dramatic presentation. He used to say, 'You have wit, description, and philosophy—those go a good way towards the production of a novel, It is worth while for you to try the experiment.'"

When she had finished the first part of *Amos Barton,* Mr. Lewes was no longer skeptical about her ability to write dialogue. The next question was whether she had the power of pathos. This was to be determined by the way in which the death of Milly was to be treated. "One night G. went to town on purpose to leave me a quiet evening for writing it. I wrote the chapter from the news brought by the shepherd to Mrs. Hackit, to the moment when Amos is dragged from the bedside, and I read it to G. when he came home. We both cried over it, and then he came up to me and kissed me, saying, 'I think your pathos is better than your fun.'"

The first part of *Amos Barton* appeared in the January number of *Blackwood.* The publisher paid the author fifty guineas. Afterwards, when the series of stories dealing with clerical life was published in book form, she was paid £120; later, when the publishing firm decided to issue a thousand copies instead of seven hundred and fifty, £60 was added to the original sum. George Eliot expressed herself as sensitive to the merits of checks for fifty guineas, but the success of her later writings was so pronounced that a check for fifty guineas would have made little impression, except a feeling of disdain.

Amos Barton was followed by *Mr. Gilfil's Love Story,* and *Janet's Repentance.* The three comprise *Scenes from Clerical Life*. The stories are based upon events which happened in the early life of the writer when she lived in Warwickshire. The village of Milby is really Nuneaton. When the villagers and country people read the *Scenes from Clerical Life* there was great excitement. Who could this *George Eliot* be? Some one who had lived among them and heard all the gossip of the neighborhood. But they could not recall any man with enough literary ability to do what had been done. Finally they did remember that a man, Liggins by name, had written poetry. The poetry was rather weak stuff, but perhaps his strength lay in fiction. Liggins was flattered by the suspicions of his neighbors. His own doubt was gradually changed to belief. Yes, he was the author of this new fiction, because every one said he was. The voice of the people is the voice of God. He was invited to write for a theological magazine. Finally George Eliot was obliged to reveal her identity when the public was about to subscribe a sum of money for the pseudo-literary Liggins who was so fastidious as to refuse money for the product of his genius. Here ends the career of Liggins, the liar.

One reason the villagers had for believing one of their own number was the author was based on the conversations in the *Scenes from Clerical Life*. Not only were they true to life, but they were conversations that had actually taken place. How did George Eliot hear them? Had she loitered in the public room of the village tavern? Mr. C. S. Olcott writes in the *Outlook*,— "The real conversations which were so cleverly reported were actually heard by Robert Evans, the father of George Eliot, who doubtless often visited the Bull in company with his neighbors. He repeated them to his wife, not realizing that the little daughter who listened so attentively was gifted with a marvelous memory, or that she possessed a genius that could transform a simple tale into a novel of dramatic power. Mary Ann Evans had moved to Coventry sixteen years before, and was therefore scarcely known in Nuneaton at the time the stories appeared. She then had no literary fame, and was no more likely to be thought of in this connection than any one of a hundred other school-girls.''

In her journal she records on October 22, 1857, —''Began my new novel, *Adam Bede.*'' For it her publishers offered her £800 for the copyright for four years; later they added £400, and still later Blackwoods, finding a ready sale for their numerous editions, proposed to pay £800 above the original price. And for the appearance of *Romola* in the *Cornhill Magazine,* Mr. George Smith offered £10,000, but £7000 was accepted. For *Middlemarch,* which appeared in separate publication, that is, independent of a magazine, she received a still larger amount. Middlemarch is considered by many critics her best work. It was very popular from the first. In a letter to John Blackwood, November, 1873, George Eliot writes, —''I had a letter from Mr. Bancroft (the American ambassador at Berlin) the other day, in which he says that everybody in Berlin reads *Middlemarch.* He had to buy two copies for his house, and he found the rector of the university, a stupendous mathematician, occupied with it in the solid part of the day.''

The public may prefer *Adam Bede* or *Middlemarch* but it is reported that George Eliot herself preferred *Silas Marner*. This is the report of Justin McCarthy, who was a frequent visitor on Sunday afternoons at the Priory, the home of George Eliot, where many distinguished visitors, such as Herbert Spencer, Tyndall, and Huxley, loved to gather. "There is a legend," writes Mr. McCarthy, "that George Eliot never liked to talk about her novels. I can only say that she started the subject with me one day. It was, to be sure, about a picture some painter had sent her, representing a scene in *Silas Marner,* and she called my attention to it, and said that of all her novels *Silas Marner* was her favorite. I ventured to disagree with her, and to say that the *Mill on the Floss* was my favorite. She entered into the discussion quite genially, just as if she were talking of the works of some stranger, which I think is the very perfection of the manner authors ought to adopt in talking about their books."

XLI

IT is said that when Victoria, late queen of England, had read *Alice in Wonderland* she was so pleased that she asked for more of the author's books. They brought her a treatise on logarithms by the Rev. C. L. Dodgson. Lewis Carroll and the Rev. C. L. Dodgson were one and the same person, although they were two dissimilar characters. The one was a popular author of nonsense that delighted children by the hundreds of thousands and the other was a scholarly mathematician.

C. L. Dodgson came of good Northern-England stock. His father, grandfather, and great-grandfather were clergymen—a contradiction, says his biographer, Mr. Collingwood, of the scandalous theory that three generations of parsons end in a fool. As a boy he kept all sorts of odd and unlikely pets. From Rugby he entered Oxford. In 1856 he was made college lecturer in mathematics, a position which he filled for a quarter of a century. That he had thoughts of lighter material than mathematics is evidenced by a short poem that appeared about this time in a college paper called *College Rhymes*. Two of the stanzas run like this:

She has the bear's ethereal grace
    The bland hyena's laugh,
The footsteps of the elephant,
    The neck of the giraffe;

I love her still, believe me,
    Though my heart its passion hides.
She is all my fancy painted her,
    But oh! how much besides.

The year 1862 saw the beginning of the world-famous *Alice*. He told the story to Dean Liddell's three daughters. "Alice," the second of the three (now Mrs. Reginald Hargreaves) thus tells the story:

"I believe the beginning of *Alice* was told one summer afternoon when the sun was so burning that we had landed in the meadows down the river, deserting the boat to take refuge in the only bit of shade to be found, and which was under a new-made hay-rick. Here from all three came the old petition of 'Tell us a story,' and so began the ever delightful tale. Sometimes to tease us—and perhaps being really tired—Mr. Dodgson would stop suddenly and say, 'And that's all till next time.' 'Oh! but it is next time,' would be the exclamation from all three; and after some persuasion the story would start afresh. Another day perhaps the story would begin in the boat, and Mr. Dodgson, in the midst of telling a thrilling adventure, would pretend to fall fast asleep, to our great dismay." . . .

"Many of Lewis Carroll's friendships with children began in a railway carriage. Once when he was traveling, a lady, whose little daughter had been reading *Alice,* startled him by exclaiming: 'Isn't it sad about poor Mr. Lewis Carroll?

He's gone mad, you know. . . . I have it on the best authority.' ''

Lewis Carroll, or rather Mr. Dodgson, did not wish his acquaintances to speak of him as the author of *Alice*. In his every-day work he wanted to be known as the serious mathematician. He was conservative in his ideas and did not look with favor upon the movement to overthrow Euclid. In 1870 he published a book entitled *Euclid and his Modern Rivals*. The London *Spectator* speaks of this as probably the most humorous contribution ever devoted to the subject of mathematics. In an academical discussion held at Oxford he once published three rules to be followed in debate. This is one of the three: ''Let it be granted that any one may speak at any length on a subject at any distance from that subject.''

XLII

WHEN a prominent literary journal at the close of the last century asked a number of distinguished Americans and Englishmen to name the ten most influential books of the century, it was interesting to note that Darwin's *Origin of Species* received more frequent mention than any other book. Five years after Charles Darwin had been buried (he was laid to rest in Westminster Abbey in 1882), his son published the *Life and Letters of Darwin*, which included an autobiographical chapter. From this work we can gather enough to show some aspects of this remarkable man.

Men of genius are often in childhood very imaginative. It is sometimes pretty difficult to distinguish between playful imagination and lying. Let us give Darwin the benefit of the doubt in this instance:

"One little event during this year (1817) has fixed itself very firmly in my mind, and I hope that it has done so from my conscience having been afterwards sorely troubled by it; it is curious as showing that apparently I was interested at this early age in the variability of plants! I told another little boy (I believe it was Leighton, who afterwards became a well-known lichenologist and botanist), that I could produce variously colored polyanthuses and primroses by watering them with certain colored fluids, which was of course a monstrous fable, and had never been tried by me.''

Darwin's school experiences were not always profitable. He says:

''I had many friends, and got together a good collection of old verses, which by patching together, sometimes aided by other boys, I could work into any subject. Much attention was paid to learning by heart the lessons of the previous day. This I could effect with great facility, learning forty or fifty lines of Virgil or Homer whilst I was in morning chapel. But this exercise was utterly useless, for every verse was forgotten in forty-eight hours. I was not idle, and with the exception of versification, generally worked conscientiously at my classics, not using cribs. The sole pleasure I ever received from such studies, was from some of the odes of Horace, which I admired greatly.''

Of his years at Cambridge he writes:

''During the three years which I spent at Cambridge my time was wasted, as far as the academical studies were concerned, as completely as at Edinburgh and at school. I attempted mathematics, and even went, during the summer of 1828, with a private tutor (a very dull man) to Barmouth, but I got on very slowly. The work was repugnant to me chiefly from my not being able to see any meaning in the very early steps in algebra. This impatience was very foolish, and in after years I have deeply regretted that I did not proceed far enough at least to understand something of the great leading principles of mathematics, for men thus endowed seem to have an extra sense. . . . In order to pass the B. A. examination, it was also necessary to get up Paley's *Evidences of Christianity,* and his *Moral Philosophy.* This was done in a thorough manner, and I am convinced that I could have written out the whole of the *Evidences* with perfect correctness, but not of course in the clear language of Paley. The logic of this book and, as I may add, of his *Natural Theology,* gave me as much delight as did Euclid. The careful study of these works, without attempting to learn any part by rote, was the only part of the academical course which, as I then felt and as I still believe, was of the least use to me in the education of my mind. I did not at that time trouble myself about Paley's premises, and taking these on trust I was charmed and convinced by the long line of argumentation."

One of the great opportunities of Darwin's life came to him when, some time after he had finished his course at Cambridge, he was offered a place as naturalist on the *Beagle,* a ship sent by the English government on a survey. At first Darwin thought he could not go because his father was opposed to the plan. Finally the father said he would consent if any man of common sense should advise his son to go. This common sense man was found in the person of his uncle, a Josiah Wedgwood, who advised the father to permit his son to go. The voyage has been described by Darwin, and thousands have been interested and profited by the reading. Some of the letters that he wrote to his friends during his trip are also very interesting. Here is one he sent to his cousin, Fox:

"My mind has been, since leaving England, in a perfect *hurricane* of delight and astonishment, and to this hour scarcely a minute has passed in idleness. . . . Geology carries the day; it is like the pleasure of gambling. Speculating, on first arrival, what the rocks may be, I often mentally cry out, three to one tertiary against primitive; but the latter has hitherto won all the bets. . . . My life, when at sea, is so quiet, that to a person who can employ himself, nothing can be pleasanter; the beauty of the sky and brilliancy of the ocean together make a picture. But when on shore, and wandering in the sublime forests, surrounded by views more gorgeous than Claude ever imagined, I enjoy a delight which none but those who have experienced it can understand. If it is to be done, it must be by studying Humboldt. At our ancient snug breakfasts, at Cambridge, I little thought that the wide Atlantic would ever separate us; but it is a rare privilege that with the body, the feelings and memory are not divided. On the contrary, the pleasantest scenes of my life, many of which have been at Cambridge, rise from the contrast of the present the more vividly in my imagination."

From Valparaiso, after he had been two years on the voyage, he writes to a friend:

"That this voyage must come to a conclusion my reason tells me, otherwise I see no end to it. It is impossible not bitterly to regret the friends and other sources of pleasure one leaves behind in England; in place of it there is much solid enjoyment, some present, but more in anticipation, when the ideas gained during the voyage can be compared with fresh ones. I find in Geology a never-failing interest, as it has been remarked, it creates the same grand ideas respecting the world which astronomy does for the universe. We have seen much fine scenery; that of the tropics in its glory and luxuriance exceeds even the language of Humboldt to describe. A Persian writer could alone do justice to it, and if he succeeded he would in England be called the 'Grandfather of all liars.' "

No one can read the life of Darwin without feeling great respect for his perseverance. His faithful devotion to his work can teach us all a useful lesson. Says his son:

"No one except my mother, knows the full amount of suffering he endured, or the full amount of his wonderful patience. For all the latter years of his life she never left him for a night, and her days were so planned that all his resting hours might be shared with her. She shielded him from every possible annoyance, and omitted nothing that might save him trouble, or prevent his becoming overtired, or that might alleviate the many discomforts of his ill-health. I hesitate to speak thus freely of a thing so sacred as the life-long devotion which prompted this constant and tender care. But it is, I repeat, a principal feature of his life, that for nearly forty years he never knew one day of the health of ordinary men, and that thus his life was one long struggle against the weariness and strain of sickness. And this cannot be told without speaking of the one condition which enabled him to bear the strain and fight out the struggle to the end."

That Darwin himself appreciated the goodness of his wife can be seen from the following tribute which has appeared in *More Letters of Charles Darwin*. It does not appear in the *Autobiography* because Mrs. Darwin was living at the time of its publication. Where in all literature can a more tender and beautiful appreciation be found?—

"You all know your mother, and what a good mother she has been to all of you. She has been my greatest blessing, and I can declare that in my whole life I have never heard her utter one word I would rather have been unsaid. She has never failed in kindest sympathy towards me, and has borne with the utmost patience my frequent complaints of ill-health and discomfort. I do not believe she has ever missed an opportunity of doing a kind action to any one near her. I marvel at my good fortune that she, so infinitely my superior in every single moral quality, consented to be my wife. She has been my wise adviser and cheerful comforter throughout life, which without her would have been during a very long period a miserable one from ill-health. She has earned the love of every soul near her."

XLIII

HUXLEY was more than one of the greatest scientists of the last century; he was a man of literary ability. By his popular lectures and clear expositions he probably did more than any other man of the century to popularize the many and important discoveries of the scientific world. At first there was much opposition to him, owing to a lack of information on the part of the public as to the import of the doctrine of evolution. Ex-President Gilman of Johns Hopkins University tells what a storm of protest was raised in America when Huxley was invited to deliver the opening address at the founding of the new university. Huxley is not even now regarded as an orthodox man, but much of the former prejudice has given way.

John Fiske, who in so many ways can be regarded as the American Huxley, has published a magazine article giving his impressions of Huxley. In this article he gives two versions of a famous Huxley anecdote. Here is one:

"It was at the meeting of the British Association at Oxford in 1860, soon after the publication of Darwin's epoch-making book, and while people in general were wagging their heads at it, that the subject came up before a hostile and fashionable audience. Samuel Wilberforce, the plausible and self-complacent Bishop of Oxford, commonly known as 'Soapy Sam,' launched out in a rash speech, conspicuous for its ignorant mis-statements, and highly seasoned with appeals to the prejudices of the audience, upon whose lack of intelligence the speaker relied. Near him sat Huxley, already known as a man of science, and known to look favorably upon Darwinism, but more or less youthful withal, only five-and-thirty, so that the bishop anticipated sport in badgering him. At the close of his speech he suddenly turned upon Huxley and begged to be informed if the learned gentleman was really willing to be regarded as the descendant of a monkey. Eager self-confidence had blinded the bishop to the tactical blunder in thus inviting a retort. Huxley was instantly upon his feet with a speech demolishing the bishop's card house of mistakes; and at the close he observed that since a question of personal preferences had been very improperly brought into a discussion of a scientific theory, he felt free to confess that if the alternatives were descent, on the one hand from a respectable monkey, or on the other from a bishop of the English church who would stoop to such misrepresentations and sophisms as the audience had lately listened to, he would declare in favor of the monkey! . . . It is curious to read that in the ensuing buzz of excitement a lady fainted, and had to be carried from the room; but the audience were in general quite alive to the bishop's blunder in manners and tactics, and, with the genuine English love of fair play, they loudly applauded Huxley. From that time forth it was recognized that he was not the sort of man to be browbeaten. As for Bishop Wilberforce, he carried with him from the affray no bitterness, but was always afterwards most courteous to his castigator.''

Huxley was a great reader of history, poetry, metaphysics, and fiction, but this is not what made him a great scientist. Original men make books, they do not need to read them. Yet Huxley loved to read. He even in his old age studied Greek to read Aristotle and the New Testament in the original. But Huxley loved things even more than books. He had little respect for mere bookish knowledge. "A rash clergyman once, without further equipment in natural science than desultory reading, attacked the Darwinian theory in some sundry magazine articles, in which he made himself uncommonly merry at Huxley's expense. This was intended to draw the great man's fire, and as the batteries remained silent the author proceeded to write to Huxley, calling his attention to the articles, and at the same time, with mock modesty, asking advice as to the further study of these deep questions. Huxley's answer was brief and to the point: 'Take a cockroach and dissect it.' ''

Huxley was fond of children and their ways. His son, Leonard, tells us that Julian, the grandchild of Huxley was a child made up of a combination of cherub and pickle. Huxley had been in his garden watering with a hose. The little four-year-old was with him. Huxley came in and said: "I like that chap! I like the way he looks you straight in the face and disobeys you. I told him not to go on the wet grass again. He just looked up boldly straight at me, as much as to say, 'What do *you* mean by ordering me about?' and deliberately walked on to the grass." In the spring the approval was not so decided. "I like that chap; he looks you straight in the face. But there's a falling off in one respect since last August—he now does what he is told."

When Julian, the grandchild, was learning to read and write, he became interested in *Water-Babies,* a story that has delighted so many children. In it he found a reference to his grandfather as one who knew much about water-babies. So he wrote to his grandfather.

Dear Grandpater, have you seen a water baby? Did you put it in a bottle? Did it wonder if it could get out? Can I see it some day? Your loving

JULIAN.

This is the answer to the letter:

March 24, 1892.

MY DEAR JULIAN:

I never could make out about that water-baby. I have seen babies in water and babies in bottles; but the baby in the water was not in the bottle and the baby in the bottle was not in the water. Ever your loving

GRANDPATER.

Huxley was also fond of cats and dogs and pets of all kind. His son tells us that once he found his father in an uncomfortable seat, while the cat had the best chair. He defended himself by saying that he could not turn the beast away. In 1893 a man, who was writing on the *Pets of Celebrities,* wrote to him for information concerning his personal likings. Huxley sent him this letter:

A long series of cats has reigned over my household for the last forty years or thereabouts; but I am sorry to say that I have no pictorial or other record of their physical and moral excellencies.

The present occupant of the throne is a large young gray tabby, Oliver by name. Not that in any sense he is a protector, for I doubt whether he has the heart to kill a mouse. However, I saw him catch and eat the first butterfly of the season, and trust that the germ of courage thus manifest may develop, with age, into efficient mousing.

As to sagacity, I should say that his judgment respecting the warmest place and the softest cushion in the room is infallible, his punctuality at meal-time is admirable, and his pertinacity in jumping on people's shoulders till they give him some of the best of what is going indicates great firmness.

XLIV

ROBERT LOUIS STEVENSON, the writer of *Treasure Island* and many other exciting romances, was an exile from home during the last few years of his life. The state of his health demanded a sunny clime and so he was forced to live in Samoa, a group of islands in the South Pacific. About three miles behind Apia, on a slight plateau seven hundred feet above the level of the sea, he cleared the forest and made a house. "I have chosen the land to be my land, the people to be my people, to live and die with," said Stevenson in his speech to the Samoan chiefs. Mr. Lloyd Osbourne, his step-son, thus describes their abode:

"Unbroken forest covered Vailima when first we saw it; not the forest of the temperate zone with its varied glades and open spaces, but the thick tangle of the tropics, dense, dark, and cold in even the hottest day, where one must walk cutlass in hand to slash the lianas and the red-edged stinging leaves of a certain tree that continually bar one's path. The murmur of streams and cascades fell sometimes upon our ears as we wandered in the deep shade, and mingled with the cooing of wild doves and the mysterious, haunting sound of a native woodpecker at work. Our Chinaman, who was with us on our first survey, busied himself with taking samples of the soil, and grew almost incoherent with the richness of what he called the 'dirty.' We, for our part, were no less enchanted with what we saw, and could realize, as we forced our way through the thickets and skirted the deep ravines, what a noble labor lay before our axes, what exquisite views and glorious gardens could be carved out of the broken mountain side and the sullen forest.''

As Stevenson was afraid that villas might be made to intervene between him and the sea, he bought much land that his view might be forever unobstructed. He entered into the work of clearing the forest with vigorous delight. For months he lived in pioneer confusion. Gangs of native workmen worked from morning to night.

''The new house was built,'' says Mr. Osbourne; ''I arrived from England with the furniture, the library, and other effects of our old home; the phase of hard work and short commons passed gradually away, and a form of hollow comfort dawned upon us. I say hollow comfort, for though we began to accumulate cows, horses, and the general apparatus of civilized life, the question of service became a vexing one. An expensive German cooked our meals and quarreled with the white house-maid; the white overseer said 'that manual labor was the one thing that never agreed with him,' and that it was an unwholesome thing for a man to be awakened in the early morning, 'for one ought to wake up natural-like,' he explained. The white carter 'couldn't bear with niggers,' and though he did his work well and faithfully, he helped to demoralize the place and loosen discipline. Everything was at sixes and sevens, when, on the occasion of Mrs. Stevenson's going to Fiji for a few months' rest, my sister and I took charge of affairs. The expensive German was bidden to depart; Mr. Stevenson discharged the carter; the white overseer (who was tied to us by contract) was bought off in cold coin, to sleep out his 'natural sleep' under a kindlier star and to engage himself (presumably) in intellectual labors elsewhere. There are two sides to 'white slavery' —that cherished expression of the labor agitator —and with the departure of our tyrants we began again to raise our diminished heads. My sister and I threw ourselves into the kitchen, and took up the labor of cooking with zeal and determination; the domestic boundaries proved too narrow for our new-found energies, and we overflowed into the province of entertainment, with decorated menus, silver plate and finger-bowls! The aristocracy of Apia was pressed to lunch with us, to commend our independence and to eat our biscuits. It was a French Revolution in miniature; we danced the carmagnole in the kitchen and were prepared to conquer the Samoan social world. One morning, before the ardor and zest of it all had time to be dulled by custom, I happened to discover a young and very handsome Samoan on our back veranda. He was quite a dandified youngster, with a red flower behind his ear and his hair limed in the latest fashion. I liked his open, attractive face and his unembarrassed manner, and inquired what propitious fate had brought him to sit upon our ice-chest and radiate good nature on our back porch. It seemed that Simele, the overseer, owed him two Chile dollars, and that he was here, bland, friendly, but insistent, to collect the debt in person. That Simele would not be back for hours in no way daunted him, and he seemed prepared to swing his brown legs and show his white teeth for a whole eternity.

" 'Chief,' I said, a sudden thought striking me, 'you are he that I have been looking for so long. You are going to stay in Vailima and be our cook!'

" 'But I don't know how to cook,' he replied.

" 'That is no matter,' I said. 'Two months ago I was as you; to-day I am a splendid cook. I will teach you my skill.'

" 'But I don't want to learn,' he said, and brought back the conversation to Chile dollars.

" 'There is no good making excuses,' I said. 'This is a psychological moment in the history of Vailima. You are the Man of Destiny.'

" 'But I haven't my box,' he expostulated.

" 'I will send for it,' I returned. 'I would not lose you for twenty boxes. If you need clothes, why there stands my own chest; flowers grow in profusion and the oil-bottle rests never empty beside my humble bed; and in the hot hours of the afternoon there is the beautifulest pool where one can bathe and wash one's lovely hair. Moreover, so generous are the regulations of Tusitala's (Stevenson's) government that his children receive weekly large sums of money, and they are allowed on Sundays to call their friends to this elegant house and entertain them with salt beef and biscuit.'

"Thus was Taalolo introduced into the Vailima kitchen, never to leave it for four years save when the war-drum called him to the front with a six-shooter and a 'death-tooth'—the Samoan war-cutlass or head-knife. He became in time not only an admirable chef, but the nucleus of the whole native establishment and the loyalest of our whole Samoan family. His coming was the turning-point in the history of the house. We had achieved independence of our white masters, and their discontented white faces had disappeared one by one. Honest brown ones now took their places and we gained more than good servants by the change."

The following incident illustrates the high regard in which Stevenson was held by the native Samoans. When Mataafa, a claimant for the throne of Upolo, was imprisoned by the European powers, Stevenson visited him in prison and gave him tobacco and other gifts to cheer the disconsolate chief. He also visited other prisoners who had sided in the affairs of Mataafa. When they were released they wished to show their gratitude in some tangible way. So they built a fine wide road to the home of the famous writer, a work which they disliked but which their love for Stevenson enabled them to accomplish. They called it "The Road of the Loving-Heart." Once when his favorite body-servant, Sosimo, had anticipated some of his master's wants and Stevenson had complimented him with, "Great is the wisdom!" "Nay," replied Sosimo with truer insight, "Great is the Love!"

Stevenson's manner of life at Vailima was somewhat like this: At six o'clock or earlier he arose and began the day's work. By dawn the rest of the household were up, and at about eight his wife's daughter began to take his dictation, working from then until noon. The afternoons were usually spent in some form of recreation— riding was a favorite pastime. He was fond of strolling through the tropical forest, and of taking part in any of the numerous outdoor sports. However, when he was in the height of literary inspiration, he stayed at his desk all day long.

On Sunday evening the household was always called together for prayers; a chapter was read from the Samoan Bible, Samoan hymns were sung and one of Stevenson's own beautiful prayers, one usually written for the occasion, was read, concluding with the Lord's Prayer in the tongue of the natives. In the dominant note of these prayers, the call for courage and cheerfulness, one can hear the cry of the dying Stevenson's need: "The day returns and brings us the petty round of irritating concerns and duties. Help us to play the man, help us to perform them with laughter and kind faces, let cheerfulness abound with industry. . . . Give us health, food, bright weather, and light hearts. . . . As the sun lightens the world, so let our loving-kindness make bright the house of our habitation."

Stevenson died as he wished—in the midst of his work. After a day spent in writing his *Weir of Hermiston,* a day full of life and gayety, he suddenly fainted and died a short time afterwards. In the prayer offered the evening before had been this sentence,—"When the day returns, return to us our sun and comforter, and call us up with morning faces and with morning hearts, eager to be happy, if happiness shall be our portion—and if the day be marked for sorrow, strong to endure it.''

On the following morning a group of powerful Samoans bore the coffin upon their shoulders to the summit of Mount Vaea, where it was the wish of Mr. Stevenson that he should rest. One of the inscriptions upon the tomb is his own noble *Requiem:*

> Under the wide and starry sky
> Dig the grave and let me lie;
> Glad did I live and gladly die,
>   And I laid me down with a will.
>
> This be the verse you grave for me:
> Here he lies where he longed to be;
> Home is the sailor, home from the sea,
>   And the hunter home from the hill.

XLV

IN four lines of oft-quoted poetry Pope has
declared that with words the same rule holds
that applies to fashion,—"Alike fantastic if
too new or old." Fashion changes, not only the
fashions of millinery but of literature also. When
the world is tired of the brilliant wit of Byron,
it turns in relief to the contemplative verse of
Wordsworth; when Longfellow and Tennyson
have had their artistic day and a thousand
imitators have produced romantic poetry, because

> Most can raise the flowers now
> For all have got the seed,—

then this same world turns with delight to the
robust poetry of Kipling. He has brought a new
dish to the banquet of life, or at least a new flavor
has been given to the old.

Kipling is a man's poet, robust and virile. As
a preface to one of his stories he wrote:

> Go stalk the red deer o'er the heather,
> Ride, follow the fox, if you can!
> But for pleasure and profit together
> Allow me the hunting of man;—

and this joy in the hunting of man is what has

made Kipling so acceptable to men. Kipling
has the defects of his virtues. There is a certain brutality in his point of view. His beautiful
Recessional is not the greater part of Kipling.
His voice "is still for war." His critics charge
him with "Jingoism." One of the most brilliant
parodies of recent times is Watson's

> Best by remembering God, say some,
> We keep our high imperial lot—
> Fortune, I think, has mainly come
> When we forgot, when we forgot!

The greater influence of Kipling, both in his
prose and poetry, is contrary to the humanitarian
spirit of the age. Le Gallienne has said,—"As a
writer Mr. Kipling is a delight; as an influence
a danger."

Mr. Kipling sprang into public notice because
he had genius and because he had a new world
to reveal to a jaded public. Mr. E. Kay Robinson was a friend and associate of Kipling when
both were in the land of mysteries, India. Mr.
Robinson went to India in 1884 and soon began
to write verses over the signature of "K. R."
Kipling was writing ballads under the initials
"R. K." The similarity of the signatures attracted Kipling and he wrote to Robinson. They
were afterwards associated in newspaper work
and became close friends. Robinson has written
about Kipling in India:

"My first sight of Kipling was at an uninteresting stage, when he was a short, square, dark
youth, who unfortunately wore spectacles instead
of eyeglasses and had an unlucky eye for color in
the selection of his clothes. He had a weakness
apparently for brown cloth with just that sugges-

tion of ruddiness or purple in it which makes
some browns so curiously conspicuous. The
charm of his manner, however, made you forget
what he looked like in half a minute. . . .

"Among Kipling's early journalistic experiences was his involuntary assumption 'for this
occasion only' of the rôle of the fighting editor.
He was essentially a man of peace, and would
always prefer making an angry man laugh to
fighting with him; but one day there called at
the office a very furious photographer. What
the paper may have said about him or his photographs has been forgotten, but never will those
who witnessed it forget the rough-and-tumble all
over the floor in which he and Kipling indulged.
The libel, or whatever it was, which had infu-
riated the photographer was not Kipling's work,
but the quarrel was forced upon him, and although he was handicapped by his spectacles and
smaller stature he made a very fine draw of it,
and then the photographer—who, it may be remarked, was very drunk—was ejected. And
Kipling wiped his glasses and buttoned his collar.

"That trick of wiping his spectacles is one
which Kipling indulged more frequently than any
man I have ever met, for the simple reason that
he was always laughing; and when you laugh till
you nearly cry your spectacles get misty. Kipling, shaking all over with laughter, and wiping
his spectacles at the same time with his hand-
kerchief, is the picture which always comes to
mind as most characteristic of him in the old
days."

With regard to Kipling's minute and exact

knowledge of details Mr. Robinson has this to say:

"To learn to write as soldiers think, he spent long hours loafing with the genuine article. He watched them at work and at play and at prayer from the points of view of all his confidants—the combatant officer, the doctor, the chaplain, the drill sergeant, and the private himself. With the navy, with every branch of sport, and with natural history, he has never wearied in seeking to learn all that man may learn at first-hand, or the very best second-hand, at any rate. . . . But most wonderful was his insight into the strangely mixed manners of life and thought of the natives of India. He knew them all through their horizontal divisions of rank and their vertical sections of caste; their ramifications of race and blood; their antagonisms and blendings of creed; their hereditary strains of calling or handicraft. Show him a native, and he would tell you his rank, caste, race, origin, habitat, creed, and calling. He would speak to the man in his own fashion, using familiar, homely figures, which brightened the other's surprised eyes with recognition of brotherhood and opened a straight way into his confidence. In two minutes the man—perhaps a wild hawk from the Afghan hills—would be pouring out into the ear of this sahib, with heaven-sent knowledge and sympathy, the weird tale of the blood feud and litigation, the border fray, and the usurer's iniquity, which had driven him so far afield as Lahore from Bajaur. To Kipling even the most suspected and suspicious of classes, the religious mendicants, would open their mouths freely.

"By the road thick with the dust of camels and thousands of cattle and goats, which winds from Lahore Fort to the River Ravi, there are walled caravanserais the distant smell of which more than suffices for most of the Europeans who pass, but sitting with the travelers in the reeking inside Kipling heard weird tales and gathered much knowledge. Under a spreading peepul tree overhanging a well by the same road squatted daily a ring of almost naked fakirs, smeared with ashes, who scowled at the European driving by; but for Kipling there was, when he wished it, an opening in the squatting circle and much to be learned from the unsavory talkers. That is how Kipling's finished word-pictures take the lifelike aspect of instantaneous photographs."

XLVI

BENJAMIN FRANKLIN had so many strong qualities, was eminent in so many lines of endeavor, that we do not always include him among the literary men of America. However, his *Autobiography* is a masterpiece. In sincerity and simplicity it is unsurpassed. This is all the more remarkable because it was written at a time when ornate writing was the fashion. A man's style is the outgrowth of his nature, and it is a striking comment upon the robust quality of Franklin's mind that his style has the simplicity of the Bible, or *Pilgrim's Progress*.

The following account, taken from his *Autobiography*, begins just after he has landed in New York, a boy of seventeen who has run away from home because he felt that his brother was not treating him fairly:

My inclinations for the sea were by this time worn out, or I might now have gratified them. But, having a trade, and supposing myself a pretty good workman, I offered my service to the printer in the place, old Mr. William Bradford, who had been the first printer in Pennsylvania, but removed from thence upon the quarrel of George Keith. He could give me no employment, having little to do and help enough already; but, says he, "My son at Philadelphia has lately lost his principal hand, Aquilla Rose, by death; if you go thither I believe he may employ you." Philadelphia was a hundred miles farther; I set out, however, in a boat for Amboy, leaving my chest and things to follow me round by sea.

In crossing the bay we met with a squall that tore our rotten sails to pieces, prevented our getting into the Kill, and drove us upon Long Island. In our way, a drunken Dutchman, who was a passenger too, fell overboard. When he was sinking, I reached through the water to his shock pate, and drew him up so that we got him in again. His ducking sobered him a little, and he went to sleep, taking first out of his pocket a book, which he desired I would dry for him. It proved to be my old favorite author, Bunyan's *Pilgrim's Progress,* in Dutch, finely printed on good paper, with copper cuts, a dress better than I had ever seen it wear in its own language. I have since found that it has been translated into most of the languages of Europe, and suppose it has been more generally than any other book, except, perhaps, the Bible. Honest John was the first that I know of who mixed narration and dialogue; a method of writing very engaging to the reader, who in the most interesting parts finds himself, as it were, brought into the company and present at the discourse. Defoe in his *Crusoe,* his *Moll Flanders, Religious Courtship, Family Instructor,* and other pieces, has imitated it with success, and Richardson has done the same in his *Pamela,* etc.

When we drew near the island we found it was

at a place where there could be no landing, there being a great surf on the stony beach. So we dropped anchor, and swung round toward the shore. Some people came down to the water edge and hallooed to us, as we did to them; but the wind was so high and the surf so loud that we could not hear so as to understand each other. There were canoes on the shore, and we made signs, and hallooed that they should fetch us, but they either did not understand us or thought it impracticable, so they went away, and night coming on, we had no remedy but to wait till the wind should abate. In the meantime, the boatman and I concluded to sleep if we could, and so crowded into the scuttle with the Dutchman, who was still wet, and the spray beating over the head of our boat leaked through to us, so that we were almost as wet as he. In this manner we lay all night, with very little rest; but the wind abating the next day, we made a shift to reach Amboy before night, having been thirty hours on the water, without victuals, or any drink but a bottle of filthy rum, the water we sailed on being salt.

In the evening I found myself very feverish, and went in to bed; but, having read somewhere that cold water, drunk plentifully, was good for a fever, I followed the prescription, sweat plentifully most of the night, my fever left me, and in the morning, crossing the ferry, I proceeded on my journey on foot, having fifty miles to Burlington, where I was told I should find boats that would carry me the rest of the way to Philadelphia.

It rained very hard all the day. I was thoroughly soaked, and by noon a good deal tired, so I stopped at a poor inn, where I stayed all night, beginning now to wish that I had never left home. I cut so miserable a figure, too, that I found, by the questions asked me, I was suspected to be some runaway servant and in danger of being taken up on that suspicion. However, I proceeded the next day, and got in the evening to an inn, within eight or ten miles of Burlington, kept by one Dr. Brown. He entered into conversation with me while I took some refreshment, and finding I had read a little, became very sociable and friendly. Our acquaintance continued as long as he lived. He had been, I imagine, an itinerant doctor, for there was no town in England, or country in Europe, of which he could not give a very particular account. He had some letters, and was ingenious, but much of an unbeliever, and wickedly undertook, some years after, to travesty the Bible in doggerel verse, as Cotton had done Virgil. By this means he set many of the facts in a very ridiculous light, and might have hurt weak minds if his work had been published; but it never was.

At his house I lay that night, and the next morning reached Burlington, but had the mortification to find that the regular boats were gone a little before my coming, and no other expected to go before Tuesday, this being Saturday; wherefore I returned to an old woman in the town of whom I had bought gingerbread to eat on the water, and asked her advice. She invited me to lodge at her house till a passage by water should offer; and, being tired with my foot traveling, I accepted the invitation. She, understanding I was a printer, would have had me stay at that town and follow my business, being ignorant of the stock necessary to begin with. She was very hospitable, gave me a dinner of ox cheek with great good will, accepting only of a pot of ale in return; and I thought myself fixed till Tuesday should come. However, walking in the evening by the side of the river, a boat came by, which I found was going toward Philadelphia, with several people in her. They took me in, and, as there was no wind, we rowed all the way, and about midnight, not having yet seen the city, some of the company were confident we must have passed it, and would row no farther. The others knew not where we were, so we put toward the shore, got into a creek, and landed near an old fence, with the rails of which we made a fire, the night being cold, in October, and there we remained till daylight. Then one of the company knew the place to be Cooper's Creek, a little above Philadelphia, which we saw as soon as we got out of the creek, and arrived there about eight or nine o'clock on the Sunday morning, and landed at the Market Street wharf.

I have been the more particular in this description of my journey, and shall be so of my first entry into that city, that you may in your mind compare such unlikely beginnings with the figure I have since made there. I was in my working dress, my best clothes being to come round by sea. I was dirty from my journey; my pockets were stuffed out with shirts and stockings, and I knew no soul, nor where to look for lodging. I was fatigued with traveling, rowing, and want of rest; I was very hungry, and my whole stock of cash consisted of a Dutch dollar and about a shilling in copper. The latter I gave the people of the boat for my passage, who at first refused it, on account of my rowing; but I insisted on their taking it, a man being sometimes more generous when he has but a little money than when he has plenty, perhaps through fear of being thought to have but little.

Then I walked up the street, gazing about, till near the market house I met a boy with bread. I had made many a meal on bread, and, inquiring where he got it, I went immediately to the baker's he directed me to, in Second Street, and asked for biscuit, intending such as we had in Boston; but they, it seems, were not made in Philadelphia. Then I asked for a threepenny loaf, and was told they had none such. So not considering or knowing the difference of money and the greater cheapness, nor the names of his bread, I bade him give me threepenny worth of any sort. He gave me, accordingly, three great puffy rolls. I was surprised at the quantity, but took it, and, having no room in my pockets, walked off with a roll under each arm, and eating the other. Thus I went up Market Street as far as Fourth Street, passing by the door of Mr. Read, my future wife's father; when she, standing at the door, saw me, and thought I made, as I certainly did, a most awkward, ridiculous appearance. Then I turned and went down Chestnut Street and part of Walnut Street, eating my roll all the way, and, coming round, found myself again on Market Street wharf, near the boat I came in, to which I went for a draught of the river water; and, being filled with one of my rolls, gave the other two to a woman and her child that came down the river in the boat with us, and were waiting to go farther.

Thus refreshed, I walked again up the street, which by this time had many clean-dressed people in it, who were all walking the same way. I joined them, and was thereby led into the great meetinghouse of the Quakers near the market. I sat down among them, and, after looking round awhile and hearing nothing said, being very drowsy through labor and want of rest the preceding night, I fell fast asleep, and continued so till the meeting broke up, when one was kind enough to rouse me. This was, therefore, the first house I was in, or slept in, in Philadelphia.

Walking down again toward the river, and looking in the faces of people, I met a young Quaker man, whose countenance I liked, and, accosting him, requested he would tell me where a stranger could get lodging. We were then near the sign of the Three Mariners. "Here," says he, "is one place that entertains strangers, but it is not a reputable house; if thee wilt walk with me I'll show thee a better." He brought me to the Crooked Billet, in Water Street. Here I got a dinner, and while I was eating it several sly questions were asked me, as it seemed to be suspected from my youth and appearance that I might be some runaway.

After dinner my sleepiness returned, and, being shown to a bed, I lay down without undressing and slept till six in the evening, was called to supper, went to bed again very early, and slept soundly till next morning. Then I made myself as tidy as I could, and went to Andrew Bradford the printer's. I found in the shop the old man,

his father, whom I had seen in New York, and
who, traveling on horseback, had got to Philadelphia before me.   He introduced me to his son,
who received me civilly, and gave me a breakfast,
but told me he did not at present want a hand,
being lately supplied with one; but there was
another printer in town, lately set up, one Kei-
mer, who, perhaps, might employ me; if not, I
should be welcome to lodge at his house, and he
would give me a little work to do now and then
till fuller business should offer.

XLVII

WASHINGTON IRVING may be called the father of American literature. It is true he is not the first writer who flourished on American soil, but in point of accomplishment he is the first literary man to impress himself upon the readers of the two continents. And what a sweet, beautiful soul he is! The only rival he has is Franklin, and Franklin is not a literary man, though he produced a literary masterpiece in his *Autobiography*. The test of a great piece of literature is, In a hundred years can it be bought in a new edition for ten cents? The New Testament can be bought for ten cents, so can the *Autobiography,* and the *Sketch Book*. These emerge from the sea of mediocrity of early American life. They abide while the works of the Michael Wigglesworths and Anne Bradstreets can be found only in the collections of the fortunate book-lover.

The early settlers believed in the virtue of large families. It is well, for otherwise Franklin and Irving would have been lost to American life. Franklin was the youngest son in a family of seventeen children, there were two girls younger (Benjamin was the eighth child of the second wife), and Irving was the eighth son and last child in a family of eleven children. It is not hard to account for Irving's first name. Nowadays when you meet a boy named Dewey or Garfield it is not difficult to guess the boy's age. Irving was born in 1783; the air was laden with the praises of the great American leader. "Washington's work is ended," said the mother, "and the child shall be named after him." Several years after this when Washington, as President, was in New York, Lizzie, the Scotch servant of the Irving family, followed the great man into a shop and said, "Please, your honor, here's a bairn was named after you." Washington placed his hand on the lad's head and gave him a fatherly blessing.

Like Lowell and Bryant, Irving was first devoted to the law, but his devotion was not of the quality that consumes. He soon strayed into pleasanter paths. In January, 1807, appeared the first number of *Salmagundi,* a humorous periodical which caused a great deal of curiosity as to the authors, whose witty articles appeared anonymously. Two years later came the droll *History of New York by Diedrich Knickerbocker,* a book in which according to Scott were to be seen traces of the wit of Swift. Scott said that he used to read it aloud to his wife and guests until "our sides were absolutely sore with laughing."

Before this work had appeared, Irving lost in three consecutive years three persons who would have rejoiced the most in his success,—his father, "the tenderest and best of sisters, a woman of whom a brother might be proud," and his sweetheart, Matilda Hoffman. She was a rare and beautiful maiden who had kindled in the heart of Irving a passion which survived her death until he himself passed away an old man. When he died his friends found her miniature and a lock of fair hair, together with the part of a manuscript written for a lady who had asked Irving why he had never married. Describing Miss Hoffman he says:

"The more I saw her, the more I had reason to admire her. Her mind seemed to unfold itself leaf by leaf, and every time to discover new sweetness. Nobody knew her so well as I, for she was generally silent. . . . Never did I meet with more intuitive rectitude of mind, more delicacy, more exquisite propriety in word, thought, and action than in this young creature. Her brilliant little sister used to say that 'people began by admiring her, but ended by loving Matilda.' For my part I idolized her." Irving then continues by giving a long account of his efforts to succeed in his literary and legal work with a view of earning a place in life so as to enable him to marry. "In the midst of this struggle and anxiety she fell into a consumption. I cannot tell you what I suffered. . . . I saw her fade rapidly away, beautiful, and more beautiful, and more angelic to the very last. I was often by her bedside, and when her mind wandered she would talk to me with a sweet, natural, and affecting eloquence that was overpowering. I saw more of the beauty of her mind in that delirious state than I ever had before. . . . I was by her when she died, and was the last she ever looked upon. . . . She was but seventeen."

So poignant was the grief of Irving that for thirty years after her death he did not like any one to mention her name to him. One day he was visiting her father when one of her nieces, taking some music from a drawer, brought with it a piece of embroidery. "Washington," said Mr. Hoffman, "this was poor Matilda's work." The effect was instantaneous. The light-hearted conversationalist of a moment before became silent and soon left the house. When in *Bracebridge Hall* he writes,—"I have loved as I never again shall love in this world—I have been loved as I shall never again be loved,"—is he not thinking of the fair Matilda? And in a note-book we find, —"She died in the beauty of her youth, and in my memory she will ever be young and beautiful."

In May, 1815, Irving went abroad for the second time. His purpose was to stay a few months; he remained seventeen years. The first sight that greeted the newly arrived American in Liverpool was the mail-coach bringing the news of the battle of Waterloo. Irving's sympathies were with Napoleon. "In spite of all his misdeeds he is a noble fellow, and I am confident will eclipse in the eyes of posterity all the crowned wiseacres that have crushed him by their overwhelming confederacy." In the year 1818 the Irving brothers went into bankruptcy. Washington's interest in the business was that of a younger brother who had little responsibility. But of late years he had been much harassed by the accumulating troubles. With the end of the business anxieties he turns to literature with a whole-souled devotion. His home friends tried to secure for him the position of Secretary of the Legation in London; his brother William wrote that Commodore Decatur was keeping open for his acceptance the office of Chief Clerk in the Navy Department; but Irving turned the offers aside. Irving is usually imaged as a sunshiny, genial, easy-going gentleman into whose blood little of the iron of firmness had been infused. The fact that he not only refused these offers but also rejected offers from Scott and Murray shows that he had will enough to keep to the bent of his genius at a time when he needed money and influence. Murray offered him a salary of £1000 a year to be the editor of a periodical.

The first number of the *Sketch Book* appeared in May, 1819, and consisted mainly in point of merit of two papers, *The Wife* and *Rip Van Winkle*. The series was finished in 1820. The work was highly successful in America, and Irving was deeply moved by the cordial expressions of praise that reached him. His manly nature is revealed in a letter to a friend in which he says, —"I hope you will not attribute all this sensibility to the kind reception I have met to an author's vanity. I am sure it proceeds from very different sources. Vanity could not bring the tears into my eyes as they have been brought by the kindness of my countrymen. I have felt cast down, blighted, and broken-spirited, and these sudden rays of sunshine agitate me more than they revive me. I hope—I hope I may yet do something more worthy of the appreciation lavished on me."

Irving had not intended to publish the *Sketch Book* in England, but owing to reprints by others he was obliged to take the matter in his own hands. Murray refused to undertake the work. Then Irving became his own publisher. But the work sold so well that Murray bought the copyright for two hundred pounds.

In 1826 we find Irving in Spain. To the American reader the name of Spain is forever associated with that of Irving, for *The Alhambra, The Conquest of Granada,* and *The Life of Columbus* are the rich evidences of his absorption of the spirit of Spain. The *Life of Columbus* was written with great care. Irving wanted to produce something that would do credit to the scholarship of his loved America. Murray paid about fifteen thousand dollars for the English copyright. For the *Conquest of Granada* he received ten thousand dollars, and for *The Alhambra* a Mr. Bentley paid five thousand.

While Irving was in Madrid one of his most welcome visitors was Longfellow, then a young man of twenty, fresh from college. Writing to his father Longfellow says,—"Mr. Rich's family is very agreeable, and Washington Irving always makes one there in the evening. This is altogether delightful, for he is one of those men who put you at ease with them in a moment. He makes no ceremony whatever with one, and of course is a very fine man in society, all mirth and good humor. He has a most beautiful countenance, and a very intellectual one, but he has some halting and hesitating in his conversation, and says very pleasant, agreeable things in a husky, weak, peculiar voice. He has a dark complexion, dark hair, whiskers already a little gray. This is a very offhand portrait of so illustrious a man."

It is interesting to compare this sketch with one that Longfellow drew from memory many years later,—"I had the pleasure of meeting Mr. Irving in Spain, and found the author, whom I had loved, repeated in the man. The same playful humor, the same touches of sentiment, the same poetic atmosphere; and what I admired still more, the entire absence of all literary jealousy, of all that mean avarice of fame which counts what is given to another as so much taken from one's self. . . . Passing his house at the early hour of six one summer morning, I saw his study window already wide open. On my mentioning it to him afterwards he said, 'Yes, I am always at work by six.' Since then I have often remembered that sunny morning and that open window, so suggestive of his sunny temperament and his open heart, and equally so of his patient and persistent toil."

Irving's career is usually looked upon as ideal. In many ways it was singularly blessed. Friends, influence, fame, and wealth were his. When an American publisher undertook the issuing of a new edition of Irving's works in 1848, there was much uncertainty as to the success of the venture, but the author received eighty-eight thousand dollars from 1848 to 1859. He also had the satisfaction of working to the last, although the last year was one of suffering. "I am rather fatigued, my dear, by my night's rest," he replied to the anxious inquiry of a niece. He had been hard at work upon his *Life of Washington*, and he sometimes feared he might have overtaxed his brain. "I do not fear death," he said, "but I would like to go down with all sails set."

This modest prayer was granted. To the day of his death he was able to receive visitors, talk intelligently, read for his own pleasure, and take short drives. The day before he died he attended church, and on coming home he remarked that he must "get a dispensation to allow whist on Sunday evenings," because he dreaded the long, lonely nights. On Monday he went to bed, and as he turned to arrange the pillows he gave a slight exclamation and instantly expired.

By his mother's side they laid him, in a cemetery overlooking the Hudson and the valley of Sleepy Hollow, a region made forever famous by the genial pen of Irving. "I could not but remember his last words to me," writes a friend who made a pilgrimage to the spot on the day of the funeral, "when his book was finished and his health was failing: 'I am getting ready to go. I am shutting up my doors and windows.' And I could not but feel that they were all open now, and bright with the light of eternal morning."

XLVIII

JAMES FENIMORE COOPER is one of the most interesting characters in the history of American authorship. Irving, Longfellow, Whittier, Lowell, Holmes, and Hawthorne early in life showed their literary bent, and lived academic and peaceful careers. They were also popular. Cooper was thirty years old before he thought of writing, and his life was embittered by the consciousness that he was the target of the most bitter criticism, both at home and abroad. Yet not one of the distinguished authors I have named is more widely known to-day than Cooper. Matthew Arnold has said somewhere that an author's place in the future is to be determined by his contemporaneous ranking in foreign lands. If that is true the names of Mark Twain, Cooper, Walt Whitman, and Poe will rank high in the annals of posterity, for their European fame is said to be the most general of any of the American writers.

There is an appealing fascination about the boyhood days of Cooper. When James was a babe of fourteen months his father moved to the headwaters of the Susquehanna. The family consisted of fifteen persons; James, the future

242

novelist, was the eleventh of twelve children. Their home was in the midst of the forest. Near by was the charming lake, Otsego. The father owned several thousand acres, and was, probably, the most prominent man in that sparsely-settled region. What boy would want a finer opportunity to indulge all the wild propensities that lurk in the untamed heart of every healthy youngster? To roam in the untracked forest, to sail the lake, to hunt, to fish, to dream of the great unknown world lying just beyond the sun-tipped trees,—what can the schools give in exchange for this? Is it surprising that the wholesomeness of the forest and the charm and freshness of God's out-of-doors found their way into the man's novels, when so many delightful boyhood experiences must have found their way into the boy's heart?

As I said, Cooper was thirty years old before he began to write. He had studied under an Episcopal rector, and was intending to enter the junior class at Yale; the rector died and Cooper entered the second term of the freshman class; for some frolic in which he was engaged he was dismissed; he then entered the navy, where he gathered valuable experience which he worked afterwards into literature; he married; resigned, and lived the quiet life of a country gentleman. One day he threw down an English novel he had been reading and said to his wife, "I believe I could write a better story myself." Now this is a feeling that many of us have had, but few of us are put to the test. Cooper's wife fortunately told him to make the trial. He did so, and *Precaution* was the result. This was published in

1820. As a novel it is a failure; as a literary document it is highly interesting. *Precaution* is a story of English life. Why should Cooper write of American life when all Americans seemed to consider American life dull and prosaic? Politically we were free; intellectually we were slaves. The English lark sang in American poetry and English lords talked in American novels. It was not until 1837 that Emerson gave that famous address, *The American Scholar,* an event which Lowell calls "without any former parallel in our literary annals," and which Holmes declared to be "our intellectual Declaration of Independence."

Precaution has been called a failure, but it was not so much of a failure that Cooper's friends discouraged him from trying again. No, it was a first attempt and gave promise of something better. Why not write about American scenes and events? The very neighborhood in which he lived had been the scene of many stirring adventures during the Revolutionary conflict. "Years before, while at the residence of John Jay, his host had given him, one summer afternoon, the account of a spy that had been in his service during the war. The coolness, shrewdness, fearlessness, but above all the unselfish patriotism of the man had profoundly impressed the Revolutionary leader who had employed him. The story made an equally deep impression upon Cooper at the time. He now resolved to take it as the foundation of the tale he had been persuaded to write."

Near the close of 1821 *The Spy* appeared. In March of the following year a third edition was on the market. The work soon appeared in Eng-

land, published by Miller, the same publisher that
had first ventured to bring Irving's *Sketch Book*
before the English public. In England the book
was at once successful. This meant much to the
American estimate of the author's ability, for
American critics were afraid to praise a work
that had not yet been applauded by England. In
this same year, 1822, a French translation appeared. In France the work was enthusiastically
received. This was the first of many translations
into many European languages. Its influence in
teaching patriotism cannot be estimated, nor can
its value as an effective retort to the sneer "Who
reads an American book?" ever be overlooked.

About the early life of Cooper there are unfortunately but few anecdotes. One reason for
this lack of *personalia* about a man who had a
most vigorous personality is due to his dying request. He enjoined upon his family that they
permit no authorized biography to appear. Because of this we have lost much that would be
valuable in estimating the character of Cooper.
There is a story that when he was a young man
he engaged in a foot-race for a prize of a basket
of fruit. "While Cooper and his competitor were
preparing to start, a little girl stood by full of
eagerness for the exciting event. Cooper quickly
turned and picked her up in his arms. 'I'll carry
her and beat you!' he exclaimed, and away they
went, Cooper with his laughing burden, the other
runner untrammeled. It is almost needless to
add that Cooper won the race, else why should
the story have been preserved?" One cannot
help speculating about the size of the girl and the
speed of the rival runner, if this story is true.

A more satisfying story is that told of Cooper's meeting with Scott. In 1826 Cooper went to Europe. With a family of ten persons he moved about for seven years. Italy, France, Germany, Switzerland, and England were visited. When in Paris the two romancers met.

"Est ce Monsieur Cooper que j'ai l'honneur de voir?"

"Monsieur je m'appelle Cooper."

"Eh bien, donc, je suis Walter Scott."

After a minute or two of French Sir Walter suddenly recollected himself and said: "Well, here have I been *parley vooing* to you in a way to surprise you, no doubt, but these Frenchmen have got my tongue so set to their lingo that I have half forgotten my own language."

I have said that Cooper was not popular. This is not putting it strong enough. He was more than unpopular; he was hated by his neighbors, and slandered by the press at home and abroad. This lamentable condition of affairs was not due to any despicable qualities in the man, for Cooper was a kind father, an affectionate husband, a good citizen, and an honest, truth-loving man. These seem admirable qualities. Of few of us can much higher praise be spoken. Why then did the citizens of Cooper's home village hold a mass meeting and pass resolutions to the effect that Cooper had rendered "himself odious to a greater portion of the citizens of this community," and why should *Fraser's Magazine,* three thousand miles away, call Cooper "a liar, a bilious braggart, a full jackass, an insect, a grub, and a reptile"?

The cause is not far to seek. Cooper was the

most disputatious man in the history of American literature. Cooper used to tell the story of the man who in an argument was met with: "Why it is as plain as that two and two make four." "But I deny that too," was the retort, "for two and two make twenty two." Cooper was himself that sort of a man. He always had a quarrel on his hands. The more pugnacious a man is, the more militant he will find society. He instituted libel suits against the most prominent editors in the country, among them Horace Greeley and Thurlow Weed. And what is more to the point,— he won his cases. But this did not make him any more popular with the press. When we remember that Billingsgate was an important part of the literary equipment of the critic of Cooper's time, we need not be surprised that Cooper's pugnacity evoked such sweet disinterestedness as Park Benjamin indulged in when he called Cooper "a superlative dolt, and a common mark of scorn and contempt of every well-informed American."

In addition to this denunciation of Cooper as a man, there have in recent years arisen severe criticisms on Cooper as a writer. "There are nineteen rules," writes Mark Twain, "governing literary art in the domain of romantic fiction— some say twenty-two. In *Deerslayer* Cooper violated eighteen of them." And then Mark Twain gives us the detailed specifications. It is very cleverly put, this criticism of Mark Twain's. But the astounding fact remains that the one rule Cooper did not violate seems to secure him a place in the Pantheon of authors. Along with Poe, and Whitman, and Mark himself, Cooper is found in various editions on the shelves of the bookdealers and in the libraries of the book-lovers from the Thames to the Volga. If Cooper had observed only one or two more of the rules of literary art, where would he stand? One is reminded of the Dutchman who was told that this clock would run eight days without winding. "Ach, Himmel, what would she do if she was woundt?"

The one literary sin that Cooper does not commit is dulness. He is interesting. Of course there are some of Cooper's works that no one cares to read now. But he is to be judged by his best, not by his worst. Balzac is something of a novelist himself, and has a right to be heard. "If Cooper," says Balzac in a passage quoted by every writer who touches upon Cooper, "had succeeded in the painting of character to the same extent that he did in the painting of the phenomena of nature, he would have uttered the last word of our art." This is no mean praise. Cooper is read because he is interesting. He shall continue to be read for another reason. He is wholesome and vigorous. The air we breathe is the air of the pine forest and the salt sea. Youth is forever attracted by the mystery and adventure of primitive life. As America becomes more and more densely settled the imagination will turn back to the early times when the bear and the deer, the settler and Indian were tracking the trail through the forest and along the shore. For this reason Cooper is likely to remain an abiding force in American literature.

XLIX

JOHN LOTHROP MOTLEY, the American historian, a writer who in his *The Rise of the Dutch Republic* produced a history as fascinating as a romance and a work that was immediately in Europe translated into three different languages, was, after graduation from Harvard, a student at Goettingen. Here he studied German so well that in after years he was asked by the emperor of Austria whether he were not a German. Here too he became acquainted with Bismarck.

That they were great friends is evident from letters by Bismarck himself. "I never pass by old Logier's House, in the Friedrichstrasse—wrote Bismarck in 1863—without looking up at the windows that used to be ornamented by a pair of red slippers sustained on the wall by the feet of a gentleman sitting in the Yankee way, his head below and out of sight. I then gratify my memory with remembrance of 'good old colony times when we were roguish chaps.'" And here is another part of a letter which illustrates that even dignitaries like to unbend and become like boys again. This letter was written by the minister of foreign affairs to the minister of the United States at the court of Vienna:

Berlin, May 23d, 1864,

Jack my Dear,— . . . what do you do that you never write a
line to me? I am working from morn to night like a nigger, and
you have nothing to do at all—you might as well tip me a line as
well as looking at your feet tilted against the wall of God knows
what a dreary color. I cannot entertain a regular correspondence;
it happens to me that during five days I do not find a quarter of
an hour for a walk; but you, lazy old chap, what keeps you from
thinking of your old friends? When just going to bed in this
moment my eye met with yours on your portrait, and I curtailed
the sweet restorer, sleep, in order to remind you of Auld Lang
Syne. Why do you never come to Berlin? It is not a quarter of
an American's holiday from Vienna, and my wife and me should
be so happy to see you once more in this sullen life. When
can you come, and when will you? I swear that I will make out
the time to look with you on old Logier's quarters, . . . and at
Gerolt's, where they once would not allow you to put your slender
legs upon a chair. Let politics be hanged and come to see me.
I promise that the Union Jack shall wave over our house, and
conversation and the best old hock shall pour damnation upon
the rebels. Do not forget old friends, neither their wives, as
mine wishes nearly as ardently as myself to see you, or at least
to see as quickly as possible a word of your handwriting.

Sei gut und komm oder schreibe.

Dein,

V. BISMARCK.

In a letter to Oliver Wendell Holmes in 1878,
Bismarck in answer to an inquiry tells how the
two became friends.

"I met Motley at Goettingen in 1832, I am not
sure if at the beginning of the Easter term or
Michaelmas term. He kept company with German students, though more addicted to study
than we members of the fighting clubs. Although not having mastered yet the German
language he exercised a marked attraction by a
conversation sparkling with wit, humor, and
originality. In autumn of 1833, having both of
us emigrated from Goettingen to Berlin for the
prosecution of our studies, we became fellow

lodgers in the house No. 161 Friedrichstrasse. There we lived in the closest intimacy, sharing meals and outdoor exercise. Motley by that time had arrived at talking fluently: he occupied himself not only in translating Goethe's poem, *Faust,* but tried his hand even in composing German verses. Enthusiastic admirer of Shakspere, Byron, Goethe, he used to spice his conversation abundantly with quotations from these his favorite authors. A pertinacious arguer, so much so that sometimes he watched my awakening in order to continue a discussion on some topic of science, poetry, or practical life cut short by the chime of the small hours, he never lost his mild and amiable temper. . . . The most striking feature of his handsome and delicate appearance was uncommonly large and beautiful eyes. He never entered a drawing-room without exciting the curiosity and sympathy of the ladies.''

While the sheets of Motley's history were passing through the press in 1856, he paid a visit to Bismarck at Frankfort:

''When I called,'' says Motley, ''Bismarck was at dinner, so I left my card, and said I would come back in half an hour. As soon as my card had been carried to him (as I learned afterwards) he sent a servant after me to the hotel, but I had gone another way. When I came back I was received with open arms. I can't express to you how cordially he received me. If I had been his brother, instead of an old friend, he could not have shown more warmth and affectionate delight in seeing me. I find I like him better even than I thought I did, and you know how high an opinion I always expressed of his talents and

disposition. He is a man of very noble character, and of very great powers of mind. The
prominent place which he now occupies as a
statesman sought *him*. He did not seek it or
any other office. The stand which he took in the
Assembly from conviction, on the occasion of the
outbreak of 1848, marked him at once to all
parties as one of the leading characters of Prus-
sia. . . .

"In the summer of 1851, he told me that the
minister, Manteuffel, asked him one day abruptly,
if he would accept the post of ambassador at
Frankfort, to which (although the proposition
was as unexpected a one to him as if I should
hear by the next mail that I had been chosen
governor of Massachusetts) he answered after
a moment's deliberation, yes, without another
word. The king, the same day, sent for him, and
asked him if he would accept the place, to which
he made the same brief answer, 'Ja.' His majesty expressed a little surprise that he made no
inquiries or conditions, when Bismarck replied
that anything which the king felt strong enough
to propose to him, he felt strong enough to
accept. I only write these details that you may
have an idea of the man. Strict integrity and
courage of character, a high sense of honor, a
firm religious belief, united with remarkable
talents, make up necessarily a combination which
cannot be found any day in any court; and I
have no doubt that he is destined to be prime
minister, unless his obstinate truthfulness, which
is apt to be a stumbling-block for politicians,
stands in his way. . . .

"Well, he accepted the post and wrote to his

wife next day, who was preparing for a summer's residence in a small house they had taken on the sea-coast, that he could not come because he was already established in Frankfort as minister. The result, he said, was three days of tears on her part. He had previously been leading the life of a plain country squire with a moderate income, had never held any position in the government or in diplomacy, and had hardly ever been to court."

L

THE YOUTH OF GEORGE TICKNOR

GEORGE TICKNOR was born in 1791. His father, he says, fitted him for college. He never went to a regular school. President Wheelock, Professor Woodward, and others connected with Dartmouth College, who were in the habit of making his father's house their home in the long winter vacations, took much notice of him; and the professor, after examining him in Cicero *Orations* and the Greek Testament, gave him a certificate of admission before he was ten years old. "Of course," he adds, "I knew very little, and the whole thing was a form, perhaps a farce. There was no thought of my going to college then, and I did not go till I was fourteen, but I was twice examined at the college (where I went with my father and mother every summer) for advanced standing, and was finally admitted as a junior, and went to reside there from Commencement, August, 1805." He learned very little at college. "The instructors generally were not as good teachers as my father had been, and I knew it." He consequently took no great interest in study, although he liked reading Horace, and had mathematics enough to enjoy calculating the great eclipse of 1806, and making a projection of it which turned out nearly right. To supply the deficiency in classical acquirements with which he left college, he was placed under Dr. John Gardiner, of Trinity Church, who was reputed a good scholar, having been bred in the mother country under Dr. Parr.

"I prepared at home what he prescribed, and the rest of my time occupied myself according to my tastes. I read with him parts of Livy, the *Annals* of Tacitus, the whole of Juvenal and Persius, the *Satires* of Horace, and portions of other Latin classics which I do not remember. I wrote Latin prose and verse. In Greek I read some books of the *Odyssey*, I don't remember how many; the *Alcestis*; and two or three other plays of Euripides; the *Prometheus Vinctus* of Æschylus; portions of Herodotus, and parts of Thucydides,—of which last I only remember how I was tormented by the account of the plague at Athens. This was the work of between two and three years."

After a year's experience in law, he decides to give up his profession and goes to Europe in order to study at Goettingen. On reaching Liverpool his first introduction is to Roscoe, and then on his way to London he stops at Hatton to visit Dr. Parr, who astonished him not a little by observing, "Sir, I would not think I had done my duty if I went to bed any night without praying for the success of Napoleon Bonaparte."

In London Mr. Ticknor formed a friendship with Lord Byron; two men more unlike in every respect can hardly be conceived of, and it is amusing to think of Byron impressing his visitor as being "simple and unaffected," or of his speaking "of his early follies with sincerity," and of his own works "with modesty." It is amusing, too, to hear that as Lady Byron is going out for a drive, "Lord Byron's manner to her was affectionate; he followed her to the door, and shook hands with her, as if he were not to see her for a month." The following curious anecdote shows that Byron was no less unpatriotic in his views than Dr. Parr himself. Mr. Ticknor is calling upon him, and Byron is praising Scott as the first man of his time, and saying of Gifford that no one could have a better disposition, when,—

"Sir James Bland Burgess, who had something to do in negotiating Jay's Treaty, came suddenly into the room, and said abruptly, 'My lord, my lord, a great battle has been fought in the Low Countries, and Bonaparte is entirely defeated.' 'But is it true?' said Lord Byron, 'is it true?' 'Yes, my lord, it is certainly true; and an aid-de-camp arrived in town last night, he has been in Downing Street this morning, and I have just seen him as he was going to Lady Wellington's. He says he thinks Bonaparte is in full retreat towards Paris.' After a moment's pause, Lord Byron replied, 'I am sorry for it;' and then, after another slight pause, he added, 'I didn't know but I might live to see Lord Castlereagh's head on a pole. But I suppose I sha'n't now.' And this was the first impression produced on his imperious nature by the news of the battle of Waterloo."

But Byron is not Mr. Ticknor's only London friend, for we read of a breakfast with Sir Humphry Davy, a "genuine bookseller's dinner" with Murray, and a visit to the author of *Gertrude of Wyoming.*

Goettingen, however, is the object of his journey, and at Goettingen he remains for the next year and a half. If he does not learn to scorn the delights of society, he has at least the resolution to live the laborious days of the earnest student. He studies five languages, and works twelve hours in the twenty-four. Greek, German, theology, and natural history seem chiefly to claim his attention, but he is also busy with French, Italian, and Latin, and manages at the same time to keep up his English reading. He is much amused with the German professors, and describes them with no little humor. There is Michaelis, who asks one of his scholars for some silver shoe-buckles, in lieu of a fee. There is Schultze, who "looks as if he had fasted six months on Greek prosody and the Pindaric meters." There is Blumenbach, who has a sharp discussion at a dinner-table, and next day sends down three huge quartos all marked to show his authorities and justify his statements.

Here is another interesting anecdote given in Ticknor's *Memoirs:*

"When I was in Goettingen, in 1816, I saw Wolf, the most distinguished Greek scholar of the time. He could also lecture extemporaneously in Latin. He was curious about this country, and questioned me about our scholars and the amount of our scholarship. I told him what I could,—amongst other things, of a fashionable, dashing preacher of New York having told me that he took great pleasure in reading the choruses of Æschylus, and that he read them without a dictionary! I was walking with Wolf at the time, and, on hearing this, he stopped, squared round, and said, 'He told you that, did he?' 'Yes,' I answered. 'Very well; the next time you hear him say it, do you tell him he lies, and that I say so.' "

During a six weeks' vacation there is a pleasant tour through Germany, and at Weimar Mr. Ticknor makes the acquaintance of Goethe, who talked about Byron, and "his great knowledge of human nature."

And now in the November of 1816, there comes an intimation that Harvard College wishes to recall Mr. Ticknor to his old home, and give him the professorship of French and Spanish literature. It was a matter of difficulty for him to make a final decision, and a year passes before he determined to accept the charge, and a year and a half more before he enters upon its duties.

Meanwhile he leaves Goettingen, visits Paris, Geneva, and Rome, and then goes on to Spain. . . . When in Spain, Mr. Ticknor is busy learning Spanish and collecting Spanish books, and here he lays the groundwork for that special literary distinction for which he is now so widely known.—Adapted from the *Athenaeum* and *Quarterly Review.*

LI

FITZ-GREENE HALLECK died at a ripe old age in 1867. On the evening of February 2d, 1869, Bryant delivered an address on the life and writings of Halleck. The address was given before the New York Historical Society and was printed the next day in the New York *Evening Post*. Here is an interesting extract from the address:

"When I look back upon Halleck's literary life I cannot help thinking that if his death had happened forty years earlier, his life would have been regarded as a bright morning prematurely overcast. Yet Halleck's literary career may be said to have ended then. All that will hand down his name to future years had already been produced. Who shall say to what cause his subsequent literary inaction was owing? It was not the decline of his powers; his brilliant conversation showed that it was not. Was it, then, indifference to fame? Was it because he had put an humble estimate on what he had written, and therefore resolved to write no more? Was it because he feared lest what he might write would be unworthy of the reputation he had been so fortunate to acquire?

"I have my own way of accounting for his literary silence in the latter half of his life. One of the resemblances which he bore to Horace consisted in the length of time for which he kept his poems by him that he might give them the last and happiest touches. He had a tenacious verbal memory, and having composed his poems without committing them to paper, he revised them in the same manner, murmuring them to himself in his solitary moments, recovering the enthusiasm with which they were first received, and in this state heightening the beauty of the thought or of the expression. I remember that once in crossing Washington Park I saw Halleck before me and quickened my pace to overtake him. As I drew near I heard him crooning to himself what seemed to be lines of verse, and as he threw back his hands in walking I perceived that they quivered with the feeling of the passage he was reciting. I instantly checked my pace and fell back, out of reverence for the mood of inspiration which seemed to be upon him, and fearful lest I should intercept the birth of a poem destined to be the delight of thousands of readers.

"In this way I suppose Halleck to have attained the gracefulness of his diction, and the airy melody of his numbers. In this way I believe he wrought up his verses to that transparent clearness of expression which causes the thought to be seen through them without any interposing dimness, so that the thought and the phrase seem one, and the thought enters the mind like a beam of light. I suppose that Halleck's time being taken up by the tasks of his vocation, he naturally lost by degrees the habit of composing in this manner, and that he found it so necessary to the perfection of what he wrote that he adopted no other in its place.

"Whatever was the reason that Halleck ceased so early to write, let us congratulate ourselves that he wrote at all. Great authors often overlay and almost smother their own fame by the voluminousness of their writings. So great is their multitude, and so rich is the literature of our language, that for frequent readings we are obliged to content ourselves with mere selections from the works of best and most beloved of our poets, even those who have not written much. It is only a few of their works that dwell and live in the general mind. Gray, for example, wrote little, and of that little one short poem, his *Elegy*, can be fairly said to survive in the public admiration, and that poem I have sometimes heard called the most popular in our language."

LII

THANATOPSIS may be said to be the most remarkable poem written by an American youth. "The unfailing wonder of it is," writes an American critic in a magazine article, "that a boy of seventeen could have written it; not merely that he could have made verse of such structural beauty and dignity, but that the thoughts of which it is compacted could have been a boy's thoughts. The poem seems to have been written while he was at his father's house in Cummington, in the summer of 1811, before he had definitely begun the study of law. Fond as he had been of showing his earlier effusions to his father and others, the consciousness of having done something different and greater must have come upon him at this time, for it was only by accident, six years after the writing of *Thanatopsis,* that his father chanced to find it and the poem now called *An Inscription Upon the Entrance to a Wood,* among some papers in a desk the boy had used while at home. Dr. Bryant read them with amazement and delight, hurried at once to the house of a neighbor, a lady of whose sympathy he felt sure, thrust them into her hands, and, with the tears running down his cheeks, said, 'Read them; they are Cullen's.'

WILLIAM CULLEN BRYANT

From a photograph from life

"Now it had happened only a short time before, that Dr. Bryant had been asked in Boston to urge his son to contribute to the newly established *North American Review,* and had written him a letter on the editor's behalf. Here was the opportunity of a proud father. Without telling his son of his discovery or his purpose, he left the poems one day, together with some translations from *Horace* by the same hand, at the office of *The North American.* The little package was addressed to his editorial friend, Mr. Willard Phillips, of whom tradition tells us that as soon as he read the poems he betook himself in hot haste to Cambridge to display his treasures to his associates, Richard H. Dana and Edward T. Channing. 'Ah, Phillips,' said Dana, when he had heard the poems read, 'you have been imposed upon. No one on this side of the Atlantic is capable of writing such verse.' But Phillips, believing Dr. Bryant to be responsible for it, declared that he knew the writer, and that Dana could see him at once if he would go to the State House in Boston. Accordingly the young men posted into town, and Dana, unconvinced after looking long and carefully at Dr. Bryant in his seat in the Senate, said, 'It is a good head, but I do not see *Thanatopsis* in it.' "

Bryant is never thought of as a humorist, and his poetry is devoid of playfulness. But in this letter to his mother, in which he announces his marriage with Frances Fairchild, we have evidence that Bryant had a strong sense of humor.

DEAR MOTHER: I hasten to send you the melancholy intelligence of what has lately happened to me.

Early on the evening of the eleventh day of the present month I was at a neighboring house in this village. Several people of both sexes were assembled in one of the apartments, and three or four others, with myself, were in another. At last came in a little elderly gentleman, pale, thin, with a solemn countenance, pleuritic voice, hooked nose, and hollow eyes. It was not long before we were summoned to attend in the apartment where he and the rest of the company were gathered. We went in and took our seats; the little elderly gentleman with the hooked nose prayed, and we all stood up. When he had finished most of us sat down. The gentleman with the hooked nose then muttered certain cabalistic expressions, which I was too much frightened to remember, but I recollect that at the conclusion I was given to understand that I was married to a young lady by the name of Frances Fairchild, whom I perceived standing by my side, and I hope in the course of few months to have the pleasure of introducing to you as your daughter-in-law, which is a matter of some interest to the poor girl, who has neither father or mother in the world.

Next to *Thanatopsis* the most widely-known and admired of Bryant's work is *To a Waterfowl*. There are two very interesting stories pertaining to this much quoted poem, one relating to the origin of the poem, the other recording its effect on two fastidious young Englishmen, Hartley Coleridge and Matthew Arnold.

Bryant was a young man with no assurance as to what the future might have in store for him. He was journeying over the hills to Plainfield to see whether there might possibly be an opening for a young lawyer. It was the 15th of December, 1816, and we can imagine that the gloom of the gathering twilight helped to deepen the youth's despondency. But before the glimmering light of evening had given place entirely to the dark of night, the sky was transfigured with the bright rays of the setting sun. The New England sky was flooded for a moment with seas of chrysolite and opal. While young Bryant stopped to enjoy the brilliant scene, a solitary bird made its way across the sky. He watched it until it was lost in the distant horizon, and then went on with new courage as he thought the thoughts so beautifully expressed in the poem which he wrote after he reached the house where he was to stay for the night.

The incident in regard to Matthew Arnold is related by Godwin in a letter to Bigelow:

"Once when the late Matthew Arnold, with his family, was visiting the ever-hospitable country home of Mr. Charles Butler, I happened to spend an evening there. In the course of it Mr. Arnold took up a volume of Mr. Bryant's poems from the table and turning to me said, 'This is the American poet, *facile princeps'*; and after a pause, he continued: 'When I first heard of him, Hartley Coleridge (we were both lads then) came into my father's house one afternoon considerably excited and exclaimed, 'Matt, do you want to hear the best short poem in the English language?' 'Faith, Hartley, I do,' was my reply. He then read a poem *To a Waterfowl* in his best manner. And he was a good reader. As soon as he had done he asked, 'What do you think of that?' 'I am not sure but you are right, Hartley, is it your father's?' was my reply. 'No,' he rejoined, 'father has written nothing like that.' Some days after he might be heard muttering to himself,

The desert and illimitable air,
Lone wandering but not lost.''

LIII

THE social experiment known as the Brook Farm enterprise is one of the most interesting episodes in American literature. Mrs. Ora G. Sedgwick is one of the many writers who have written about the place and its inhabitants. She went there in June, 1841, and lived for some time at the Hive, the principal community edifice. She was then but a girl of sixteen, but the impressions on her youthful mind were strong enough to enable her recently to describe her life there. As to Curtis she has this to say:

"The arrival of George William Curtis, then a youth of eighteen, and his brother Burrill, two years his senior, was a noteworthy event in the annals of Brook Farm, at least in the estimation of the younger members. I shall never forget the flutter of excitement caused by Mr. Ripley's announcing their expected coming in these words: 'Now we're going to have two young Greek gods among us.' . . . On a bright morning in May, 1842, soon after Mr. Ripley's announcement, as I was coming down from the Eyrie to the Hive, I saw Charles A. Dana with two strange young men approaching my 'magic gate' from the direction of the Hive. Arriving at the gate before me, Mr. Dana threw it open with the flourish peculiar to his manner, and stood holding it back. His companions stood beside him, and all three waited for me to pass through. I saw at a glance that these must be 'the two young Greek gods.' They stood disclosed, not like Virgil's Venus, by their step, but by their beauty and bearing. Burrill Curtis was at that time the more beautiful. He had a Greek face, of great purity of expression, and curling hair. George too was very handsome—not so remarkably as in later life, but already with a man's virile expression.

"About George William Curtis there was a peculiar personal elegance and an air of great deference in listening to one whom he admired or looked up to. There was a certain remoteness (at times almost amounting to indifference) about him, but he was always courteous. His friends were all older than himself, and he appeared much older in manners and conversation than he was in years; more like a man of twenty-five than a youth of eighteen."

Mrs. Sedgwick also gives us a charming glimpse at the great American novelist, Hawthorne:

"I do not recollect Hawthorne's talking much at the table. Indeed, he was a very taciturn man. One day, tired of seeing him sitting immovable on the sofa in the hall, as I was learning some verses to recite at the evening class for recitation formed by Charles A. Dana, I daringly took my book, pushed it into his hands, and said, 'Will you hear my poetry, Mr. Hawthorne?' He gave me a sidelong glance from his very shy eyes, took the book, and most kindly heard me. After that he was on the sofa every week to hear me recite.

"One evening he was alone in the hall, sitting on a chair at the farther end, when my room mate, Ellen Slade, and myself were going upstairs. She whispered to me, 'Let's throw the sofa pillows at Mr. Hawthorne.' Reaching over the bannisters, we each took a cushion and threw it. Quick as a flash he put out his hand, seized a broom that was hanging near him, warded off our cushions, and threw them back with sure aim. As fast as we could throw them at him he returned them with effect, hitting us every time, while we could hit only the broom. He must have been very quick in his movements. Through it all not a word was spoken. We laughed and laughed, and his eyes shone and twinkled like stars. Wonderful eyes they were, and when anything witty was said I always looked quickly at Mr. Hawthorne; for his dark eyes lighted up as if flames were suddenly kindled behind them, and then the smile came down to his lips and over his grave face.

"My memories of Mr. Hawthorne are among the pleasantest of my Brook Farm recollections. His manners to children were charming and kind. I saw him one day walking, as was his custom, with his hands behind his back, head bent forward, the two little Bancrofts and other children following him with pleased faces, and stooping every now and then with broad smiles, after which they would rise and run on again behind him. Puzzled at these maneuvers, I watched closely, and found that although he hardly moved a muscle except to walk, yet from time to time he dropped a penny, for which the children scrambled.''

LIV

HAWTHORNE AND THE SCARLET LETTER

ON June 8, 1849, Hawthorne walked out of the Salem Custom House—a man without a job. Taylor's Whig administration had come in, so our Democratic friend, Mr. Hawthorne, walked out. The job he left was not in our modern eyes a very lucrative one, it was worth $1,200 a year and Hawthorne had had it for three years. But he went out "mad," for he knew he had not meddled in politics and he thought that as an author—even if he was the "most obscure man of letters in America"—he was entitled to some consideration.

And then there were the wife and children! As he walked home to tell them the doleful news, he was much depressed by thoughts of them. He had paid his old debts; but he had saved nothing. He seemed to lack money, friends, and influence. He had written to a friend in Boston,—"I shall not stand upon my dignity; that must take care of itself. . . . Do not think anything too humble to be mentioned to me. The intelligence has just reached me, and Sophia has not yet heard it. She will bear it like a woman,—that is to say better than a man." What a noble tribute to woman's fortitude! Hawthorne's belief in the sustaining love of his wife reminds us of a tradition which says that he never read a letter from his wife without first washing his hands. To him the act was sacred, and like a priest of old before handling the symbols of love he performed the rites of purification.

His son tells us how the wife met the news with which he greeted her on his arrival at home, "that he had left his head behind." She exclaimed, "Oh, then you can write your book!" And when he with the prudence of a practical man wanted to know where the bread and rice were to come from while he was writing the book, she like all good wives—of olden times, at least —brought forth a "pile of gold" which she had saved from the household weekly expenses. When the pile of gold had been subjected to mathematical accuracy it dwindled to $150, but it was enough to tide over immediate wants.

It was in the early winter that James T. Fields, the publisher who plays such a prominent part in the early history of American literature, descended upon the quiet Salem household like the "godmother in a fairy story." Fields has told the story of his visit: "I found him alone in a chamber over the sitting-room of the dwelling; and as the day was cold, he was hovering near a stove. We fell into talk about his future prospects, and he was, as I feared I should find him, in a very desponding mood. 'Now,' said I, 'is the time for you to publish, for I know during these years in Salem you must have got something ready for the press.' 'Nonsense,' said he, 'what heart had I to write anything, when my publishers have been so many years trying to sell a small edition of the *Twice-told Tales.*' I still pressed upon him the good chances he would have now with something new. 'Who would risk publishing a book for me, the most unpopular writer in America?' 'I would,' said I, 'and would start with an edition of 2,000 copies of anything you would write.' 'What madness!' he exclaimed. 'Your friendship for me gets the better of your judgment.' 'No, no!' he continued, 'I have no money to indemnify a publisher's losses on my account.' I looked at my watch, and found that the train would be soon starting for Boston, and I knew that there was not much time to lose in trying to discover what had been his literary work during these last few years in Salem. I remember that I pressed him to reveal to me what he had been writing. He shook his head and gave me to understand that he had produced nothing. At that moment I caught sight of a bureau or set of drawers near where we were sitting; and immediately it occurred to me that hidden in that article of furniture was a story or stories by the author of *Twice-told Tales;* and I became so positive of it that I charged him vehemently with the fact. He seemed surprised, I thought, but shook his head again; and I rose to take my leave, begging him not to come into the cold entry, saying I would come back and see him again in a few days. I was hurrying down the stairs when he called after me from the chamber, asking me to stop a moment. Then quickly stepping into the entry with a roll of MS. in his hands, he said: 'How in heaven's name did you know this thing was there? As you found me out, take what was written, and tell me, after you get home and have time to read it, if it is good for anything. It is either very good or very bad—I don't know which!' On my way to Boston I read the germ of *The Scarlet Letter.*"

Hawthorne's original plan was to write a number of stories, of which this particular one was to be the longest. He was going to call his book of tales, *Old-Time Legends: together with Sketches, Experimental and Ideal,*—a title which Woodberry calls "ghostly with the transcendental nonage of his genius." Fields urged that the tale be made longer and fuller and that it be published by itself. So the original plan was changed, as was also the title. This was wise, for the cumbersome original title would have killed any book, but the present title is nothing short of a stroke of genius.

About this time Hawthorne's friends, under the leading of Hillard, sent a kind letter and a considerable sum of money. Hawthorne replied, —"I read your letter in the vestibule of the Post Office; and it drew—what my troubles never have —the water to my eyes; so that I was glad of the sharply-cold west wind that blew into them as I came homeward, and gave them an excuse for being red and bleared." After saying it was sweet to be remembered, but bitter to need their aid, he concludes,—"The money, dear Hillard, will smooth my path for a long time to come. The only way in which a man can retain his self-respect, while availing himself of the generosity of his friends, is by making it an incitement to his utmost exertion, so that he may not need their help again. I shall look upon it so—nor

will shun any drudgery that my hand shall find
to do, if thereby I may win bread.''

Four days after this letter was written, on
February 3, 1850, he finished *The Scarlet Letter*.
He writes to a friend saying he read the last
scene to his wife, or rather tried to read it, ''for
my voice swelled and heaved, as if I were tossed
up and down on an ocean as it subsides after a
storm.'' Mrs. Hawthorne told a friend that her
husband seemed depressed all during that winter.
''There was a knot in his forehead all the time,''
said his wife. One day he told her he had a
story that he wished to read to her. He read
part of the work one evening. The next evening
he continued. His wife followed the story with
intense interest. Her excitement arose until
when he was reading near the end of the book,
where Arthur and Hester and the child meet in
the forest, Mrs. Hawthorne sank from her low
stool to the floor and said she could endure no
more. Hawthorne stopped and said in wonder,
—''Do you really feel it so much? Then there
must be something in it.''

Mrs. Hawthorne relates that on the day after
the MS. was delivered to Fields, this publisher
returned and when admitted to the house caught
up her boy in his arms and said,—''You splendid
little fellow, do you know what a father you
have?'' Then he ran upstairs to talk to Hawthorne, calling to her as he went that he had sat
up all night to read the story. Soon her husband
came down and walked about the room with a
new light in his eyes.

Early in April the book was issued in an edition of 5,000 copies; this was soon exhausted, and

Hawthorne was well started on that career of literary fame which led Mr. Hamilton W. Mabie, a hundred years after the birth of Hawthorne, to call him "the foremost literary artist of America."

The Scarlet Letter, as Hawthorne himself tells us, is a story of "human frailty and sorrow." It is the story of one who has brooded long and faithfully upon the problem of evil. In it we read that man is the master of his fate. The great difference between ancient and modern literature is this: the old dramatists seem to believe that somewhere there is a power above and beyond the control of man, a blind, unreasoning force that seems to play with man as the football of chance. Whatever may be done by man will prove unavailing if Fate or Destiny has decreed otherwise. Out of such a philosophy of life comes the story of Œdipus. The modern conception is that expressed by Shakspere:

> The fault, dear Brutus, is not in our stars,
> But in ourselves, that we are underlings.

Still later Henley in his one great poem has expressed the thought with vigor,—

> Out of the night that covers me,
> Black as the pit from pole to pole,
> I thank whatever gods there be
> For my unconquerable soul!

With unfaltering aim Hawthorne shows that each character works out its own destiny. That man is helpless, the sport of gods, the football of Fate, is disproved by the patient transformation in the character of Hester.

Some one has well characterized *The Scarlet*

Letter as "a drama of the spirit." It is a story such as only one who had brooded deeply on the problem of evil could write. Hawthorne was a "solitary brooder upon life." Every one who knew him testified to this impression. When William Dean Howells, a young man from Ohio, knocked at the door of the Wayside Cottage, a letter of introduction in his hand, and a feeling of hero-worship in his heart, he was ushered into the presence of the great romancer, who advanced "carrying his head with a heavy forward droop" and with pondering pace. His look was "somber and brooding—the look of a man who had dealt faithfully and therefore sorrowfully with that problem of evil which forever attracted and forever evaded Hawthorne."

Hawthorne impressed all who met him with his reserve and shyness. Many stories are told to illustrate this quality. Hawthorne was once a visitor at a club where a number of literary men had gathered. The taciturnity of Hawthorne was more impressive than the loquacity of the witty Holmes. After Hawthorne had left Emerson said, "Hawthorne rides his dark horse well." George William Curtis relates this anecdote:

" . . . I recall the silent and preternatural vigor with which, on one occasion, he wielded his paddle to counteract the bad rowing of a friend who conscientiously considered it his duty to do something and not let Hawthorne work alone, but who with every stroke neutralized all Hawthorne's efforts. I suppose he would have struggled until he fell senseless rather than to ask his friend to desist. His principle seemed to be, if a man cannot understand without talking to him, it is quite useless to talk, because it is immaterial whether such a man understands or not."

Hawthorne's father was a man of the sea, a man of few words, and it is sometimes said that the romancer inherited his shy and reserved disposition from his father. But his mother was not behind the father in reserve. After her husband's death she shut herself up in Hindoo-like seclusion and lived the life of a hermit for more than forty years.

Hawthorne gives us an interesting account of his boyhood in an autobiographical note to his friend Stoddard. "When I was eight or nine years old, my mother, with her three children, took up her residence on the banks of the Sebago Lake, in Maine, where the family owned a large tract of land; and here I ran quite wild . . . fishing all day long, or shooting with an old fowling-piece; but reading a good deal too, on the rainy days, especially in *Shakspere* and *The Pilgrim's Progress.*"

More pertinent as to his habits of loneliness is the following account of how he lived for nine or ten years after his graduation from Bowdoin. "I had always," he writes, "a natural tendency (it appears to have been on the paternal side) toward seclusion; and this I now indulged to the utmost, so that, for months together, I scarcely held human intercourse outside of my own family, seldom going out except at twilight, or only to take the nearest way to the most convenient solitude, which was oftenest the seashore. . . . Having spent so much of my boyhood and youth from my native place, I had very few acquaintances in Salem, and during the nine or ten years that I spent there, in this solitary way, I doubt whether so much as twenty people in the town were aware of my existence.''

Such was the solitariness of the youthful Hawthorne. Is it surprising that in the fiction of the mature man there should be a pervading sense of remoteness, of silences that fascinate, of mysteries that charm?

LV

LIVING at Oxford, writes Max Müller, I have had the good fortune of receiving visits from Emerson, Dr. Wendell Holmes, and Lowell, to speak of the brightest stars only. Each of them stayed at our house for several days, so that I could take them in at leisure, while others had to be taken at one gulp, often between one train and the next. Oxford has a great attraction for all Americans, and it is a pleasure to see how completely they feel at home in the memories of the place. The days when Emerson, Wendell Holmes, and Lowell were staying with us, the breakfasts and luncheons, the teas and dinners, and the delightful walks through college halls, chapels and gardens are possessions forever. . . .

I do not wonder that philosophers by profession had nothing to say to his (Emerson's) essays because they did not seem to advance their favorite inquiries beyond the point they had reached before. But there were many people, particularly in America, to whom these rhapsodies did more good than any learned disquisitions or carefully arranged sermons. There is in them what attracts us so much in the ancients, freshness, directness, self-confidence, unswerving loyalty to truth, as far as they could see it. He had no one to fear, no one to please. Socrates or Plato, if suddenly brought to life in America, might have spoken like Emerson, and the effect produced by Emerson was certainly like that produced by Socrates in olden times.

What Emerson's personal charm must have been in earlier life we can only conjecture from the rapturous praises bestowed on him by his friends, even during his lifetime. . . . And his influence was not confined to the American mind. I have watched it growing in England. I can still remember the time when even experienced judges spoke of his essays as mere declamations, as poetical rhapsodies, as poor imitations of Carlyle. Then gradually one man after another found something in Emerson which was not to be found in Carlyle, particularly his loving heart, his tolerant spirit, his comprehensive sympathy with all that was or was meant to be good and true, even though to his own mind it was neither the one nor the other. . . .

Another eminent American who often honored my quiet home at Oxford was James Russell Lowell, for a long time United States minister in England. He was a professor and at the same time a politician and a man of the world. Few essays are so brimful of interesting facts and original reflections as his essays entitled *Among my Books*.

Lowell's conversation was inexhaustible, his information astonishing. Pleasant as he was, even as an antagonist, he would occasionally lose his temper and use very emphatic language. I was once sitting next to him when I heard him stagger his neighbor, a young lady, by bursting out with, "But, madam, I do not accept your major premise!" Poor thing, she evidently was not accustomed to such language, and not acquainted with that terrible term. She collapsed, evidently quite at a loss as to what gift on her part Mr. Lowell declined to accept.

Sometimes even the most harmless remark about America would call forth very sharp replies from him. Everybody knows that the salaries paid by America to her diplomatic staff are insufficient, and no one knew it better than he himself. But when the remark was made in his presence that the United States treated their diplomatic representatives stingily, he fired up, and discoursed most eloquently on the advantages of high thoughts and humble living. . . .

I lost the pleasure of shaking hands with Longfellow during his stay in England. Though I have been more of a fixture at Oxford than most professors, I was away during the vacation when he paid his visit to our university, and thus lost seeing a poet to whom I felt strongly attracted, not only by the general spirit of his poetry, which was steeped in German thought, but as the translator of several of my father's poems.

I was more fortunate with Dr. Wendell Holmes. His arrival in England had been proclaimed beforehand, and one naturally remained at home in order to be allowed to receive him. His hundred days in England were one uninterrupted triumphal progress. When he arrived at Liverpool he found about three hundred invitations waiting for him. Though he was accompanied by a most active and efficient daughter, he had at once to engage a secretary to answer this deluge of letters. And though he was past eighty, he never spared himself, and was always ready to see and to be seen. He was not only an old, but a ripe and mellow man. There was no subject on which one could touch which was not familiar to the autocrat of the breakfast table. His thoughts and his words were ready, and one felt that it was not for the first time that the subject had been carefully thought out and talked out by him. That he should have been able to stand all the fatigue of the journey and the constant claims on his ready wit seemed to me marvelous. I had the pleasure of showing him the old buildings of Oxford. He seemed to know them all, and had something to ask and say about every one. When we came to Magdalen College, he wanted to see and to measure the elms. He was very proud of some elms in America, and he had actually brought some string with which he had measured the largest tree he knew in his own country. He proceeded to measure one of our finest elms in Magdalen College, and when he found that it was larger than his American giant, he stood before it admiring it, without a single word of envy or disappointment.

I had, however, a great fright while he was staying at our house. He had evidently done too much, and after our first dinner party he had feverish shivering fits, and the doctor whom I sent for declared at once that he must keep perfectly quiet in bed, and attend no more parties of any kind. This was a great disappointment to myself and to a great many of my friends. But at his time of life the doctor's warning could not be disregarded, and I had, at all events, the satisfaction of sending him off to Cambridge safe

and sound. I had him several days quite to myself, and there were few subjects which we did
not discuss. We mostly agreed, but even where
we did not, it was a real pleasure to differ from
him. We discussed the greatest and the smallest
questions, and on every one he had some wise and
telling remarks to pour out. I remember one
conversation while we were sitting at an old
wainscoted room at All Souls', ornamented with
the arms of former fellows. It had been at first
the library of the college, then one of the fellows' rooms, and lastly a lecture room. We
were deep in the old question of the true relation
between the divine and human in man, and here
again, as on all other questions, everything
seemed to be clear and evident to his mind. Perhaps I ought not to repeat what he said to me
when we parted: "I have had much talk with
people in England; with you I have had a real
conversation." We understood each other and
wondered how it was that men so often mis-
understood one another. I told him that it was
the badness of our language, he thought it was
the badness of our tempers. Perhaps we were
both right. With him again good-by was good-by
for life, and at such moments one wonders indeed how kindred souls became separated, and
one feels startled and repelled at the thought
that, such as they were on earth, they can never
meet again. And yet there is continuity in the
world, there is no flaw, no break anywhere, and
what has been will surely be again, though how
it will be we cannot know, and if only we trust
in the wisdom that pervades the whole universe,
we need not know.

LVI

IN 1860 William Dean Howells, now one of the foremost literary influences in the English-speaking world, was a young man writing for the *Ohio State Journal* of Columbus. Several of his poems had been kindly received and published by the *Atlantic Monthly,* so that the young lady from New England who screamed with surprise at seeing the *Atlantic* on a western table and cried, "Why, have you got the *Atlantic Monthly out here?*" could be met with, "There are several contributors to the *Atlantic* in Columbus." The several were Howells and J. J. Piatt. But to be an accepted contributor to the *Atlantic* was not enough. Howells must see the literary celebrities of New England. Emerson and Bayard Taylor he had seen and heard in Columbus, but Longfellow, Hawthorne, Lowell, Holmes, and Whittier were the literary saints at whose shrine he wished to burn the sacred incense of his adoring soul.

From Hawthorne he received a card introducing him to Emerson. Emerson was then about sixty, although nothing about him suggested an old man. After some conversation on general topics, Emerson began to talk of Hawthorne, praising Hawthorne's fine personal qualities. "But his last book," he added, reflectively, "is mere mush." This criticism related to the *Marble Faun*. Of course, such a comment shocked Howells, whose sense of literary values was much keener than Emerson's. "Emerson had, in fact," writes Howells, "a defective sense as to specific pieces of literature; he praised extravagantly, and in the wrong place, especially among the new things, and he failed to see the worth of much that was fine and precious beside the line of his fancy."

Then Emerson made some inquiry about a Michigan young man who had been sending some of his poetry to Emerson. Howells was embarrassed to be obliged to say that he knew nothing of the Michigan poet. Later Emerson asked whether he had become acquainted with the poems of Mr. William Henry Channing. Howells replied that he knew them only through the criticism of Poe.

"Whose criticisms?" asked Emerson.

"Poe's," replied Howells.

"Oh," Emerson cried after a thoughtful moment, "you mean *the jingle man!*"

This was a moment of confusion and embarrassment for Howells. Had the vituperative pen of Poe ever thrown off more stinging criticism than that? "*The jingle man!*"

Emerson turned the conversation to Howells himself and asked him what he had written for the *Atlantic*. Howells replied, and Emerson took down the bound volumes and carefully affixed Howells' initials to the poems. "He followed me to the door, still speaking of poetry, and as he took a kindly enough leave of me, he said one might very well give a pleasant hour to it now and then." This was a shock to Howells. "A pleasant hour!" Howells was intending to consecrate all time and eternity to it, and here is the Sage of Concord coolly speaking of poetry as though it were some trifling diversion, like billiards or whist.

Later in life when Howells resided in Cambridge he had abundant opportunity to become acquainted with Longfellow, whom in *Literary Friends and Acquaintance* he calls the "White Mr. Longfellow."

"He was the most perfectly modest man I ever saw, ever imagined, but he had a gentle dignity which I do not believe any one, the coarsest, the obtusest, could trespass upon. In the years when I began to know him, his long hair and the beautiful beard which mixed with it were of iron-gray, which I saw blanch to a perfect silver, while that pearly tone of his complexion, which Appleton so admired, lost itself in the wanness of age and pain. When he walked, he had a kind of spring in his gait, as if now and again a buoyant thought lifted him from the ground. It was fine to meet him coming down a Cambridge street; you felt that the encounter made you a part of literary history, and set you apart with him for the moment from the poor and mean. When he appeared in Harvard Square, he beatified if not beautified the ugliest and vulgarest looking spot on the planet outside of New York. You could meet him sometimes at the market, if you were of the same provision-man as he, for Longfellow remained as constant to his tradespeople as to any other friends. He rather liked to bring his proofs back to the printer himself, and we often found ourselves together at the University Press, where *The Atlantic Monthly* used to be printed. But outside of his own house Longfellow seemed to want a fit atmosphere, and I love best to think of him in his study, where he wrought at his lovely art with a serenity expressed in his smooth, regular, and scrupulously perfect handwriting. It was quite vertical, and rounded, with a slope neither to the right nor left, and at the time I knew him first, he was fond of using a soft pencil on printing paper, though commonly he wrote with a quill. Each letter was distinct in shape, and between the verses was always the exact space of half an inch. I have a good many of his poems written in this fashion, but whether they were the first drafts or not I cannot say; very likely not. Towards the last he no longer sent the poems to the magazines in his own hand, but they were always signed in autograph.

"I once asked him if he were not a great deal interrupted, and he said, with a faint sigh, Not more than was good for him, he fancied; if it were not for the interruptions, he might overwork. He was not a friend to stated exercise, I believe, nor fond of walking, as Lowell was; he had not, indeed, the childish associations of the younger poet with the Cambridge neighborhoods; and I never saw him walking for pleasure except on the east veranda of his house, though I was told he loved walking in his youth. In this and in some other things Longfellow was more European than American, more Latin than Saxon.

He once said quaintly that one got a great deal of exercise in putting on and off one's overcoat and overshoes. . . .

"He was patient, as I said of all things, and gentle beyond all mere gentlemanliness. But it would have been a great mistake to mistake his mildness for softness. It was most manly and firm, and of course, it was braced with the New England conscience he was born to. If he did not find it well to assert himself, he was prompt in behalf of his friends, and one of the fine things told of him was his resenting some things said of Sumner at a dinner in Boston during the old pro-slavery times; he said to the gentlemen present that Sumner was his friend, and he must leave their company if they continued to assail him.

"But he spoke almost as rarely of his friends as of himself. He liked the large, impersonal topics which could be dealt with on their human side, and involved characters rather than individuals. This was rather strange in Cambridge, where we were apt to take our instances from our environments. It was not the only thing he was strange in there; he was not to that manner born; he lacked the final intimacies which can come only of birth and lifelong association, and which make the men of the Boston breed seem exclusive when they least feel so; he was Longfellow to the friends who were James, and Charles, and Wendell to one another. He and Hawthorne were classmates at college, but I never heard him mention Hawthorne; I never heard him mention Whittier or Emerson. I think his reticence about his contemporaries was largely due to his reluctance from criticism: he was the finest artist of them all, and if he praised he must have praised with the reservations of an honest man. Of younger writers he was willing enough to speak. No new contributor made his mark in the magazine unnoted by him, and sometimes I showed him verse in manuscript which gave me peculiar pleasure. I remember his liking for the first piece that Mr. Maurice Thompson sent me, and how he tasted the fresh flavor of it and inhaled its wild new fragrance."

LVII

WE have passed the hundredth anniversary of the birth of Longfellow, and he still remains the favorite American poet. Not that Longfellow is one of the great world poets; Longfellow himself would have been offended with that eulogistic extravagance which would place him among the few immortals. He is not a Homer, nor a Dante, nor a Shakspere. No, he is not even a Wordsworth in philosophic insight into nature, nor a Shelley in power to snatch the soul into the starry empyrean, nor a Tennyson in variety and passion, nor a Milton in grandeur of poetic expression. He is—only Longfellow. But that means he has his own peculiar charm. It is idle to detract from the fame of one man because he is not some one else. Roast beef may be more nutritious than strawberries, but that is no criticism upon the flavor of the strawberry. Longfellow is not Milton, but then neither is Milton Longfellow:

> If I cannot carry forests on my back
> Neither can you crack a nut.

Of late years the critics have been finding fault with Longfellow. They have said that really

HENRY WADSWORTH LONGFELLOW
From a wood engraving of a life photograph

Longfellow is no poet. Frederic Harrison calls Evangeline "goody, goody dribble!" and Quiller-Couch in his anthology gives three pages to Longfellow and seven to Wilfred Scawen Blunt —but who is Blunt? When I was in Berlin I found in a German history of English and American Literature one-half a page devoted to Longfellow and ten pages to Poe. Perhaps some of this criticism is but the natural reaction following the extreme praise that ensued after the death of Longfellow in 1882.

But Longfellow is surviving all derogatory criticism. He is still the poet with the universal appeal. It is altogether probable that he is more widely read to-day than any other American poet. Even foreigners still express their affection for this poet of the domestic affections. In 1907 Sir Henry Mortimer Durand, the English Ambassador to the United States, made an address in which he made graceful acknowledgement of his debt to this American poet:

"I owe much of the pleasure of my life to American writers of every shade of thought. . . . But I owe to one American writer much more than pleasure. Tastes differ and fashions change, and I am told that the poetry of Longfellow is not read as it used to be. Men in my own country have asked me whether the rivers of Damascus were not better than all the waters of Israel, whether Shakspere, and Milton, and Shelley, and Keats were not enough for me, that I need go to Longfellow. And Americans have seemed surprised that I did not speak rather of Lowell and Bryant and others. Far be it from me to say a word against any of them. I have loved them all from my youth up, every one of them in his own way, and Shakspere as the master and compendium of them all. No one, I suppose, would place Longfellow as a poet quite on the same level with some of them. But the fact remains that, for one reason or another, perhaps in part from early associations, Longfellow has always spoken to my heart. Many a time, in lands far away from the land he loved so well, I have sought for sympathy in happiness and in sorrow—

> Not from the grand old masters,
> Not from the bards sublime,
> Whose distant footsteps echo
> Through the corridors of time—

but from that pure and gentle and untroubled spirit."

Professor E. A. Grosvenor, of Amherst, years ago published an article on Longfellow that was widely copied. It is an interesting account of a conversation in 1879 on board the Messageries steamer *Donai,* bound from Constantinople to Marseilles. On board many nationalities were represented. The story is a fine illustration of the wide-spread popularity of the American poet.

"One evening, as we were quitting the Straits of Bonifacio, some one remarked at dinner that, though Victor Hugo was born in Paris, the earliest impressions of his life were received in Corsica, close to which we were passing. Ten or twelve of us lingered after the meal was finished to talk of the great French poet. One of the party spoke of him as embodying, more than any other writer, the humanistic tendencies of the nineteenth century and as the exponent of what is best in humanity.

"We had been talking in French, when the Russian lady exclaimed in English to the gentleman who had last spoken, 'How can you, an American, give to him the place that is occupied by your own Longfellow? Longfellow is the universal poet. He is better known, too, among foreigners than any one except their own poets! Then she commenced repeating in rich, mellow tones:

> I stood on the bridge at midnight,
>   As the clocks were striking the hour,
> And the moon rose over the city
>   Behind the dark church tower.

I recall how her voice trembled over the words:

> And the burden laid upon me
>   Seemed greater than I could bear.

and how it swelled out in the concluding lines:

> As the symbol of love in Heaven,
>   And its wavering image here.

It was dramatic and never to be forgotten. Then she added, 'I long to visit Boston that I may stand on the Bridge.'

"In the company was an English captain returning from the Zulu war. He was the son of that member of Parliament who had been the chief supporter of the claimant in the famous Tichborne case, and who had poured out his money like water in behalf of the man whom he considered cruelly wronged. The captain was a typical British soldier, with every characteristic of his class. Joining our steamer at Genoa, he had so far talked only of the Zulus and, with bitter indignation, of the manner in which the Prince Imperial had been deserted by British soldiers to be slain by savages. As soon as the Russian lady had concluded he said: 'I can give you something better than that,' and began in a voice like a trumpet:

> Tell me not in mournful numbers
> Life is but an empty dream.

His recitation of the entire poem was marked by the common English upheaval and down-letting of the voice in each line; but it was evident that he loved what he was repeating.

"Then a tall, lank, gray-haired Scotchman, who knew no French, who had hardly mingled with the other passengers, and who seemed always communing with himself, suddenly commenced:

> There is no flock, however watched and tended,
> But one dead lamb is there.

He repeated only a few stanzas, but could apparently have given the whole poem, had he wished.

"For myself, I know that my contribution was *My Lost Youth*, beginning

> Often I think of the beautiful town,
>   That is seated by the sea;
> Often in thought go up and down
> The pleasant streets of that dear old town
>   And my youth comes back to me.

Never did the distance from an early home seem so great to one, New England born, as in that strange company, gathered from many lands, each with words upon the lip which the American had first heard in childhood.

"A handsome, olive-cheeked young man, a Greek from Manchester, educated and living in

England, said, 'How do you like this?' Then he began to sing:

> Stars of the summer night,
> Far in yon azure deeps,
> Hide, hide your golden light!
> She sleeps!
> My lady sleeps!
> Sleeps!

So he rendered the whole of that exquisite serenade—dear to American college students—with a freedom and a fire which hinted that he had sung it at least once before on some more appropriate occasion. Perhaps to some dark-eyed maiden of that elegant Greek colony of Manchester it had come as a revelation, and perhaps she had first heard it sung in front of her father's mansion and had looked down, appreciative but unseen, from above.

"The captain of the *Donai* was not her regular commander, but an officer of the national French navy, who was in charge only for a few voyages. A thorough Frenchman, no one would have accused him of knowing a word of any tongue, save his own. Versatile, overflowing with wit and *bons mots*, it must have wearied him to be silent so long. To our astonishment, in accents so Gallic that one discerned with difficulty that he was attempting English, he intoned:

> Zee seds of neet fair valeeng fast,
> Ven t'rough an Alpeen veelage past
> A yout, who bore meed snow and eece
> A bannair veed dees strange deveece
> Excelsiorr!

" 'Eh, voila,' he exclaimed with satisfaction, 'J'ai appris cela a l'école. C'est tout l'anglais que je sais.'

" '*Mais, commandant,*' said the Russian lady, '*ce n'est pas l'anglais du tout ce que vous venez de dire là.*'

" '*Ah, oui, madame, ça vient de votre Longfellow.*'

"None of the other passengers contributed, but already six nationalities had spoken—Scotch, Russian, Greek, French, English, and American. As we arose from the table and went up on deck to watch the lights glimmering in Napoleon's birthplace, Ajaccio, the Russian lady said: 'Do you suppose there is any other poet of any country, living or dead, from whom so many of us could have quoted? Not one. Not even Shakspere or Victor Hugo or Homer.' "

LVIII

HENRY DAVID THOREAU

DURING his lifetime Thoreau published but two books,—*Walden,* and the *Week on the Concord and Merrimack Rivers,*—and these had but limited sale while the author was living. Over seven hundred copies of the *Week on the Concord and Merrimack Rivers* were returned to Thoreau by his publisher. Thoreau must have had a helpful sense of humor, for after lugging the burden upstairs he complacently remarks,—"I have now a library of nearly nine hundred volumes, over seven hundred of which I wrote myself." In recent times a costly edition of all Thoreau's writings has been published. He is one of the rare spirits whose fame increases with the years. But of all his voluminous writings *Walden,* so it seems to me, is the most readable, the freshest, the most stimulating. Higginson says that it is, perhaps, the only book yet written in America that can bear an annual reading.

Walden is a record of Thoreau's sojourn for about two years in the woods by Walden Pond. He went about two miles from his mother's door, built a little house or hut, and there lived, reading his favorite books, philosophizing, studying nature, and to a great extent avoiding society. Some people have condemned him as selfish, others have defended him. His best defense is his work. If anything so fresh and readable as *Walden* be the result, we might be willing to deny ourselves the society of some of our urban friends, without charging them with selfishness. Thoreau is sometimes called a "wild man"; in a sense, he is untamed. He himself confessed,— "There is in my nature, methinks, a singular yearning toward all wildness." Yet he was a true lover of men. He hated slavery and went to jail rather than pay his taxes, because he disbelieved in supporting a government that upheld slavery. When his friend, the philosophic Emerson, peered into the prison cell and said,— "Henry, why are you here?" the quick retort was,—"Why are you not here?"

It must be remembered that Thoreau lived in a time of social experiment. Hawthorne had thrown in his lot for a brief time with the Brook Farm idealists. Why should not Thoreau make an experiment of his own? Why not live the simple life before Wagner wrote about it? He was tired of the conventionalities of society, of the incessant interruptions to steady thought. Society is naught but a conspiracy to compel imitation. "The head monkey of Paris puts on a traveler's cap, and all the monkeys in America do the same." So Thoreau moves out into the woods by the side of Walden Pond. Before he can live there he must build his house:

"Near the end of March, 1845, I borrowed an axe and went down to the woods by Walden Pond, nearest to where I intended to build my house, and began to cut down some tall arrowy pines, still in their youth, for timber. It is difficult to begin without borrowing, but perhaps it is the most generous course thus to permit your fellow-men to have an interest in your enterprise. The owner of the axe as he released his hold on it, said that it was the apple of his eye; but I returned it sharper than I received it."

His house, when finished, was ten feet wide and fifteen long. The exact cost was twenty-eight dollars, twelve and one-half cents. In *Walden* he gives an itemized account of the cost. And then he adds, with a twinkle of his eye, I think,— "I intend to build me a house which will surpass any on the main street in Concord in grandeur and luxury, as soon as it pleases me as much and will cost me no more than my present one."

Thoreau also finds some satisfaction that his house cost him less than the year's rent of a college room at Harvard; for there the mere rent of a student's room, "which is only a little larger than my own, is thirty dollars each year, though the corporation had the advantage of building thirty-two side by side and under one roof."

In this book he gives a very interesting account of what his food cost him during the eight months from July 4 to March 1. Here is his list:

Rice	$1.73½
Molasses	1.73
Rye meal	1.04¾
Indian meal	.99¾
Pork	.22
Flour	.88
Sugar	.80
Lard	.65

Apples	$ .25
Dried apple	.22
Sweet potatoes	.10
One pumpkin	.06
One watermelon	.02
Salt	.03

"Yes," says he, "I did eat $8.74, all told; but I should not thus unblushingly publish my guilt, if I did not know that most of my readers were equally guilty with myself, and that their deeds would look no better in print." In this connection one may call to mind a reported saying of Mrs. Emerson's to the effect that Henry never got very far away from the sound of the dinner horn. It is not hard to imagine that the hospitable Emerson often invited the kindred-spirited Thoreau into his house for a warm and abundant dinner. Another writer recently has advanced also this thought: Thoreau was not so much of a selfish hermit as it might appear. He went into the woods to make his house or hut a station on the underground railroad. If this be true, a new and different light is thrown upon Thoreau's conduct.

Thoreau was a great lover of nature and the things of nature loved him. Dr. Channing gives us this glimpse of the man:

"Thoreau named all the birds without a gun, a weapon he never used in mature years. He neither killed nor imprisoned any animal, unless driven by acute needs. He brought home a flying squirrel, to study its mode of flight, but quickly carried it back to the wood. He possessed true instincts of topography, and could conceal choice things in the bush and find them again. ... If Thoreau needed a box in his walk, he would strip a piece of birch bark off the tree, fold it, when cut straightly, together, and put his tender lichen or brittle creature therein.''

Emerson supplements this picture with the following account of a visit he once made to Walden:

''The naturalist waded into the pool for the water plants, and his strong legs were no insignificant part of his armor. On this day he looked for the menyanthes and detected it across the wide pool; and, on examination of the floret, declared that it had been in flower five days. He drew out of his breast-pocket a diary, and read the names of all the plants that should bloom that day, whereof he kept account as a banker does when his notes are due. . . . He could pace rods more accurately than another man could measure them with rod and chain. He could find his way in the woods at night better by his feet than by his eyes. He knew every track in the snow and on the ground, and what creature had taken the path in the snow before him.''

Thoreau could write the most beautiful descriptions when he was so inclined. Here is an exquisite description of a snowstorm.

''Did you ever admire the steady, silent, windless fall of the snow, in some lead-colored sky, silent save the little ticking of the flakes as they touched the twigs? It is chased silver, molded over the pines and oak leaves. Soft shades hang like curtains along the closely-draped wood-paths. Frozen apples become little cider-vats. The old crooked apple-trees, frozen stiff in the pale, shivering sunlight, that appears to be dying of consumption, gleam forth like the heroes of one of

Dante's cold hells; we would mind any change in the mercury of the dream. The snow crunches under the feet; the chopper's axe rings funereally through the tragic air. At early morn the frost on button-bushes and willows was silvery and every stem and minutest twig and filamentary weed came up a silver thing, while the cottage smoke rose salmon-colored into that oblique day. At the base of ditches were shooting crystals, like the blades of an ivory-handled penknife, the rosettes and favors fretted of silver on the flat ice. The little cascades in the brook were ornamented with transparent shields, and long candelabrums and spermaceti-colored fools'-caps and plated jellies and white globes, with the black water whirling along transparently underneath. The sun comes out, and all at a glance, rubies, sapphires, diamonds, and emeralds start into intense life on the angles of the snow crystals."

LIX

THERE has been great difference of opinion concerning the genius of Poe. His life also has been the subject of much controversy. By some Poe is painted as a fiend incarnate, by others as a man more sinned against than sinning. When Howells visited Emerson he was surprised to hear the Concord Sage refer to Poe as the "jingle man," but then Emerson himself had been treated rather contemptuously by Poe, and that, together with Emerson's lack of appreciation of melody, may account for the "jingle man" expression.

It is not strange that Poe has been the subject of bitter criticism. He himself was bitter and unjust in his criticisms of others. He once wrote: "Bryant is not *all* a fool. Mr. Willis is not *quite* an ass. Mr. Longfellow *will* steal, but, perhaps, he cannot help it." The man who will write like that must expect similar vituperation in return. To have friends, a man must be friendly. Poe was lacking in those warm human sympathies that attract our fellow-men. The human touch lacking in his art is also lacking in his life. "Except the wife who idolized him," writes Mr. Woodberry in his excellent Life of Poe, "and the mother who cared for him, no one touched his heart in the years of his manhood, and at no time was love so strong in him as to rule his life; as he was self-indulgent, he was self-absorbed, and outside of his family no kind act, no noble affection, no generous sacrifice is recorded of him.''

In *Scribner's Magazine,* 1878, Mrs. Susan T. Weiss in writing of the *Last Days of Edgar Allan Poe,* one of the most accurate accounts of this period of the poet's life, gives us a more pleasing impression. We quote the following extracts:

It was a day or two after his arrival that Poe, accompanied by his sister, called on us. . . . The remembrance of that first meeting with the poet is still as vividly impressed upon my mind as though it had been but yesterday. A shy and dreamy girl, scarcely more than a child, I had all my life taken an interest in those strange stories and poems of Edgar Poe; and now, with my old childish impression of their author scarcely worn off, I regarded the meeting with an eager, yet shrinking anticipation. As I entered the parlor, Poe was seated near the window, quietly conversing. His attitude was easy and graceful, with one arm lightly resting on the back of his chair. His dark curling hair was thrown back from his broad forehead—a style in which he habitually wore it. At sight of him, the impression produced upon me was of a refined, high-bred, and chivalrous gentleman. I use this word ''chivalrous'' as exactly descriptive of something in his whole *personnel,* distinct from either polish or high-breeding, and which, though instantly apparent, was yet an effect too subtle to be described.

He rose on my entrance, and, other visitors being present, stood with one hand on the back of his chair, awaiting my greeting. So dignified was his manner, so reserved his expression, that I experienced an involuntary recoil, until I turned to him and saw his eyes suddenly brighten as I offered my hand; a barrier seemed to melt between us, and I felt that we were no longer strangers. . . .

While upon this subject, I venture, though with great hesitation, to say a word in relation to Poe's own marriage with his cousin, Virginia Clemm. I am aware that there exists with the public but one view of this union, and that so lovely and touching in itself, that to mar the picture with even a shadow inspires almost a feeling of remorse. Yet since in the biography of a distinguished man of genius truth is above all things desirable, and since in this instance the facts do not redound to the discredit of any party concerned, I may be allowed to state what I have been assured is truth.

Poets are proverbial for uncongenial marriages, and to this Poe can scarcely be classed as an exception. From the time when as a youth of nineteen he became a tutor to his sweet and gentle little cousin of six years old, he loved her with the protective tenderness of an elder brother. As years passed he became the subject of successive fancies or passions for various charming women; but she gradually budding into early womanhood experienced but one attachment—an absorbing devotion to her handsome, talented, and fascinating cousin. So intense was this passion that her health and spirits became seriously affected, and her mother, aroused to painful solicitude, spoke to Edgar about it. This was just as he was preparing to leave her house, which had been for some years his home, and enter the world of business. The idea of this separation was insupportable to Virginia. The result was that Poe, at that time a young man of twenty-eight, married his little, penniless, and delicate child-cousin of fourteen or fifteen, and thus unselfishly secured her own and her mother's happiness. In his wife he had ever the most tender and devoted of companions; but it was his own declaration that he ever missed in her a certain intellectual and spiritual sympathy necessary to perfect happiness in such an union. . . . He was never a deliberately unkind husband, and toward the close of Mrs. Poe's life he was assiduous in his tender care and attention. Yet his own declaration to an intimate friend of his youth was that his marriage "had not been a congenial one;" and I repeatedly heard the match ascribed to Mrs. Clemm, by those who were well acquainted with the family and the circumstances. In thus alluding to a subject so delicate, I have not lightly done so, or unadvisedly made a statement which seems refuted by the testimony of so many who have written of the "passionate idolatry" with which the poet regarded his wife. I have heard the subject often and freely discussed by Poe's most intimate friends, including his sisters, and upon this authority I speak. Lovely in person, sweet and gentle in disposition, his young wife deserved, doubtless, all the love that it was in his nature to bestow. Of his unvarying filial affection for Mrs. Clemm, and of her almost angelic devotion to himself and his interests, there can be no question.

Once in discussing *The Raven,* Poe observed that he had never heard it correctly delivered by even the best readers—that is, not as he desired that it should be read. That evening, a number of visitors being present, he was requested to recite the poem, and complied. His impressive delivery held the company spell-bound, but in the midst of it, I, happening to glance toward the open window above the level roof of the green-house, beheld a group of sable faces the whites of whose eyes shone in strong relief against the surrounding darkness. These were a number of our family servants, who having heard much talk about "Mr. Poe, the poet," and having but an imperfect idea of what a poet was, had requested permission of my brother to witness the recital. As the speaker became more impassioned and excited, more conspicuous grew the circle of white eyes, until when at length he turned suddenly toward the window, and, extending his arm, cried, with awful vehemence, "Get thee back into the tempest, and the night's Plutonian shore!" there was a sudden disappearance of the sable visages, a scuttling of feet, and the gallery audience was gone. Ludicrous as was the incident, the final touch was given when at that moment Miss Poe, who was an extraordinary character in her way, sleepily entered the room, and with a dull and drowsy deliberation seated herself on her brother's knee. He had subsided from his excitement into a gloomy despair, and now, fixing his eyes upon his sister, he concluded:

And the raven never flitting, still is sitting, *still* is sitting,
On the pallid bust of Pallas, just above my chamber door;
And its eyes have all the seeming of a demon that is dreaming—

The effect was irresistible; and as the final "nevermore" was solemnly uttered the half-suppressed titter of two very young persons in a corner was responded to by a general laugh. Poe remarked quietly that on his next delivery of a public lecture "he would take Rose along, to act the part of the raven, in which she seemed born to excel." . . .

It is with feelings of deep sadness, even after the lapse of so many years, that I approach the close of these reminiscences.

Poe one day told me that it was necessary that he should go to New York. He must make certain preparations for establishing his magazine, the *Stylus*, but he should in less than two weeks return to Richmond, where he proposed henceforth to reside. He looked forward to this arrangement with great pleasure. "I mean to turn over a new leaf; I shall begin to lead a new life," he said, confidently. He had often spoken to me of his books,—"few, but *recherché*,"—and he now proposed to send certain of these by express, for my perusal. "You must annotate them extensively," he said. "A book wherein the minds of the author and the reader are thus brought in contact is to me a hundredfold increased in interest. It is like flint and steel." One of the books which he desired me to read was Mrs. Browning's poems, and another one of Hawthorne's works. I remember his saying of the latter that he was "indisputably the best prose writer in America;" that "Irving and the

rest were mere commonplace beside him;" and
that "there was more inspiration of true genius
in Hawthorne's prose than in all Longfellow's
poetry." This may serve to give an idea of his
own opinion of what constitutes genius, though
some of Longfellow's poems he pronounced
"perfect of their kind."

The evening of the day previous to that appointed for his departure from Richmond, Poe
spent at my mother's. He declined to enter the
parlors, where a number of visitors were assembled, saying he preferred the more quiet
sitting-room; and here I had a long and almost
uninterrupted conversation with him. He spoke
of his future, seeming to anticipate it with an
eager delight, like that of youth. He declared
that the last few weeks in the society of his old
and new friends had been the happiest that he
had known for many years, and that when he
again left New York he should there leave behind
all the trouble and vexation of his past life. . . .

In speaking of his own writings Poe expressed
his conviction that he had written his best poems,
but that in prose he might yet surpass what he
had already accomplished. . . .

He was the last of the party to leave the house.
We were standing on the portico, and after going
a few steps he paused, turned, and again lifted
his hat, in a last adieu. At the moment, a brilliant meteor appeared in the sky directly over
his head, and vanished in the east. We com-
mented laughingly upon the incident; but I remembered it sadly afterward.

That night he spent at Duncan's lodge; and as
his friend said, sat late at his window, medita-

tively smoking, and seemingly disinclined for conversation. On the following morning he went into the city, accompanied by his friends Dr. Gibbon Carter and Dr. Mackenzie. The day was passed with them and others of his intimate friends. Late in the evening he entered the office of Dr. John Carter, and spent an hour in looking over the day's papers; then taking Dr. Carter's cane he went out, remarking that he would step across to Saddler's (a fashionable restaurant) and get supper. From the circumstance of his taking the cane, leaving his own in its place, it is probable that he had intended to return; but at the restaurant he met with some acquaintances who detained him until late, and then accompanied him to the Baltimore boat. According to their account he was quite sober and cheerful to the last, remarking, as he took leave of them, that he would soon be in Richmond again.

. . . Three days after, a friend came to me with the day's issue of the *Richmond Dispatch*. Without a word she pointed to a particular paragraph, where I read,—"Death of Edgar A. Poe, in Baltimore."

Poe had made himself popular in Richmond, people had become interested in him, and his death cast a universal gloom over the city. His old friends, and even those more recently formed, and whom he had strangely attached to himself, deeply regretted him. Mr. Sully came to consult with me about a picture of *The Raven* which he intended to make; and in the course of the conversation expressed himself in regard to his lost friend with a warmth of feeling and appreciation not usual to him. The two had been schoolmates; and the artist said: "Poe was one of the most warm-hearted and generous of men. In his youth and prosperity, when admired and looked up to by all his companions, he invariably stood by me and took my part. I was a dull boy at learning, and Edgar never grudged time or pains in assisting me." In further speaking, he said, with a decision and earnestness which impressed me, "It was Mr. Allan's cruelty in casting him upon the world, a beggar, which ruined Poe. Some who had envied him took advantage of his change of fortune to slight and insult him. He was sensitive and proud, and felt the change keenly. It was this which embittered him. By nature no person was less inclined to reserve or bitterness, and as a boy he was frank and generous to a fault." In speaking of his poems, Mr. Sully remarked: "He has an eye for dramatic, but not for scenic or artistic effect. Except in *The Raven*, I can nowhere in his poems find a subject for a picture."

In closing these reminiscences, I may be allowed to make a few remarks founded upon my actual personal knowledge of Poe, in at least the phase of character in which he appeared to me. What he may have been to his ordinary associates, or to the world at large, I do not know; and in the picture presented to us by Dr. Griswold,—half maniac, half demon,—I confess, I cannot recognize a trait of the gentle, grateful, warm-hearted man whom I saw amid his friends, —his careworn face all aglow with generous feeling in the kindness and appreciation to which he was so little accustomed. His faults were sufficiently apparent; but for these a more than ordinary allowance should be made, in consideration of the unfavorable influences surrounding him from his very birth. He was ever the sport of an adverse fortune. Born in penury, reared in affluence, treated at one time with pernicious indulgence and then literally turned into the streets, a beggar and an outcast, deserted by those who had formerly courted him, maliciously calumniated, smarting always under a sense of wrong and injustice,—what wonder that his bright, warm, and naturally generous and genial nature should have become embittered? What wonder that his keenly sensitive and susceptible poetic temperament should have become jarred, out of tune, and into harsh discord with himself and mankind? Let the just and the generous pause before they judge; and upon their lips the breath of condemnation will soften into a sigh of sympathy and regret.

LX

POOR Artemus! says Haweis in his lecture on the American humorist, I shall not see his like again, as he appeared for a few short weeks before an English audience at the Egyptian Hall, Piccadilly.

Sometimes, as to looks, profoundly dejected, at others shy or reproachful; nervously anxious to please (apparently), yet with a certain twinkle at the back of his eye which convinced you of his perfect *sang froid,* and one thing always—full, unescapably full, of fun. . . .

When Artemus arrived here in 1866 he was a dying man.

I can see him now, as he came on the narrow platform in front of his inferior panorama, and stole a glance at the densely packed room and then at his panorama.

His tall, gaunt, though slender figure, his curly light hair and large aquiline nose, which always reminded me of a macaw; his thin face flushed with consumption, his little cough, which seemed to shake him to pieces, and which he said "was wearing him out," at which we all laughed irresistibly, and then felt ashamed of ourselves, as well we might; but he himself seemed to enjoy

313

his cough. It was all part of that odd, topsy-turvy mind in which everything appeared most natural upside down!

On first entering he would seem profoundly unconscious that anything was expected of him, but after looking at the audience, then at his own clothes, and then apologetically at his panorama, he began to explain its merits.

The fact is Artemus intended having the finest scenes that could be painted, but he gave that up on account of the expense, and then determined to get the worst as the next best thing for his purpose.

When anything very bad came up he would pause and gaze admiringly at the canvas, and then look round a little reproachfully at the company.

"This picture," he would say, "is a great work of art; it is an oil painting done in petroleum. It is by the Old Masters. It was the last thing they did before dying. They did this, and then they expired. I wish you were nearer to it so you could see it better. I wish I could take it to your residences and let you see it by daylight. Some of the greatest artists in London come here every morning before daylight with lanterns to look at it. They say they never saw anything like it before, and they hope they never shall again!"

Certain curious brown splotches appearing in the foreground, Artemus pointed gravely to them, and said:

"These are intended for horses; I know they are, because the artist told me so. After two years, he came to me one morning and said, 'Mr.

Ward, I cannot conceal it from you any longer; they are horses.' "

Apropos of nothing he observed:

"I really don't care for money; I only travel around to show my clothes."

This was a favorite joke of his. He would look with a piteous expression of discomfort and almost misery at his black trousers and swallow-tail coat, a costume in which he said he was always most wretched.

"These clothes I have on," he continued, "were a great success in America." And then quite irrelevantly and rather hastily, "How often do large fortunes ruin young men! I should like to be ruined, but I can get on very well as I am!"

So the lecture dribbled on with little fragments of impertinent biography, mere pegs for slender witticisms like this:

"When quite a child I used to draw on wood. I drew a small cartload of raw material over a wooden bridge, the people of the village noticed me, I drew their attention, they said I had a future before me; up to that time I had an idea it was behind me."

Or this:

"I became a man. I have always been mixed up with art. I have an uncle who takes photographs, and I have a servant who takes anything he can set his hands on."

With one more example from his life among the Mormons, which, perhaps, though brief, includes a greater variety of wit and humor than any single passage I could select, I must conclude my memorial glimpses of this incomparable and lamented humorist.

"I regret to say that efforts were made to make a Mormon of me while I was in Utah.

"It was leap year when I was there, and seventeen young widows—the wives of a deceased Mormon (he died by request)—offered me their hearts and hands. I called upon them one day, and taking their soft, white hands in mine—which made eighteen hands altogether—I found them in tears. And I said 'Why is this thus?—what is the reason of this thusness?'

"They hove a sigh—seventeen sighs of different size. They said—

" 'Oh, soon thou wilt be gonested away!'

"I told them that when I got ready to leave a place I usually wentested. They said—'Doth not like us?'

"I said, 'I doth, I doth!' I also said, 'I hope your intentions are honorable, as I am a lone child and my parents are far, far away!'

"They then said, 'Wilt not marry us?'

"I said, 'Oh no, it cannot was.'

"Again they asked me to marry them, and again I declined. When they cried—

" 'Oh, cruel man: this is too much—oh, too much!'

"I told them it was on account of the muchness that I declined."

LXI

EDMUND GOSSE VISITS WHITTIER

IN December of 1884, Mr. Edmund Gosse, one of the most distinguished of English critics, visited Whittier at a house called Oak Knoll, in Massachusetts, where he was then staying with friends. We quote brief extracts from a report of that visit as published in *Good Words,* an English magazine:

"Doubtless in leafy season Oak Knoll may have its charms, but it was distinctly sinister that December morning. We rang, and after a long pause the front door opened slightly, and a very unprepossessing dog emerged, and shut the door (if I may say so) behind him. We were face to face with this animal, which presented none of the features identified in one's mind with the idea of Mr. Whittier. It sniffed unpleasantly, but we spoke to it most blandly and it became assured that we were not tramps. The dog sat down, and looked at us; we had nowhere to sit down, but we looked at the dog. Then, after many blandishments, but feeling very uncomfortable, I ventured to hold the dog in conversation while I rang again. After another pause the door was slightly opened, and a voice of no agreeable timbre asked what we wanted. We explained,

317

across the dog, that we had come by appointment to see Mr. Whittier. The door was closed a second time, and, if our carriage had still been waiting, we should certainly have driven back to Danvers. But at length a hard-featured woman grudgingly admitted us, and showed us, growling as she did it, into a parlor.

"Our troubles were then over, for Mr. Whittier himself appeared, with all that report had ever told of a gentle sweetness and dignified cordial courtesy. He was then seventy-seven years old, and, although he spoke of age and feebleness, he showed few signs of either; he was, in fact, to live eight years more. Perhaps because the room was low, he seemed surprisingly tall; he must, in fact, have been a little less than six feet high. The peculiarity of his face rested in the extraordinary large and luminous black eyes, set in black eyebrows, and fringed with thick black eye-lashes curiously curved inward. . . .

"His generosity to those much younger and less gifted than himself is well known, and I shall not dwell on the good-natured things which he proceeded to say to his English visitor. He made no profession, at any time, of being a critic, and his formula was that such and such verse or prose had given him pleasure—'I am grateful to thee for all that enjoyment' was his charming way of being kind. . . . He spoke with great emotion of Emerson—'the noblest human being I have known,' and of Longfellow, 'perhaps the sweetest. But you will see Holmes,' he added. I said that it was my great privilege to be seeing Dr. Holmes every day, and that the night before he had sent all sorts of affectionate messages by me to Mr. Whittier. The latter expressed great curiosity to see Holmes's short *Life of Emerson* which, in fact, was published five or six days later. . . . Mr. Whittier greatly surprised me by confessing that he was quite color-blind. He exemplified his condition by saying that if I came to Amesbury I should be scandalized by one of his carpets. It appeared that he was never permitted, by the guardian goddess of his hearth, to go 'shopping' for himself, but that once, being in Boston, and needing a carpet, he had ventured to go to a store and buy what he thought to be a very nice, quiet article, precisely suited to adorn a Quaker home. When it arrived at Amesbury there was a universal shout of horror, for what had struck Mr. Whittier as a particularly soft combination of browns and grays proved, to normal eyes, to be a loud pattern of bright red roses on a field of the crudest cabbage-green.''

LXII

IN the *New England Magazine* Charlotte Forten Grimke writes entertainingly of Whittier. From this article we are permitted to quote the following extracts:

"And so it happened that, one lovely summer day, my friend and I found ourselves on the train, rapidly whirling eastward, through the pleasant old town of Newburyport, across the 'shining Merrimac,' on our way to the poet's home in Amesbury. Arriving at the station, we found Mr. Whittier awaiting us, and a walk of a few minutes brought us to his house on Friend Street. Amesbury, a busy manufacturing town, pleasantly situated on the Merrimac, impressed me at first as hardly retired enough for a poet's home; for fresh in my recollection were Longfellow's historic house, guarded by stately poplars, standing back from the quiet Cambridge street, and Lowell's old mansion, completely buried in its noble elms; and each of these had quite realized my ideal of the home of a poet. But the little house looked very quiet and homelike; and when we entered it and received the warm welcome of the poet's sister, we felt, as all felt who entered that hospitable door, the very spirit of

JOHN GREENLEAF WHITTIER
From a photograph

peace descending upon us. The house was then white (it was afterwards painted a pale yellow), with green blinds, and a little vine-wreathed piazza on one side, upon which opened the glass door of 'the garden room,' the poet's favorite sitting-room and study. The windows of this room looked out upon a pleasant, old-fashioned garden. The walls on both sides of the fireplace were covered with books. The other walls were hung with pictures, among which we noticed 'The Barefoot Boy,' a painting of Mr. Whittier's birthplace in Haverhill, a copy of that lovely picture, 'The Motherless,' under which were written some exquisite lines by Mrs. Stowe, and a beautiful little sea-view, painted by a friend of the poet. Vases of fresh, bright flowers stood upon the mantelpiece. After we had rested we went into the little parlor, where hung the portrait of the loved and cherished mother, who some years before had passed away to the 'Better Land.' Hers was one of those sweet, aged faces which one often sees among the Friends,—full of repose, breathing a benediction upon all around. There were other pictures and books, and upon a table in the corner stood Rogers' 'Wounded Scout.'

"At the head of the staircase hung a great cluster of pansies, purple and white and gold. Mr. Whittier called our attention to their wonderful resemblance to human faces,—a resemblance which we so often see in pansies, and which was brought out with really startling distinctness in this picture.

"In the cool, pleasant chamber assigned to us, pervaded by an air of Quaker serenity and purity, was a large painting of the poet in his youth.

This was the realization of my girlish dreams. There were the clustering curls, the brilliant dark eyes, the firm, resolute mouth. He looked like a youthful Bayard, 'without fear and without reproach,' ready to throw himself unflinchingly into the most stirring scenes of the battle of life.

"We were at once greatly interested in Miss Whittier, and impressed by the simplicity and kindness of her manner. We saw the soul's beauty shining in her soft, dark eyes, and in the smile which, like her brother's, was very winning, and we felt it in the music of her gentle voice and the warm pressure of her hand. There was a refreshing atmosphere of unworldliness about her. She had rarely been away from her home, and although her brother's fame obliged her to receive many strangers, she had never, as she told us, been able to overcome a shyness of disposition, except in the case of a very few friends. She was naturally witty and original, and when she did shake off her shyness, had a childlike way of saying bright things which was very charming. She and her brother had lived together, alone since their mother's death, and in their mutual devotion have been well compared to Charles Lamb and his sister.

"We spent a delightful evening in the garden-room in quiet, cheerful talk. In society Mr. Whittier had the reputation of being very shy, and he was so among strangers; but at times, in the companionship of his friends, no one could be more genial. He had even a boyish frankness of manner, a natural love of fun, a keen appreciation of the humorous, which the sorrows and poor health of many years failed to subdue.

That night he talked to us freely of his childhood, of the life on the old farm in Haverhill, which he has so vividly described in *Snow-Bound,* and showed us a venerable book, *Davideis,* being a history of David written in rhyme, the quaintest and most amusing rhyme, by Thomas Ellwood, a friend of Milton. It was the first book of 'poetry,' he told us, that he read when a boy. He entertained us with stories of people who came to see him. He had many very interesting and charming visitors, of course, but there were also many exceedingly queer ones, and these, he said with a queer smile, generally 'brought their carpet bags!' He said he was thankful to live in such a place as Amesbury, where people did not speak to him about his poems, nor think of him as a poet. Sometimes he had amused himself by tracking the most persistent of the lion-hunters, and found that the same individuals went to Emerson and Longfellow and other authors, and made precisely the same speeches. Emerson was not much annoyed by them; he enjoyed studying character in all its phases.

Begging letters and begging visits were also very frequent, and his sister told us that her brother had frequently been victimized in his desire to help those whose pitiful stories he believed. One day he received a letter from a man in a neighboring town, asking him for a loan of ten dollars, and assuring him that he should blow his brains out if Mr. Whittier did not send him the money. The tone of the letter made him doubt the sincerity of the writer, and he did not send the money, comforting himself, he said, with the thought that the man really had no brains to blow out. 'I must confess, however,' he added, 'I looked rather anxiously at the newspapers for the next few days, but seeing no news of a suicide in the neighboring town, I was relieved.'

"His sister once told us of an incident which occurred during the war, which pleased them very much. One night, at a late hour, the door-bell rang, and her brother, on answering it, found a young man in an officer's uniform standing at the door. 'Is this Mr. Whittier?' he asked. 'Yes.' 'Well, sir,' was the quick reply, 'I only wanted to have the pleasure of shaking hands with you.' And with that he seized the poet's hand, shook it warmly, and rushed away, before Mr. Whittier had recovered from his surprise.

"In subsequent visits to Mr. Whittier, he was sometimes induced to talk about his poems, although that was a subject on which he rarely spoke. On my friend's once warmly praising *Maud Muller,* he said decidedly that he did not like the poem, because it was too sad; it ministered to the spirit of unrest and dissatisfaction which was only too prevalent. With *My Psalm* he felt much better satisfied, because it was more hopeful. His favorite poets were Wordsworth and Burns. He once showed us an autograph letter of Burns, which he prized very highly, and a number of beautiful photographs of Scotch scenery, the gift of a sturdy old Scotchman, a neighbor of his and also an ardent admirer of Burns.

"Our conversation occasionally touched on the subject of marriage, and I remember his asking us if we could imagine why there should be so much unhappiness among married people, even

among those who seemed to have everything calculated to make them happy, and who really
loved each other. He said he had pondered over
the subject a good deal, and had finally concluded that it was because they saw too much of
each other. He did not believe it was well for
any two human beings to have too much of each
other's society. We told him that, being a much-
to-be-commiserated bachelor, he was not competent authority on that subject.

"Among the most intimate of his friends were
Mr. and Mrs. James T. Fields, Colonel Higginson, Charles Sumner, and Bayard Taylor. To
the two latter, and also to Emerson, he has alluded very beautifully in one of his most characteristic poems, *The Last Walk in Autumn*.

"On visiting the poet after my return from
the South, for a vacation, I found a new inmate
of the house, a gray and scarlet parrot, named
Charlie, a great pet of the poet and his sister,
and far-famed for his wit and wisdom. He could
say many things with great distinctness, and
although at first refusing rather spitefully to
make my acquaintance, when I invited him to
come into the kitchen and get his supper he at
once hopped upon my hand and behaved in the
most amicable manner. It was very comical to
see him dance to a tune of Mr. Whittier's whist-
ling. His master told us that he would climb
toilsomely up the spout, pausing at every step or
two to say, in a tone of the deepest self-pity,
'Poor Charlie!' and when he reached the roof
screaming impertinently at the passers-by. The
Irish children said that he called them 'Paddies,'
and threatened him with dire vengeance. Mr.

Whittier said he did not know; he 'could believe anything of that bird.' Charlie's favorite amusement was shaking the unripe pears from the trees in the garden; and when he saw Miss Whittier approaching, he would steal away with drooping head, like a child caught in a naughty action. This gifted bird afterwards died, and was much missed by the poet, who alluded to him in the poem entitled *The Common Question*.

"Mr. Whittier showed me a couple of stuffed birds which had been sent to him by the Emperor of Brazil, after reading his *Cry of a Lost Soul,* in allusion to the bird in South American forests which has so intensely mournful a note that the Indians give it a name which signifies a lost soul. The first birds which were sent did not reach him, and the Emperor on hearing it sent two more. The bird is larger than a mocking bird, and has sober gray plumage, very unlike the bright-hued creatures usually seen in tropical forests.

"The Emperor was a warm admirer of Mr. Whittier, and one of the first persons for whom he inquired on reaching Boston was the poet. There was some delay about their meeting and Dom Pedro became very impatient. At last they met in a house in Boston. Dom Pedro expressed great delight at meeting the poet, and talked with him a long time, paying very little attention to any one else. On leaving, he asked Mr. Whittier to accompany him downstairs, and before entering his carriage threw his arms around the astonished poet and embraced him warmly.

"Rare and beautiful were the qualities which met in Mr. Whittier: a singularly unworldly and sweet disposition, and unwavering love of truth

and justice, a keen sense of humor, the highest
type of courage, and a firm faith in God's goodness, which no amount of suffering ever shook.
For years he was an invalid, a martyr to severe
headaches. He once told me that he had not for
a long time written anything without suffering.
The nearest and dearest of his earthly ties had
been severed by death. But he never rebelled.
His life exemplified the spirit of resignation
which is breathed throughout so many of his
poems.

> All as God wills, who wisely heeds
> To give or to withhold,
> And knoweth more of all my needs
> Than all my prayers have told.

"My husband and I made our last visit to him
two years ago, at Oak Knoll. He gave us his
customary warm greeting and, although in extremely feeble health, was as sweet and genial
in spirit and as entertaining in conversation as
ever. He took us into his cosey little library,
and talked about his books and pictures and old
friends, and promised to send us his latest photograph,—which he afterwards did. Fearing to
weary him, we stayed but a short time. So frail
he looked, that in parting from him our hearts
were saddened by the thought that we might not
look upon that dear face again. And so it proved.
I shall ever remember him as I saw him then, in
his beautiful country home, surrounded by devoted friends, awaiting calmly the summons to
enter into rest—in that serene and lovely old
age which comes only to those gifted ones whose
lives are the embodiment of all that is noblest
and best and sweetest in their poetry.

"Farewell, beloved, revered friend! Thou art gone to join the loved ones who beckoned to thee from those blessed shores of Peace. To thee, how great the gain! To us, how infinite the loss! But thy influence shall remain with us. Still shalt thou

> . . . be to other souls
> The cup of strength in some great agony,
> Enkindle generous ardor, feed pure love,
> Beget the smiles that have no cruelty—
> Be the sweet presence of a good diffused,
> And in diffusion ever more intense.

LXIII

HENRY WARD BEECHER

IT would be no compliment to call Henry Ward
Beecher the American Spurgeon. He may
be that, but he is more. If we can imagine
Mr. Spurgeon and Mr. John Bright with a cau-
tious touch of Professor Maurice and a strong
tincture of the late F. W. Robertson—if, I say,
it is possible to imagine such a compound being
brought up in New England and at last securely
fixed in a New York pulpit, we shall get a product
not unlike Henry Ward Beecher. . . .

Mr. Beecher was brought up in the country.
His novel, *Norwood*—not very readable, by the
way, although full of charming passages—
abounds in woods and streams, hills and dales,
and flowers. "The willows," he tells us somewhere, "had thrown off their silky catkins, and
were in leaf; the elm was covered with chocolate-
colored blossoms, the soft maple drew bees to its
crimson tassels." Would that all preachers and
writers used no more offensive and superfluous
flowers of speech than such as these. . . .

When he wants to illustrate the comfort of a
powerful, unseen, though protective love, he tells
us how, as a boy, he woke up one midsummer
night and listened, with a sense of half-uneasy

awe, to the wild cry of the marsh birds, whilst
the moonlight streamed full into his room; and
then, as he grew more and more disturbed, he
suddenly heard his father clear his throat
"a-hem," in the next room, and instantly that
familiar sound restored his equanimity. The
illustration is simple, but it hits the mark and
goes home. His affectionate tributes to his
father and mother are constantly breaking forth
in spite of himself. "I thank God," he says,
"for two things. First, that I was born and bred
in the country, of parents that gave me a sound
constitution and a noble example. I never can
pay back what I got from my parents. Next I
am thankful that I was brought up in circumstances where I never became acquainted with
wickedness." How delightful it is to think of a
man who, without a taint of conscious insincerity,
but simply out of the fulness of his heart, can get
up before four thousand people, and say:

"I never was sullied in act, nor in thought
when I was young. I grew up as pure as a
woman. And I cannot express to God the thanks
which I owe to my mother, and to my father, and
to the great household of sisters and brothers
among whom I lived. And the secondary knowledge of those wicked things which I have gained
in later life in a professional way, I gained under
such guards that it was not harmful to me." . . .

He has a wonderful way of importing his leisure hours into the pulpit, and making the great
cooped-up multitude feel something of the joy
and freshness of his own exhilaration. One
golden day above others seems to have dwelt in
his mind. He refers to it again and again.

"When I walked one day on the top of Mt. Washington—glorious day of memory! Such another day I think I shall not experience till I stand on the battlements of the New Jerusalem —how I was discharged of all imperfections; the wide far-spreading country which lay beneath me in beauteous light, how heavenly it looked, and I communed with God. I had sweet tokens that he loved me. My very being rose right up into his nature. I walked with him, and the cities far and near of New York, and all the cities and villages which lay between it and me, with their thunder, the wrangling of human passions below me, were to me as if they were not."

Some of his sermons are full of vacation-rambles. He passes through woods and gardens and plucks flowers and fragrant leaves, which will all have to do service in Brooklyn Church; he watches the crowded flight of pigeons from the treetops, and thinks of men's riches that so make themselves wings and fly away. As he scales the mountains and sees the summer storms sweep through the valleys beneath him, he thinks of the storms in the human heart—"many, many storms there are that lie low and hug the ground, and the way to escape them is to go up the mountain sides and get higher than they are."

Mr. Beecher's travels in Europe were not thrown away upon his ardent and artistic temperament. He has stood before the great pictures to some purpose, and has not failed to read their open secret.

"Have you ever stood in Dresden to watch that matchless picture of Raphael's, the 'Madonna di San Siste'? Engravings of it are all through the world; but no engraving has ever reproduced the mother's face. The Infant Christ that she holds is far more nearly represented than the mother. In her face there is a mist. It is wonder, it is love, it is adoration, it is awe—it is all these mingled, as if she held in her hands her babe, and yet it was God! That picture means nothing to me as it does to the Roman Church; but it means everything to me, because I believe that every mother should love the God that is in her child, and that every mother's heart should be watching to discern and see in the child, which is more than flesh and blood, something that takes hold of immortality and glory.''

—Selected from the *Contemporary Review*.

LXIV

THE London *Times*, sometimes nicknamed the *Thunderer*, was for many years the most influential paper in the world. Emerson in his *English Traits* says, "No power in England is more felt, more feared, or more obeyed." In view of the high position of this paper it is a matter of interest to our American students of literature to read what this paper had to say on the death of Lowell.

Here follows the larger part of the editorial from the *Times:*

The death of Mr. Lowell will probably be more keenly and widely felt in England than would be that of any other American, or, indeed, of any other man who was not a fellow-countryman of our own. To very many in England it will be counted as a grave personal loss; and thousands more will miss in him one whom through his writings they had admired, felt with, laughed with, as with a friend. For a long time past, in fact ever since he quitted the Legation, his long annual visits to London have been regarded by a wide circle as one of the events of the year, and he himself as one of the most valued guests. We had hoped that this last June would again see him in

333

his old London haunts, bright, genial, interesting as ever; but a cruel fate decided that this was not to be, and neither the Old World nor the New should know him more. Never a strong man, he has succumbed, at a ripe age, it is true, but prematurely, as all will think who knew how fresh his intelligence and his sympathies were to the last. With him there passes away one of the very few Americans who were the equals of any son of the Old World—of any Frenchman or any Englishman—in that indefinable mixture of qualities, which we sum up for want of a better word, under the name of culture. How did he arrive at it? The answer is, by natural gifts, by constant play of mind with mind in talk, and by reading. On those who casually met Mr. Lowell in society, he certainly did not make the impression of a book-worm, or of a man to whom books were indispensable; but none the less is it true that whenever official business was not too heavy he invariably read for a *minimum* of four hours a day. This did not include the time that he gave to ephemeral literature; it was the time that he spent in the serious reading of books, generally old books. How many of us, not professed students, can show a record as good, or half as good? He read quickly, too, in various languages, his favorites being the English of the Elizabethans, Spanish, old French, and modern French. His excellent memory and wonderful assimilative power built up this reading into the mental endowments that all the world admired.

When Mr. Lowell came to England as the representative of the United States under the last Republican administration, London felt a sympathetic curiosity as to the author of the famous *Biglow Papers* and of so much excellent prose criticism. In a very short time the feeling warmed into admiration and friendship. The official world spoke well of the way in which the new minister performed his duties—generally not very heavy, but always demanding tact and prudence—of his position as minister. Menacing sounds, indeed, began to be heard from across the ocean, when the Irish Fenians, who control so much of the press of the United States, began to raise the cry that Mr. Lowell sacrificed the interests of their dynamitard friends to a brutal British government; but, as the Washington officials took no notice, nobody here paid much attention to the matter. In social life, the new minister began to be a power. He went everywhere—to the houses of the great, to the houses of the men of letters, and to places where such people most do congregate. His talk was excellent give-and-take. He was neither a professional anecdotist, like another famous American talker, Mr. Chauncey Depew, nor a man on the watch for something to disagree with, like Mr. Blaine, nor even, as was his admirable successor, Mr. Phelps, a man of long silences broken by flashes of humor. Mr. Lowell seemed to know everything and have his knowledge always to hand; he was quick in repartee; he mixed anecdote with reflection in the happiest manner; he laughed at others' jests, and they laughed at his. Still, one had to be a little careful with him, for there were points on which he was extremely sensitive. Nobody, for example, must talk in his presence of *Americanisms,* or hint that the standard of language and literature observed in America showed any deflection from the best standard of the race. . . .

On one occasion Mr. Lowell was sorely tempted to make his permanent home here. Just about the time of his ceasing to be minister, he was seriously sounded as to his willingness to be nominated to the new post of professor of English language and literature at Oxford. Had he consented to stand, not even a board determined to sink literature in philology could have passed over his claims. But he declined, for two reasons. There were claims of family, over in Massachusetts, and, greatly as he loved the mental atmosphere of England, he thought it his duty not to accept a definitely English post. And the sense of duty is strong in that old Puritan stock from which he sprang.

. . . But the distinguishing feature of Mr. Lowell was his adding to these high literary gifts the strong practical side which made of him a social power and a diplomatist. Naturally, such a man made a mark by his speeches, and happy was the audience, at the unveiling of a monument or at a literary dinner, that had the privilege of listening to Mr. Lowell. Seldom in England, where this kind of speaking is not cultivated as an art, have we witnessed such a perfect union of self-possession, sense, and salt. The speech on Henry Fielding, the speech in which he compared the sound of London to "the roaring loom of time," the address on Democracy—to mention but a few—will not be easily forgotten. Nor will those who had the privilege of experiencing it, in however slight a degree, forget the sweet affectionateness which, in spite of an occasional irritability and over-sensitiveness, was at the root of Mr. Lowell's character. Corrupt politicians disliked him and feared the barbed arrows of his indignant wit; but he goes to the grave mourned by all that is best in America, and he takes with him the heart-felt regard as well as the admiration, of this elder branch of our common English race.

LXV

THE WRITING OF "AMERICA"

THE Rev. Dr. Samuel F. Smith, author of *America,* died in Boston in 1895. On April 3, of the same year, he had received a grand public testimonial in Music Hall in recognition of his authorship of *America.* In the souvenir of that occasion Dr. Smith tells how he came to write the poem that made him famous.

"In the year 1831 William C. Woodbridge, of New York, a noted educator, was deputed to visit Germany and inspect the system of the public schools, that if he should find in them any features of interest unknown to our public schools here they might be adopted in the schools of the United States. He found that in the German schools much attention was given to music; he also found many books containing music and songs for children. Returning home, he brought several of these music-books, and placed them in the hands of Mr. Lowell Mason, then a noted composer, organist, and choir leader. Having himself no knowledge of the German language he brought them to me at Andover, where I was then studying theology, requesting me, as I should find time, to furnish him translations of the German words, or to write new hymns and songs adapted to the German music.

"On a dismal day in February, 1832, looking over one of these books, my attention was drawn to a tune which attracted me by its simple and natural movement and its fitness for children's choirs. Glancing at the German words at the foot of the page, I saw that they were patriotic, and I was instantly inspired to write a patriotic hymn of my own.

"Seizing a scrap of waste paper, I began to write, and in half an hour I think the words stood upon it substantially as they are sung to-day. I did not know at the time that the tune was the British *God Save the King*. I do not share the regrets of those who deem it an evil that the national tune of Britain and America is the same. On the contrary, I deem it a new and beautiful tie of union between the mother and the daughter, one furnishing the music (if, indeed, it is really English), and the other the words.

"I did not propose to write a national hymn. I did not think that I had done so. I laid the song aside, and nearly forgot that I had made it. Some weeks later I sent it to Mr. Mason, and on the following Fourth of July, much to my surprise, he brought it out at a children's celebration in the Park Street Church, in Boston, where it was first sung in public."

LXVI

ELIZABETH STUART PHELPS AND HER FIRST STORY

SOME years ago the author of *Gates Ajar* told in an American magazine how she began her literary career. From this account we quote:
"The town of Lawrence was three miles and a half from Andover. Up to the year 1860 we had considered Lawrence chiefly in the light of a place to drive to. . . . Upon the map of our young fancy the great mills were sketched in lightly; we looked up from the restaurant ice-cream to see the hands pour out for dinner, a dark and restless, but a patient, throng, used in those days, to standing eleven hours and a quarter—women and girls—at their looms, six days of the week, and making no audible complaints; for socialism had not reached Lawrence, and anarchy was content to bray in distant parts of the geography at which the factory people had not arrived when they left school. . . .

". . . One January evening, we were forced to think about the mills with curdling horror that no one living in that locality when the tragedy happened will forget.

"At five o'clock the Pemberton Mills, all hands being at the time on duty, without a tremor of warning, sank to the ground.

"At the erection of the factory a pillar with a defective core had passed careless inspectors. In technical language the core had 'floated' an eighth of an inch from its position. The weak spot in the too thin wall of the pillar had bided its time, and yielded. The roof, the walls, the machinery fell upon seven hundred and fifty living men and women, and buried them. Most of these were rescued, but eighty-eight were killed. As the night came on, those watchers on Andover Hill who could not join the rescuing parties, saw a strange and fearful light at the north.

"Where we were used to watching the beautiful belt of the lighted mills blaze—a zone of laughing fire from east to west, upon the horizon bar—a red and awful glare went up. The mill had taken fire. A lantern, overturned in the hands of a man who was groping to save an imprisoned life, had flashed to the cotton, or the wool, or the oil with which the ruins were saturated. One of the historic conflagrations of New England resulted.

"With blanching cheeks we listened to the whispers that told us how the mill-girls, caught in the ruins beyond hope of escape, began to sing. They were used to singing, poor things, at their looms —mill-girls always are—and their young souls took courage from the familiar sound of one another's voices. They sang the hymns and songs which they had learned in the schools and churches. No classical strains, no 'music for music's sake,' ascended from that furnace; no ditty of love or frolic, but the plain, religious outcries of the people: *Heaven is my Home, Jesus, Lover of my Soul,* and *Shall we Gather at the River?* Voice after voice dropped. The fire raced on.   A few brave girls still sang:

> Shall we gather at the river,
> There to walk and worship ever?

"But the startled Merrimac rolled by, red as blood beneath the glare of the burning mills, and it was left to the fire and the river to finish the chorus.

"At the time this tragedy occurred, I felt my share of its horror, like other people; but no more than that.   My brother, being of the privileged sex, was sent over to see the scene, but I was not allowed to go.

"Years after, I cannot say just how many, the half-effaced negative came back to form under the chemical of some new perception of the significance of human tragedy.

"It occurred to me to use the event as the basis of a story.   To this end I set forth to study the subject.   I had heard nothing in those days about 'material,' and conscience in the use of it, and little enough about art.   We did not talk about realism then.   Of critical phraseology I knew nothing, and of critical standards only what I had observed by reading the best fiction.   Poor novels and stories I did not read.   I do not remember being forbidden them; but, by that parental art finer than denial, they were absent from my convenience.

"It needed no instruction in the canons of art, however, to teach me that to do a good thing, one must work hard for it.   So I gave the best part of a month to the study of the Pemberton Mill tragedy, driving to Lawrence, and investigating every possible avenue of information left at that too long remove of time which might give the data. I visited the rebuilt mills, and studied the machinery. I consulted engineers and officials and physicians, newspaper men, and persons who had been in the mill at the time of its fall. I scoured the files of old local papers, and from these I took certain portions of names, actually involved in the catastrophe, though, of course, fictitiously used. When there was nothing left for me to learn on the subject, I came home and wrote a little story called 'The Tenth of January,' and sent it to the *Atlantic Monthly,* where it appeared in due time.

"This story is of more interest to its author than it can possibly be now to any reader, because it distinctly marked for me the first recognition which I received from literary people."

LXVII

NEXT to Poe, Sidney Lanier ranks as the foremost of the poets of the South. In character Lanier is one of the rarest and purest of souls. His life was so chaste, his ideals so high, his devotion to his art so unselfish that he has been called "the Sir Galahad among American poets." Dr. Gilman, who in his capacity as president of Johns Hopkins University had frequent opportunities to observe Lanier, who was an instructor in this institution, has made the following comment,—"The appearance of Lanier was striking. There was nothing eccentric or odd about him, but his words, manners, ways of speech, were distinguished. I have heard a lady say that if he took his place in a crowded horse-car, an exhilarating atmosphere seemed to be introduced by his breezy ways."

He was born in Georgia in 1842. After graduation from a small college in his native state and then serving as tutor for a short time, he entered the Confederate army. During his war experiences, whether in the field or in prison, he studied poetry and played the flute. These two arts were his passions for life. While yet in his college days he had acquired a fine reputation as

344

a flute-player. At eighteen he was said to be
the best flute-player in Georgia. One of his college friends at the time made record of his admiration in writing,—"Tutor Lanier is the finest
flute-player you or I ever saw. It is perfectly
splendid—his playing. He is far-famed for it.
His flute cost fifty dollars, and he runs the notes
as easily as any one on the piano."

The passionate love of his sensitive soul is revealed in this poetic description of a visit to the
opera:

"I have just come in from the *Tempest* at the
Grand Opera House . . . and my heart is so full.
. . . In one interlude between the scenes we had
a violin solo, adagio, with soft accompaniment
by orchestra. As the fair tender notes came,
they opened like flower-buds expanding into flowers under the sweet rain of the accompaniment.
Kind heavens! My head fell on the seat in front,
I was weighed down with great loves and great
ideas and divine inflowings and devout outflow-
ings, and as each note grew and budded, and became a bud again and died into a fresh birth in
the next bud tone, I also lived these flower-tone
lives, and grew and expanded, and folded back
and died and was born again, and partook of the
unfathomable mysteries of flowers and tones."
And at another time he writes in the same vein,
—" 'Twas opening night of Theodore Thomas'
orchestra at Central Park Garden, and I could
not resist the temptation to go and bathe in the
sweet amber seas of this fine orchestra, and so I
went, and tugged me through a vast crowd, and,
after standing some while, found a seat, and the
baton waved, and I plunged into the sea, and lay

and floated. Ah! the dear flutes and oboes and horns drifted me hither and thither, and the great violins and small violins swayed me upon waves, and overflowed me with strong lavations, and sprinkled glistening foam in my face, and in among the clarinetti, as among waving water-lilies with plexile stems, pushed my easy way, and so, even lying in the music waters, I floated and flowed, my soul utterly bent and prostrate.'' Who has ever written more expressively of that ecstasy that lays hold of the sensuous soul of the lover of fine music?

Lanier is one of the heroic souls of song. Like Stevenson he was cheery enough to jest about his poverty. His contest with the demon of Want seems to have been fiercer even than was the warfare waged by the gay romancer. Lanier wishes to meet Charlotte Cushman, but he is not sure that he can; he must sell a poem or two to get the price of a suitable new dress coat. ''Alas,'' he writes to the lady herself, in that gay spirit of humor which is the strong defense of some sensitive souls, ''with what unspeakable care I would have brushed this present garment of mine in days gone by, if I had dreamed that the time would come when so great a thing as a visit to *you* might hang upon the little length of its nap! Behold, it is not only in man's breast that pathos lies, and the very coat lapel that covers it may be a tragedy.''

The poetic temperament is commonly supposed to be at variance with domestic tranquillity. The domestic life of Lanier is a contradiction to that popular belief. He ends one of his letters to his wife with this petition,—''Let us lead them (the children) to love everything in the world, above the world, and under the world adequately; that is the sum and substance of a perfect life. And so God's divine rest be upon every head under the roof that covers thine this night, prayeth thy husband.''

In his letter to Gibson Peacock, January 6, 1878, we have a charming picture of the delight of a man who has at last found a place to nest his family, after some years of forlorn wanderings and uncertainties:

'' . . . I have also moved my family into our new home, have had a Christmas tree for the youngsters, have looked up a cheap school for Harry and Sidney, have discharged my daily duties as first flute of the Peabody Orchestra, have written a couple of poems and part of an essay on Beethoven and Bismarck, have accomplished at least a hundred thousand miscellaneous nothings. . . . We are in a state of supreme content with our new home; it really seems to me as incredible that myriads of people have been living in their own homes heretofore; as to the young couple with a first baby it seems impossible that a great many other couples have had similar prodigies. Good heavens! how I wish that the whole world had a home.

''I confess that I am a little nervous about the gas bills, which must come in, in the course of time; and there are the water rates, and several sorts of imposts and taxes; but then the dignity of being liable to such things is a very supporting consideration. No man is a Bohemian who has to pay a water tax and a street tax. Every day when I sit down in my dining-room—*my* dining-room! I find the wish growing stronger that each poor soul in Baltimore, whether saint or sinner, could come and dine with me. How I would carve out the merry-thoughts for the old hags! How I would stuff the big wan-eyed rascals till their rags ripped again! There was a knight of old times who built the dining-hall of his castle across the highway, so that every wayfarer must perforce pass through; there the traveler, rich or poor, found always a trencher and wherewithal to fill it. Three times a day in my own chair at my own table, do I envy that knight and wish that I might do as he did.''

LXVIII

THE story of "Mark Twain's Debts" is told in *The Bookman* by Frederick A. King. We are permitted to tell the story in Mr. King's own words:

An anecdote is recorded of Mark Twain and General Grant, who, in company with William D. Howells, once sat together at luncheon, spread in the General's private office in the purlieus of Wall Street, in the days when war and statesmanship had been laid aside, and the hero of battles and civic life was endeavoring to retrieve his scattered fortunes by a trial of business.

"Why don't you write your memoirs?" asked Mark Twain, mindful of how much there was to record, and how eager would be the readers of such a work.

But the General with characteristic modesty demurred, and the point was not pressed. This was several years before the failure of the firm of Ward and Grant, which swept away the General's private fortune, leaving him an old man, broken in health, and filled with anxiety about the provision for his family after he should be gone.

When the evil days at last came, some mem-

ory of the suggestion dropped by his friend, the
humorist—who could be immensely serious, too,
when need be—may have led to the task that, in
added contention with pain and suffering, con-
constituted the last battle that the General should
fight.

Whatever the influence moving General Grant
to the final decision to compose his memoirs, it
happened, to his great fortune, that Mark Twain
again called, and found that the work he had long
ago suggested was at last in progress; but also
that the inexperienced writer, modestly under-
estimating the commercial value of his forth-
coming work, was about to sign away the puta-
tive profits. Fifty thousand dollars offered for
his copyright seemed a generous sum to the unlit-
erary General Grant, and it took the vehement
persuasion of one who was himself a publisher
to convince him that his prospective publishers
would not hesitate at quadrupling that sum
rather than lose the chance of publishing the
book.

When the conjecture was proven true, the
General with characteristic generosity, withdrew
the contract from his prospective publishers and
placed it in the hands of the firm that Mark
Twain headed. All the provisions were amply
fulfilled; for when Mark Twain paid his last visit
to the stricken author at the place of sojourn on
Mount McGregor, he brought to the now speech-
less sufferer the smile of happiness and satisfaction by saying: "General, there is in the bank
now royalties on advanced sales aggregating
nearly $300,000. It is at Mrs. Grant's order."

The anecdote is given at this length because,

taken in connection with subsequent events dealing with General Grant's benefactor, it points a forceful illustration of the irony of fortune. There came a day when the very instrument by which Mark Twain was enabled to provide a peaceful close to the life of a brave warrior, and to guarantee affluence for his family, delivered himself a stroke that dissipated his own fortune at a time when age is supposed to have absorbed the vigor for a new grapple with destinies.

In 1884 the publishing firm of C. L. Webster and Company was organized to publish the works of Mark Twain. Of this firm Mark Twain was president; but he took little active part in the management of its affairs. Able to conceive in broad outlines successful policies, he was singularly deficient in the power to handle the details of their execution. On April 18, 1894, the firm whose business enterprises had always figured in large sums through the immense popularity of the author-publisher's own works, the *Memoirs of General Grant,* and the *Life of Pope Leo,* made an assignment for the benefit of its creditors. The bankrupt firm acknowledged liabilities approximating $80,000. What in the ordinary view of commercial affairs would have furnished but one item in the list of failures which record the misfortunes of ninety per cent who engage in business, became in this instance a notable case through the eminence of the chief actor.

What might he have done?

The law could lay claim upon his personal assets. To surrender these possessions proved no act of self-sacrifice, considering his wife's fortune, upon which the law had no claim. His wife, however, joined him in the act of renunciation, and they stood together penniless. Beyond this point there could be no legal, and, to many minds, no moral responsibility for the debts of his firm. One can speculate upon the force of the temptation to take advantage of the position. Mark Twain was sixty years old, and ill at that. Having sacrificed all he possessed to meet the demands of his creditors, he might justly claim the benefit of what remained of capacity for wealth-producing labor. His own words in reply to a slander which insinuated that he had set to work again for his own benefit are splendid for inspiration and honesty:

"The law recognizes no mortgage on a man's brain, and a merchant who has given up all he has may take advantage of the laws of insolvency, and start free again for himself; but I am not a business man, and honor is a harder master than the law. It cannot compromise for less than a hundred cents on the dollar."

. . . The great parallel case to the one here under examination is that of Sir Walter Scott, who lost his all through the failure of his printers, the Ballantynes, and between January, 1826, and January, 1828, earned for his creditors nearly £40,000. In the early stages of this trial he suffered acutely from the attitude of his friends, and he records in his diary how some would smile as if to say: "Think nothing about it, my lad; it is quite out of our thoughts;" how others adopted an affected gravity "such as one sees and despises at a funeral," while the best bred "just shook hands and went on."

How the world treated Mark Twain we learn
from the speech at the banquet given by the Lotus
Club on his return from his arduous journey
around the world: ''There were ninety-six creditors in all, and not by a finger's weight did ninety-
five out of the ninety-six add to the burden of
that time.''

'' 'Don't you worry, and don't you hurry,' was
what they said.'' With the courage of a man
buffeted, but not beaten, he gathered himself up
for ''one more last try for fortune and fair
fame.'' In the latter part of 1895 he started out
on a tour of the English-speaking countries of
the world to give lectures and readings from his
own works.

There were misgivings, of course, as to the
success of the venture. Here was a field not
absolutely untried, but not hitherto cultivated to
the point of assured success. In 1873 he had
made a lecture tour in England and in 1885 had
given platform readings in company with George
W. Cable. But age had sapped the zest for public appearance, and he was skeptical of his power
to move people with interest in his books. Moreover, there was a further thing to be considered,
a possible impediment to success among the English colonies which he proposed to visit. His
popularity with Englishmen had never been
great, owing to the liberties he had taken with
that nation's people in *Innocents Abroad.*

The latter apprehension was the more remote,
however, for, starting from New York, he had a
continent to traverse before embarking for the
shores that held for him an uncertain welcome.
To test his ability to interest an audience, to ''try

23

it on the dog," as they say in theatrical parlance, he subjected himself to the severest test possible, crossed to Randall's Island and read before a company of boys. Unsophisticated by the lecturer's reputation as a humorist, the boys proved to be the organs of sincerest testimony to the permanence of the old power to amuse, and the first public appearance in Cleveland, Ohio, was undertaken with fewer misgivings.

From Vancouver, Mark Twain sailed for Sidney and gave readings before the English-speaking communities of Australia; then continued on to Tasmania, New Zealand, Ceylon, India and South Africa.

His fears as to his welcome among Englishmen were proved to be groundless. In Australia, great as was his success as a lecturer, his personal success outweighed even that, and the market on his books was exhausted. We cannot follow him on this trip of mingled arduous labor and personal satisfaction. The humorous reactions of his homely vision upon the quaint, the bizarre, the pretentious, aspects of life in remote parts of the world may be read in his own record of this journey, *Following the Equator*. There are few things to record of this great effort to pay his debts.

In India he was taken ill, but the disease was not severe. In June, 1897, when he had circled the globe and had settled for a time in London, cablegrams came from that city announcing his mental and physical collapse. The English-speaking world was stricken with sympathy, and the New York *Herald* at once began a subscription fund for his relief. The report was contradicted at once, but admiration for the author's strenuous effort seemed to grow, and the *Herald* fund was assuming generous proportions when the following characteristic message declining to accept the relief came from the proposed bene-ficiary:

I was glad when you instituted that movement, for I was tired of the fact and worry of debt, but I recognized that it is not permissible for a man whose case is not hopeless to shift his burden to other men's shoulders.

In November of the same year a report was circulated that he was out of debt, but from Vienna, whither he had gone to live, came a laconic cablegram nailing the optimistic impeach-ment:

Lie. Wrote no such letters. Still deeply in debt.

Nearly half of the original indebtedness needed to be paid, and here, with scarcely an opposing voice in judgment, he might have waived the claim upon himself for his firm's responsibilities, but he avowed that he would pay dollar for dol-lar.

The time of accomplishment was not long in coming. When the undertaking was begun, it was with the resolution to clear up the debt in three years. Allowing for the unexpected, it was feared it would take four, then at the age of sixty-four a new start in life would be open to the author, who might point to a considerable occupancy of space on library shelves and regard a life work accomplished. It took but two years and a half to pay the debt. He began the effort the latter part of 1895 and finished it in the early part of 1898.

His return to America and his home in 1900 was, in the unromantic procedure of our self-conscious days, of the nature of a triumph. He was formally welcomed by the Lotus Club, and, of course, as delicately as might be, he was praised for his honesty. His reply to compliment was a generous recognition of social virtue, which renders easier such an effort as he made. Said he:

Your president has referred to certain burdens which I was weighted with. I am glad he did, as it gives me an opportunity which I wanted. To speak of those debts—you all knew what he meant when he referred to it, and to the poor bankrupt firm of C. L. Webster and Company. No one has said a word about those creditors. There were ninety-six creditors in all, and not by a finger's weight did ninety-five out of the ninety-six add to the burden of that time. They treated me well; they treated me handsomely. I never knew I owed them anything; not a sign came from them.

The story is one of simple elements, and suits the prosaic character of our age. It does not match Sir Walter's for romance. There was no such brain-racking work; no forcing of the phantasmal multitude of the poet's brain to dance to pay the expenses of the funeral; no mediæval castle to sacrifice; no tragic failure of the ultimate goal. What there is of real romance seems obscured by the facts of more or less safe speculation upon assured futures. It was a safe business venture.

The hero was not unworthy of the praises which his peers at the Lotus dinner were glad to lavish. Said St. Clair McKelway:

"He has enough excess and versatility to be a genius. He has enough quality and quantity of virtues to be a saint. But he has honorably transmuted his genius into work, whereby it has been brought into relations with literature and with life. And he has preferred warm fellowship to cool perfection, so that sinners love him and saints are content to wait for him.''

LXIX

HAMLIN GARLAND is one of the writers whose name suggests the great Northwest. He was born in Wisconsin in 1860, went to Iowa and later to Dakota, striving at an early age to wrest a living from the soil. At ten years of age he plowed seventy acres of land. His vivid descriptions of Western farm-life are not the results of reading and casual observation, supplemented by a vivid imagination; they are the products of actual experiences.

In a personal interview with Mr. Garland, Frank G. Carpenter gives us the following interesting particulars:

"The conversation here turned to Mr. Garland's literary work, and he told me how he was first led to write by reading Hawthorne's *Mosses from an Old Manse*. This book so delighted him that he wanted to write essays like it for a living, and he practised at this during the intervals of his school-teaching and studying for years. It was not until he was older that he attempted fiction or poetry. The story of his first published article is a curious one. Said he:

" 'My first literary success was a poem which I wrote for *Harper's Weekly,* entitled 'Lost in

358

the Norther.' It was a poem describing a bliz-
zard and the feelings of a man lost in it. I received twenty-five dollars for it.'

" 'That must have been a good deal of money
to you then, Mr. Garland?'

" 'It was,' was the reply. 'It was my first
money in literature, and I spent it upon my
father and mother. I paid five dollars for a
copy of Grant's *Memoirs,* which I sent father, and
with the remaining twenty dollars I bought a
silk dress for my mother. It was the first silk
dress she had ever had.'

" 'When did you write your first fiction?'

" 'My mother got half of the money I received
for that,' replied Mr. Garland, 'as it was due to
her that I wrote it. I had been studying in
Boston for several years, when I went out to
Dakota to visit my parents. The night after I
arrived I was talking with mother about old
times and old friends. She told me how one
family had gone back to New York for a visit,
and had returned very happy, in getting back to
their Western home. As she told the story, the
pathos of it struck me. I went into another
room and began to write. The story was one of
the best chapters of my book *Main-Traveled
Roads.* I read it to mother, and she liked it, and
upon telling her that I thought it was worth at
least seventy-five dollars, she replied: "Well, if
that is so, I think you ought to *divvy* with me,
for I gave you the story." "I will," said I, and
so, when I got my seventy-five dollars, I sent her
a check for thirty-seven dollars and fifty cents.
I got many other good suggestions during that
trip to Dakota. I wrote poems and stories.

Some of the stories were published in *The Century,* and I remember that I received six hundred dollars within two weeks from its editors. It was perhaps a year later before I published my first book. It had a good sale, and I have been writing from that day to this.'

"Hamlin Garland spends a part of every year in the West. He has bought the old home place where he was born in Wisconsin, and he has there a little farm of four acres, upon which he raises asparagus, strawberries, onions, and bushels of other things. His mother lives with him. During my talk with him the other night he said: 'I like the West and the Western people. I have been brought up with them, and I expect to devote my life to writing about them. I spend a portion of each summer on the Rocky Mountains, camping out. I like to go where I can sleep in the open air and have elbow-room away from the crowded city.' "

LXX

I N 1900, Stephen Crane, while yet barely thirty, died. His early passing away was widely regarded as a loss to American literature. In England he was especially admired as a vigorous writer. His *The Red Badge of Courage* won him wide recognition as a keen analyst. Old soldiers who read the story could not believe that it was written by a boy who was born after the war had ended. By many critics his stories of boyhood are considered the writings that shall be longest remembered. Shortly before his death Mr. Crane wrote the following letter to the editor of a Rochester daily:

"My father was a Methodist minister, author of numerous works of theology, and an editor of various periodicals of the church. He was a graduate of Princeton, and he was a great, fine, simple mind. As for myself, I went to Lafayette College, but did not graduate. I found mining-engineering not at all to my taste. I preferred base-ball. Later I attended Syracuse University, where I attempted to study literature, but found base-ball again much more to my taste. My first work in fiction was for the New York *Tribune,* when I was eighteen years old. During this time, one story of the series went into the *Cosmopolitan*. At the age of twenty I wrote my first novel—*Maggie*. It never really got on the market, but it made for me the friendship of William Dean Howells and Hamlin Garland, and since that time I have never been conscious for an instant that those friendships have at all diminished. After completing *Maggie,* I wrote mainly for the New York *Press* and for *The Arena*. In the latter part of my twenty-first year I began *The Red Badge of Courage,* and completed it early in my twenty-second year. The year following I wrote the poems contained in the volume known as *The Black Riders*. On the first day of last November I was precisely twenty-nine years old and had finished my fifth novel, *Active Service*. I have only one pride, and that is that the English edition of *The Red Badge of Courage* has been received with great praise by the English reviewers. I am proud of this simply because the remoter people would seem more just and harder to win.''

In another letter to the same editor he writes about his literary sincerity:

''The one thing that deeply pleases me is the fact that men of sense invariably believe me to be sincere. I know that my work does not amount to a string of dried beans—I always calmly admit it—but I also know that I do the best that is in me without regard to praise or blame. When I was the mark for every humorist in the country, I went ahead; and now when I am the mark for only fifty per cent of the humorists of the country, I go ahead; for I understand that a man is born into the world with his own pair of eyes, and he is not at all responsible for his vision—he is merely responsible for his quality of personal honesty. To keep close to this personal honesty is my supreme ambition."

LXXI

EUGENE FIELD

THE general public will always remember Eugene Field as the author of *Little Boy Blue,* the many friends of Field, in addition to their memory of him as the charming poet of childhood, will always think of him as the irrepressible prince of merry-makers. To perpetrate a joke Field spared neither labor nor his friends. Many of his pranks were mere whimsicalities, innocent pleasantries that hurt no one. He would spend three hours in illustrating a letter to a friend, filling the letter with gossipy trivialities and using six different kinds of ink to make it look grotesque.

During the last years of Field's too brief life he was importuned so frequently for the facts concerning his career that he printed a brief biography or *Auto-Analysis,* as he called it. This contains a generous portion of fiction mingled with some fact. He begins his autobiography with:

"I was born in St. Louis, Mo., September 3, 1850. . . . Upon the death of my mother (1856), I was put in the care of my (paternal) cousin, Miss Mary Field French, at Amherst, Mass.

"In 1865 I entered the private school of Rev.

364

James Tufts, Monson, Mass., and there fitted for
Williams College, which institution I entered as
a freshman in 1868. Upon my father's death, in
1869, I entered the sophomore class of Knox College, Galesburg, Ill., my guardian, John W.
Burgess, now of Columbia College, being then a
professor in that institution. But in 1870 I went
to Columbia, Mo., and entered the State University there, and completed my junior year with
my brother. In 1872 I visited Europe, spending
six months and my patrimony in France, Italy,
Ireland, and England. In May, 1873, I became a
reporter on the St. Louis *Evening Journal*. In
October of that year I married Miss Julia Suther-
land Comstock (born in Chenango Co., N. Y.), of
St. Joseph, Mo., at that time a girl of sixteen.
We have had eight children—three daughters
and five sons.''

This is not all of the autobiography. There
are about a thousand words more. The reason
Field attended three collegiate institutions is that
his mischievous pranks made him *persona non
grata* to the college authorities. In after years
the old historian of Knox College wrote: ''He
was prolific of harmless pranks and his school
life was a big joke.''

The gay irresponsibility of Field is early illustrated in the reckless manner in which he
spent ''six months and his patrimony'' in Europe.
In 1872 Field received $8,000, the first portion of
his patrimony. He proposed to a young friend,
Comstock, the brother of Julia, whom he later
married, that they go to Europe. Field offered
to bear all the expenses of the trip. They went
and for six months they had a glorious time.

Soon the money was gone; he telegraphed for more; was obliged to sell the odd curios he had gathered to pay his way home. This expenditure of his money in a trip abroad is not so unprofitable a venture as it appears. The elder Field had left a fortune valued at $60,000; Eugene's share was to be about $25,000. In two years he spent about $20,000. His brother Roswell, more prudent, lived for several years on his share but finally, owing to the depreciation of real estate values, saw his fortune dwindle away. He is said to have envied the shrewdness of Eugene in spending his money when he had it.

Field had the highest respect for womankind. In his *Auto-Analysis* he writes: "I am fond of companionship of women, and I have no unconquerable prejudice against feminine beauty. I recall with pride that in twenty-two years of active journalism I have always written in reverential praise of womankind." This respect for womankind, however, did not prevent him from playing pranks upon his wife. On their wedding journey he delighted to tease his young Julia by ordering at Delmonico's "boiled pig's feet à la St. Jo." A few years later a quartet was accustomed to meet at Eugene's home. Field did not sing with the quartet but as a fifth member acted as reader or reciter in their little entertainments. Eugene delighted to tease his wife by walking into the parlor when the quartet was practicing at his home and saying: "Well, boys, let us take off our coats and take it easy; it's too hot." When this was done, Eugene would blaze forth in the brilliancy of a red flannel undershirt, with white cuffs and collar pinned to his shirt.

When Carl Schurz was making his senatorial campaign in Missouri, Field was sent with the party to report the meetings. Field, although greatly admiring Schurz, took great delight in misreporting Schurz, whose only comment would be: "Field, why will you lie so outrageously?" One evening when a group of German serenaders had assembled in front of the hotel to do honor to Schurz, Field rushed out and pretending to be Schurz, addressed them in broken English. At another time, at a political meeting, Field suddenly stepped out to the front and began:

"Ladies and Shentlemen: I haf such a pad colt dot et vas not bossible for me to make you a speedg to-night, but I haf die bleasure to introduce to you my brilliant chournalistic friendt Euchene Fielt, who will spoke you in my blace."

While in Denver Field worked upon the *Tribune*. Over his desk hung,—"This is my busy day," and on the wall,—"God bless our proofreader, He can't call for him too soon." In his office he kept an old bottomless black-walnut chair. Across its yawning chasm he would carelessly thrown old newspapers. As it was the only unoccupied chair in the room, the casual visitor would drop unsuspectingly into the trap. The angry subscriber who had come to wreak vengeance upon the writer of irritating personalities could not withstand the apparently sincere apologies which Field lavished upon his victim. It was so humiliating to a man of Field's sensibilities to be obliged to receive such important visitors in an office whose very furniture indicated the poverty of the newspaper.

In 1883 Field moved to Chicago, where the rest

of his life was passed. Mr. Stone, one of the proprietors of *The News,* had gone to Denver to have a personal interview with Field, whose work had attracted attention in the newspaper world. Field stipulated that he was to have a column a day for his own use. The Chicago public soon was attracted by the brilliant versatility of the writer of "Sharps and Flats," the title of the column written by Field.

Some months after Field had moved to Chicago he concluded that the general public ought to know that he had arrived. It was a cold morning in December. "So he arrayed himself in a long linen duster, buttoned up from knees to collar, put an old straw hat on his head, and taking a shabby book under one arm and a palm-leaf fan in his hand, he marched all the way down Clark Street, past the City Hall, to the office. Everywhere along the route he was greeted with jeers or pitying words, as his appearance excited the mirth or commiseration of the passers-by. When he reached the entrance to the *Daily News* office he was followed by a motley crowd of noisy urchins whom he dismissed with a grimace and the cabalistic gesture with which Nicholas Koorn perplexed and repulsed Antony Van Corlear from the battlement of the fortress of Rensellaerstein. Then closing the door in their astonished faces, he mounted the two flights of stairs to the editorial rooms, where he recounted, with the glee of the boy he was in such things, the success of his joke."

Field had execrable taste in dress and he knew it. Consequently he enjoyed presenting neckties to his friends. His biographer, Slason Thompson, who worked in the same newspaper office, separated only by a low thin partition, relates that in the afternoon about two o'clock Field would stick his head above the partition and say,— "Come along, Nompy, and I'll buy you a new necktie," and when Thompson would decline the offer, Field would mildly respond, "Very well, if you won't let me buy you a necktie, you must buy me a lunch," and off to the coffee-house they would march, where the bill would be paid by Thompson, for Field was indeed through life the gay knight he styled himself, *sans peur and sans monnaie.*

LXXII

O. HENRY AS A PRISONER

WHENEVER I enter Columbus, Ohio, from the south on The Hocking Valley Railroad I think of O. Henry as I see the cold gray stone walls of a Federal prison, for it was to this prison that O. Henry was assigned when he was sentenced March 25, 1898, to spend five years in a Federal prison. On account of good behavior he was given his freedom after three years and three months of imprisonment.

We are not going to discuss whether or not this man, who later became one of the world's most popular story writers, was guilty of embezzlement. In a letter to his mother-in-law, Mrs. G. P. Roach, written just after being sentenced, he wrote: "Right here I want to state solemnly to you that in spite of the jury's verdict I am absolutely innocent of wrong doing in that bank matter, except so far as foolishly keeping a position that I could not successfuly fill."

After entering the Ohio prison he was asked: "What is your occupation?"

"I am a newspaper reporter," he answered.

"What else can you do?"

"I am a registered pharmacist."

Here was a man the prison authorities could

370

use. In C. Alphonso Smith's *O. Henry Biography*, published by Doubleday, Page and Company there is an interesting letter* written by Dr. J. M. Thomas, who was head physician during O. Henry's imprisonment:—

Druggists were scarce and I felt I was fortunate in securing the services of Sydney Porter, for he was a registered pharmacist and unusually competent. In fact, he could do anything in the drug line. Previous to his banking career in Texas he had worked in a drug store in North Carolina, so he told me. While Porter was drug clerk Jimmie Consedine, one time proprietor of the old hotel Metropole in New York, was a muse. Consedine spent all his time painting. Out of this came a falling out with O. Henry. Consedine painted a cow with its tail touching the ground. Porter gave a Texas cowman's explanation of the absurdity of such a thing and won Consedine's undying hatred.

After serving some time as drug clerk O. Henry came to me and said: "I have never asked a favor of you before but there is one I should like to ask now. I can be private secretary to the steward outside (meaning that he would be outside the walls and trusted). It depends on your recommendation." I asked him if he wanted to go. When he said he did, I called up the steward, Mr. C. N. Wilcox, and in twenty minutes O. Henry was outside.

He did not associate very much with any of the other inmates of the prison except the western outlaws. Very few of the officers or attendants

*Republished by permission.

at the prison ever saw him. Most convicts would tell me frankly how they got into jail. They did not seem to suffer much from mortification. O. Henry, on the other hand, was very much weighed down by his imprisonment. In my experience of handling over ten thousand prisoners in the eight years I was physician at the prison, I have never known a man who was so deeply humiliated by his prison experience as O. Henry. He was a model prisoner, willing, obedient, faithful. His record is clear in every respect. It was very seldom that he mentioned his imprisonment or in any way discussed the subject. One time we had a little misunderstanding about some alcohol which was disappearing too rapidly for the ordinary uses to which it was put. I requested that he wait for me one morning so that I could find out how much alcohol he was using in his night rounds, and after asking him a few questions he became excited when he thought I might be suspicioning him. "I am not a thief," he said, "and I never stole a thing in my life. I was sent here for embezzling bank funds, not one cent of which I ever got. Some one else got it all, and I am doing time for it."

You can tell when a prisoner is lying as well as you can in the case of anybody else. I believed O. Henry implicitly. I soon discovered that he was not the offender in the matter of the alcohol. But the question disturbed him and he asked me once or twice afterward if I really thought that he ever stole anything.

Once in a long while he would talk about his supposed crime and the great mistake he made in going to Central America as soon as there was any suspicion cast on him. When he disappeared suspicion became conviction. After his return from Central America, when he was tried, he never told anything that would clear himself. While he was in Central America he met Al Jennings who was likewise a fugitive from justice. After they returned to the States they renewed their friendship at the prison, where both eventually landed. Jennings was also one of the trusted prisoners and in the afternoon they would often come into my office and tell stories.

O. Henry liked the western prisoners, those from Arizona, Texas, and Indian Territory, and he got stories from them all and retold them in the office. Since reading his books I recognize many of the stories I heard there. As I mentioned before, he was an unusually good pharmacist and for this reason was permitted to look after the minor ills of the prisoners at night. He would spend two or three hours on the range or tiers of cells every night and knew most of the prisoners and their life stories.

The Gentle Grafter portrays the stories told him on his night rounds. I remember having heard him recount many of them. He wrote quite a number of short stories while in prison and it was a frequent thing for me to find a story written on scrap paper on my desk in the morning, with a note telling me to read it before he sent it out. We would often joke about the price the story would bring, anything from twenty-five to fifty dollars. He wrote them at night in from one to three hours, he told me.

LXXIII

JACK LONDON belongs to the great majority whose fame steadily diminishes after death. Neither steadily nor as a whole did he look at life. He belongs to that class that violently protests against the established order of things without being able to point the way to a better. He is an iconoclast, a revolutionist. Intense in all that he felt and did, he was not destined always to express that intensity with the skill of the artist and the poise of a philosopher.

His early life was a life of struggle, a life of unconventionality. His education was desultory, his literary training insufficient, and yet his *Call of the Wild* is one of the books destined to survive. It is true that in his story of the wonderful dog that later becomes a wolf, he sentimentalizes and gives to the dog the psychology of the human being, belonging to the school of Ernest Seton-Thompson rather than that of John Burroughs, yet the story is so well told that we overlook the improbability. Perhaps the story made its wide appeal because in man there still resides the instinct that draws one toward the primitive and savage.

It is always interesting to learn how young

writers make a beginning in the art of authorship. In *John Barleycorn** Jack London has given a vivid account of his early struggles in learning to write.

"I sought odd jobs. I worked days, and half-days, at anything I could get. I mowed lawns, trimmed hedges, took up carpets, beat them, and laid them again. Further, I took the civil service examinations for mail carrier and passed first. But alas, there was no vacancy, and I must wait. And while I waited, and in between the odd jobs I managed to procure, I started to earn ten dollars by writing a newspaper account of a voyage I had made, in an open boat down the Yukon, of nineteen hundred miles in nineteen days. I didn't know the first thing about the newspaper game, but I was confident I'd get ten dollars for my article.

"But I didn't. The first San Francisco newspaper to which I mailed it never acknowledged receipt of the manuscript, but held on to it. The longer it held on to it, the more certain I was that the thing was accepted.

"And here is the funny thing. Some are born to fortune, and some have fortune thrust upon them. But in my case I was clubbed into fortune, and bitter necessity wielded the club. I had long since abandoned all thought of writing as a career. My honest intention in writing that article was to earn ten dollars. And that was the limit of my intention. It would help to tide me along until I got steady employment. Had a vacancy occurred

*Permission to quote granted by *The Century Co.*

in the post office at that time, I should have jumped at it.

"But the vacancy did not occur, nor did a steady job; and I employed the time between odd jobs writing a twenty-one-thousand-word serial for the *Youth's Companion*. I turned it out and typed it in seven days. I fancy that was what was the matter with it, for it came back.

"It took some time for it to go and come, and in the meantime I tried my hand at short stories. I sold one to the *Overland Monthly* for five dollars. The *Black Cat* gave me forty dollars for another. The *Overland Monthly* offered me seven dollars and a half, pay on publication, for all the stories I should deliver. I got my bicycle, my watch, and my father's mackintosh out of pawn and rented a typewriter. Also, I paid up the bills I owed to the several groceries that allowed me a small credit. I recall the Portuguese groceryman who never permitted my bill to go beyond four dollars. Hopkins, another grocer, could not be budged beyond five dollars.

"And just then came the call from the post office to go to work. It placed me in a most trying predicament. The sixty-five dollars I could earn regularly every month was a terrible temptation. I couldn't decide what to do. And I'll never be able to forgive the postmaster of Oakland. I answered the call, and I talked to him like a man. I frankly told him the situation. It looked as if I might win out at writing. The chance was good, but not certain. Now, if he would pass me by and select the next man on the eligible list, and give me a call at the next vacancy—

"But he shut me off with: 'Then you don't want the position?'

" 'But I do,' " I protested. " 'Don't you see, if you will pass me over this time—' "

" 'If you want it you will take it,' " he said coldly.

"Happily for me, the cursed brutality of the man made me angry.

" 'Very well,' " I said. " 'I won't take it.' "

Shortly after the death of Jack London there appeared in the *New Statesman* a personal sketch by Oliver Madox Hueffer. We quote extracts from it:

"Jack London was the ideal yarn-spinner—his spoken stories were even better than his written—and one reason why I think him likely to be numbered as among the writers of real mark was that he was perfectly unconscious of it. Like Peter Pan, he never grew up, and he lived his own stories with such intensity that he ended by believing them himself. In the newspaper biographies I see that he is credited with having followed an infinity of occupations; quite a number of them he knew only as does the amateur, and if he followed them at all it was for no more than an experimental month or so. . . .

Among the apocryphal legends attached to his name, and founded very possibly on his own statements, was that of his almost superhuman drunkenness. That at one time or another he drank too much I can believe—certainly in all the time of our acquaintance he never showed any sign of it. He was by no means a teetotaler; but I never saw him drunk. Nor did he ever boast of his drinking prowess in my presence. If he ever did, I am sure it was in the spirit of the child who declares he has robbed an orchard—because the feat strikes him as picturesque. Another well-known American writer once told me, on London's own authority, that he regarded himself as having been saved from a drunkard's grave by his wife, who, knowing of his weakness, made him promise, before their marriage, that he would get drunk every Thursday until she gave him leave to stop —with the result that he found compulsory drunkenness so unbearable that he besought her permission to become a total abstainer. I can well imagine his telling the story, even perhaps coming in the end to believe it; not for one moment do I believe it myself. I fear I may have given an impression of him merely as of a picturesque liar. That he was not. He was at least as truthful as —possibly more so than—his neighbors, but he had a passion for romance—even as evidenced in things in which the ordinary man can see nothing romantic—so that he lived in a world of his own, of which the less clairvoyant had little or no idea. It bubbled out in his life as it bubbled out in his books, and it is on that lack of effort that his claim to fame will probably rest. . . . In his forty-one years of life he turned out an amazing amount of work; he was as industrious as that other great story-teller Alexandre Dumas—and there is nothing among it which cannot rank as a story. Almost invariably it is also a good story, though, like other men, he turned out his fair share of pot-boilers. Romance, especially if carried out in real life, is occasionally expensive. At Glenellen, his home in California, for instance, he built himself a lordly pleasure house. I forget how many thousands of dollars it cost, and it was burned down, uninsured, the day before he was to have moved into it. He himself believed that an incendiary was responsible, as there had been labor troubles during the building of it, and his lust of life was such that he could never hear of any kind of activity without wishing to take his share in it.

Jack London was, above all things, a worshipper of the Anglo-Saxon. I do not know his own descent; in person he was more Celtic than Teutonic —small, dark, full of movement, with eyes that could glow like topazes when something exciting was toward. Certainly he was not Jewish, as some have thought, and his name was his father's before him. When I last saw him *The Valley of the Moon* was, or was to be, for I forget if it was actually published, the greatest of his works—a judgment in which I do not agree with him. It was, fundamentally, an appeal to the Anglo-Saxon not to allow himself to be pushed out of the most fertile valleys of the Pacific by the lesser breeds without the law. Characteristically, it suggests no way in which this ideal is to be attained. So it was with his incursions into Communism and the various other 'isms which find their place in the fertile Californian mind. He examined them all; occasionally plunged into them—experimentally—and towards them all his attitude was the same childish excitement: " 'Say, what do you think about that?' "

LXXIV

THE son of an Irishman with a trace of Romany blood, his mother a Greek, his wife a Japanese,—such was Lafcadio Hearn, born in 1850 on Lefcada, one of the Ionian Isles. Although his very earliest years were passed in Greece, England, and France, landing in New York when he was nineteen, and his last years, the productive literary years, were spent in Japan, he is usually listed as an American writer. His literary friends and publishers were American; he began his career as writer in the United States, living in New York, New Orleans, Cincinnati, and Philadelphia.

In 1890 we find Hearn in Japan, where he is to become the great interpreter of the Japanese spirit. At first he is extremely enthusiastic over the rare qualities he finds in the Oriental civilization. He writes to Elizabeth Bisland,—"What I love in Japan is the Japanese,—the poor simple humanity of the country. It is divine. There is nothing in the world approaching the natural charm of them. No book ever written has reflected it. And I love their gods, their customs, their dress, their bird-like quavering songs, their houses, their superstitions, their faults."

Such whole-hearted enthusiasm naturally could not endure. Thirteen years later, after he had been unjustly dropped from the governmental University in which he had been teaching, he writes to a friend about securing employment for a year or two in America, while he can supervise the education of his oldest son, a sensitive, gentle, and backward boy,—"A being entirely innocent of evil—what chance for him in such a world as Japan."

F. Hadland Davis writing an article on Hearn for *The Japan Magazine* of Tokyo, seventeen years after the death of Hearn—he died in 1904—has these discriminating observations;—

"His character was so sensitive, so wayward, so eerie, so childlike, so wrapped about with mystery, that no one, so far, has been able to describe him with any degree of completeness. . . .

"Even Mrs. Hearn's wonderful reminiscences of her husband are elusive, for we catch only a glimpse of this shy, fleeting figure. . . .

"Mrs. Hearn used to tell her husband Japanese ghost stories. They were told on dreary evenings, and in a room that was dimly lighted. Mrs. Hearn wrote:

" 'When I tell him stories I always tell him at first the mere skeleton of the story. If it is interesting, he puts it down in his notebook and makes me repeat several times.

'And when the story is interesting, he instantly becomes exceedingly serious; the color of his face changes; his eyes wear the look of fearful enthusiasm.

'As I went on, as usual, with the story of Oka-chinsan, his face gradually became pale; his eyes

were fixed: I feel a sudden awe. When I finished
the narrative he became a little relaxed and said it
was very interesting. 'O blood!' he repeatedly
said; and asked me several questions regarding
the situations, actions, and so forth, involved in
the story. 'In what manner was "O blood!" exclaimed? In what manner of voice? What do
you think of the sound of "geta" at that time?
How was the night? I think so and so. What do
you think? and so forth.' Thus he consulted me
about various things besides the original story
which I told from the book. If any one happened
to see us thus talking from outside, he would
surely think that we were mad. . . .'

"Hearn never invented a story of his own. He
borrowed his material, but so far from leaving a
debt we usually associate with plagiarism, he ran-
sacked his store of words with so much diligence,
and arranged and re-arranged them with so much
artistry, that the material, fusty enough in the
original, glows with the lustre of Chinese silk.

"Lamb claimed that the value of a book lent to
Coleridge was enhanced considerably when it was
returned with the magic of his marginal notes.
And so it was with Hearn. He borrowed a good
deal of his literary material, but he had the art
of jeweling dull phrases and of giving a ghostly
perfume to the most acrid passages. He borrowed
nothing that his genius did not beautify a thou-
sandfold. . . .

"When Hearn praised, he praised wholeheart-
edly. He has never excelled the following in
warmth of eulogy: 'I have a book for you—an
astounding book,—a godlike book. . . . It is the
finest book on the east ever written: and though

very small contains more than all my library of Oriental books.' The volume was Percival Lowell's *The Soul of the Far East.* He wrote with the same generous abandon: 'Never in this world will I be able to write one page to compare with a page of his. He makes me feel so small, that after reading him I wonder why I am such an ass as to write at all.'

Such enthusiasm is interesting rather than valuable. It is only when Hearn's opinions are analytical, are not emotional, that they become worthy of honest criticism. He has dealt as justly with Zola and Ebers as he has written extravagantly of Gautier and Flaubert. . . .

"Now and again, made a little dizzy by Hearn's literary frenzies, we stumble upon a good thing such as the following remark on Carlyle:

" 'Assuredly Carlyle is no sweet pill to swallow; and he never guides you anywhere. He is hard reading; one feels as if traveling over broken rocks, and boulders hidden by scrub. But there are lightning flashes in that apocalyptic style of his which reveal infinite things. I read only for the flashes. Even then, only a little at a time every day. Did you ever know the agony of trying to read *Sartor Resartus* for pleasure?'

" 'The new poetry is simply rotten!' wrote Hearn, 'morbidly and otherwise. . . . There is no joy in this new world—and scarcely any tenderness: the language is the language of art, but the spirit is of Holbein and Gothic ages of religious madness.' In spite of this observation, he finally preferred Dobson, and Watson, and Lang to Wordsworth, Keats, or Shelley. Hearn quoted Watson's line on Wordsworth: 'It may be thought has broadened since he died!' and playfully added: 'Well, I should smile. His deepest truths have become platitudes.' Hearn wrote of Swinburne: 'There is non-sense in Swinburne, but he is merely a melodist and colorist. He enlarges the English tongue,—shows its richness, unsuspected flexibility, admirable sponge-power of beauty-absorption. . . .' His criticism of Whitman was sound and neatly expressed. He wrote:

"Whitman's gold seems to me in the ore: his diamonds and emeralds in the rough. . . . Whitman's is indeed a titanic voice; but it seems to me the voice of the giant beneath the volcano,—half stifled, half uttered—roaring betimes because articulation is impossible. . . .

"The wonder is that this sensitive writer, who rushed from one shrine of praise to another, from Gautier to Kipling, and from Kipling to Herbert Spencer, should have been able to form an individual style of his own that is either the man himself, or his dream of the beautiful that came to him in the States, in the West Indies, and in Japan—that dream of poetic prose. He wrote: 'Then I stopped thinking. For I saw my home—and the lights of its household gods—and my boy stretching out his hands to me—and all the simple charm and love of Old Japan. And the fairy-world seized my soul again, very softly and sweetly—as a child might a butterfly.' That is our last impression of Lafcadio Hearn, for it was from such thoughts as these that he dreamed his dream, called up to a weary and cynical and hustling world the ghostly magic of the Land of the Gods."

WALT WHITMAN

LXXV

WHEN Walt Whitman's *Leaves of Grass* first appeared about eight hundred copies were printed. There were twelve poems in it, the first one beginning,—

> I celebrate myself;
> And what I assume you shall assume;
> For every atom belonging to me as good belongs to you.

A presentation copy was sent by the author to Emerson who sent a congratulatory letter in which he said: "I find it the most extraordinary piece of art and wisdom that America has yet contributed. . . . I greet you at the beginning of a great career." Not all critics were so appreciative. Whittier threw his presentation copy, so it is said, into the fire. The London *Critic,* with that fine discrimination and delicacy of expression characteristic of the critic of several generations ago, declared that "Walt Whitman is as unacquainted with art as a hog is with mathematics."

His poetry is most unusual, his personality most striking, and yet his life rather commonplace. He had scant schooling. When he was twelve years old he became errand boy in a lawyer's office. At twenty-one he was editor, compositor, and distributor of a country newspaper. "I went to New York, bought a press and types, hired some little help, but did most of the work myself, including the press work. . . . I bought a good horse, and every week went all around the country serving my papers, devoting one day and night to it. I never had happier jaunts." In 1847 he was editor of the *Brooklyn Eagle;* a year later he made a memorable trip to New Orleans. During the Civil War he had valuable experience as a volunteer nurse in the hospitals. At that time he wrote home, "I fancy the reason I am able to do some good in the hospitals among the poor, languishing, and wounded boys, is that I am so large and well, —indeed like a great wild buffalo with much hair." He at one time estimated that he had helped about eighty thousand sick and wounded.

In his later years Walt Whitman lived in Camden, N. J. A very interesting account of visits to his home is given in *Scribner's Magazine** by William R. Thayer.

"UNION LEAGUE, PHILADELPHIA
"August 2, 1885.

"While the recollection of it is still fresh I want to give you a description of an hour I spent one day last week with the most singular personage among American writers. Do you guess whom I mean? or shall I tell you?—Walt Whitman. The afternoon was hot and bright and as I crossed the Delaware by ferry to Camden and walked along the straight, level streets I wondered what I should say in explanation of my intrusion, but as soon as I reached the house I lost my perplexity.

*Permission to reprint granted.

Even the exterior of Whitman's home, situated at 328 Mickle Street, is simple and friendly enough to dispel formality. The house, or rather cottage, is only two stories high and less than five paces wide. It is of wood, and is shaded by a tree on the sidewalk. The front door was open, and when I rang, a comely housekeeper opened an inside summer door, through the slats of which I had already seen her ironing at the end of a corridor.

"I asked if Mr. Whitman was able to see visitors—he had had a slight sunstroke a few days before—and she said: 'Certainly.' Having seated me in the little parlor—a sort of double room, the back part of which does service as a chamber, being furnished with a bed and a few wooden chairs —she disappeared, and presently I heard rumbling as of slow movements overhead. I looked at the things about me—all simple, neat, and cosey —and felt half-ashamed to have disturbed the old man. Soon I heard shuffling steps and the regular clacking of a stick on the entry floor, and in a moment Whitman moved into sight through the doorway. Very cordial was his handshake, and ere I had made a short apology for interrupting him, his 'Glad to see yer' put me quite at ease. He sat in a wicker-bottomed rocking-chair near one window, and I about six feet from him near the other.

"I wish I could draw him for you, because if there be to-day a patriarchal-looking man, it is he. . . . Mr. Thayer's first visit led to others. At a later time he observes:

"Walt did not always care to admit the sources from which he borrowed freely. One day, for instance, he talked about Shakespeare's historical plays, which, he said, showed that Shakespeare was at heart a democrat, and that he had written the plays in order to discredit monarchy and kings and the robber barons, and all that other old feudal nonsense. I discovered afterward that he had appropriated this fantastic notion from his own staunch champion, William D. O'Connor. . . .

"Being myself already saturated with Emerson, and persuaded that the essence of Walt's gospel of Americanism, and democracy, and, above all, of the supreme value of the individual had been proclaimed by Emerson in imperishable pages long before Walt began his *Leaves of Grass,* I was curious from the outset to see whether he would acknowledge any obligations. My own theory was and is that somewhere in the late forties Walt came upon Emerson's *Essays,* devoured and absorbed them, found in them a revelation which interpreted American life to him, and deliberately adopted the teachings as if they had been original with himself. When he came to write, he put them in his own language, laying emphasis on this or that particular which most appealed to him, and giving free rein to his wonderful pictorial talent. And just as the disciple usually exaggerates or distorts some non-essential in his master's teaching, so Walt, bent on glorifying the individual, no matter how insignificant it might be, glorified rubbish as if it were the finest gold of the spirit.

"At one time, when I was wrestling with the old serpents of fatalism and evil, it occurred to me to go over and consult Walt. Ought not he, if any one, with his genial poise and his apparent acceptance of whatever fortune brought him, to solve these insistent questions?

"I attacked him rather too suddenly, in the stand-and-deliver fashion of a much-perplexed visitor at the Delphic oracle, craving an immediate reply. I asked him how he explained this terrible reality of evil, when the burden of every page of *Leaves of Grass* and of his other writings and sayings was: 'Life's all right.' And I began to cite the misery—whether of body or of soul—the pain and sorrow and sin and injustice—from which nobody escapes.

"He did not let me go on long, but showed a little impatience, and replied almost testily: 'Oh, you can't tackle it that way! This ain't a matter to be settled by yes or no. What you call evil is all a part of it. If you have a hill, you've got to have a hollow. I wish some one—I've often thought of doing it myself—would crack up the good of evil—how it helps us along—how it all fits in.'

" 'That is just what Emerson once said,' I interrupted.

" 'Did he?' said Walt, with what seemed to me unexpected interest. 'Did he? Where did he say that?'

"I told him the essay which contains the well-known passage, and I think I also quoted the familiar 'Evil is good in the making.' It seemed to me that Walt was uncomfortable, as if I had unwittingly startled him into furnishing the clew to his inspiration; and whenever in subsequent talks I referred to Emerson's ideas, I thought that he feigned ignorance of them. In early manhood, he made no secret of his discipleship to Emerson,

whom he called 'master' in a famous letter. He
sent one of the first copies of *Leaves of Grass* to
Emerson, violated common propriety by printing
in the New York *Tribune* Emerson's commenda-
tion and by stamping a sentence from it on the
next edition of the *Leaves*. Later, when he came
to be accepted himself as a prophet, I suspect that
he was glad to forget that he had ever called any
one 'master.' In my frontal attack on the problem of evil, I made no further progress with Walt
that day or later. He was neither a philosopher
nor a theologian and I doubt whether he had ever
felt the problem poignantly. For practical living
he found it wise to turn away from or to dodge
the grisly questions which challenged too rudely
his pantheistic optimism. . . .

"Indeed, it was plain enough that Walt regarded me, as a college graduate, with a certain
suspicion and lack of sympathy. His self-ap-
pointed mission being to break down all conven-
tions and to shout his 'barbaric yawp over the
roofs of the world,' he naturally looked upon a
college as the last citadel of convention and therefore as his special enemy. Although in England
his readers came mostly from the university and
literary circles, over here the colleges, partly
from prudery and partly from pedantry, had been
very slow even to mention him. At Harvard, in my
time, for instance, a professor might casually refer to *Leaves of Grass,* but when the student went
to the library to consult the book, he found that
it was catalogued with two blue stars, which meant
that it was kept under lock and key in the 'inferno'
devoted to obscene productions.

"One day after I had been warmly praising

Walt's poems on the Civil War, I said that I thought what he had written about Lincoln would stand along with James Russel Lowell's 'Commemoration Ode' as the highest poetic tributes to the martyr President. He surprised me a little by saying that he had never read Lowell; that he supposed that he was one of those academic 'fellers,' who breathed the fetid air of college lecture-rooms and gave it out in his poems; that he was not a 'critter' for us. I replied that although Lowell was a bookman, he was much more; at the very top of our writers for humor and a splendid force for patriotism before and during the war. 'You ought at least to read the *Ode,* I said emphatically, 'and you would see that he isn't the anaemic fellow you imagine. Much of his other poetry also is fine, some of it very good; and although he isn't a poet of the first class—who is in our time?—he stands well in the second class.'

" 'You wouldn't persuade me to eat a second-class egg, would yer?' said Walt. 'I don't care for second-class poetry, either.' . . .

"I talked with him frequently about Lincoln, whom I took it for granted he must have known well; but he surprised me by saying that although he 'loafed a good deal around the White House,' he never ran across the President but twice, and he heard Lincoln speak only twice—once of an evening from a balcony about some battle news. 'He had rather a high voice with carrying power, but on the whole pleasant and impressive.' . . .

"I heard him say nothing that can add to his well-known and, in their way, unsurpassed descriptions of hospital scenes; but he made one characteristic remark which may be worth repeating.

" 'The human critter,' he said, 'has become too self-restrained. He thinks it isn't manly to show his emotions, and so he tries to keep as hard and mum as a statue. This is all wrong. The Greeks howled when they were hurt and bawled with rage when they were angry. But our soldiers in the war would clinch their teeth and not let out a sign of what they were suffering, no matter how badly they were wounded; and so they often died because the surgeons couldn't tell where they'd been hit.'

"Walt, himself, according to those who knew him in early and middle life, was preternaturally emotional and never attempted to check or to disguise the expression of his feeling at the moment. His disapproval of discipline, which has been one of the chief gains made by normal, civilized men since the Homeric age, harmonizes, therefore, with the rest of his philosophy of unrestraint.

"Of references to passing political affairs, I recall only one, bearing on President Harrison: 'I guess he is the smallest egg ever laid in Uncle Sam's basket.'

"I never saw him show resentment, even under unusual provocation. Thus, when Swinburne recanted in his customary vitriolic language his former bombastic laudation, I ventured to ask Walt whether he had seen the ferocious article in the *Fortnightly Review*. 'Yes,' he said with a tranquillity more effective than sarcasm; 'yes, and I rather guess Swinburne has soured a little on me.' "

LXXVI

WHEN Joseph Conrad passed away in 1924 he had established his reputation as one of the great romantic writers of his generation, but nothing that he ever wrote is stranger, more romantic than his own career. It was in 1878 that a Polish boy, shy in manner, slight in stature, knowing no English, landed in the English north seaport of Lowestoft, eager to sign as seaman under the British flag. He had already had two years of experience as a sailor aboard French craft in the Mediterranean, and so he had little difficulty in finding a place on a Lowestoft coaster, "Skimmer of the Seas."

This Polish lad, Joseph Conrad Korzeniowski, advanced from forecastle to quarter-deck in the world of seamanship; he also advanced from the apprenticeship of an unknown, struggling underpaid writer to a mastership in the world of English letters. Before his death his original manuscripts were sold at public auction for over $100,-000.

The transition from sailing to writing is not so inexplicable as it might appear. Percy A. Hutchison in commenting upon an article (probably the last ever written by Conrad for a magazine) appearing in the *National Geographic Magazine* gives this explanation:

"Conrad, who had received his certificate as master mariner a few years earlier (i. e. before 1888), was in command of a sailing-ship loading at Sydney, Australia, for Mauritius. 'All of a sudden,' Conrad writes, 'all the deep-lying, historic sense of the exploring adventures in the Pacific surged up to the surface of my being. Almost without reflection I sat down and wrote a letter to my owners, suggesting, instead of the usual southern route, I take the ship to Mauritius by way of Torres Strait. I ought to have received a severe rap on the knuckles for submitting such an unheard-of proposition.' "

"Dangerous waters, Torres Strait, for sailing-vessels, because of the calms that prevail there; as dangerous, almost, as the Sargosso Sea; and except for the Spanish explorer, Torres, for whom the Strait is named, and James Cook, the English explorer, perhaps never traversed by any European sailing-ship. Yet Conrad was bent on attempting the passage, and for the reason, the sole reason, that in spirit he was one with the great explorers who were dead; their imagination was his imagination, their courage his courage. 'I was never lonely at sea,' he writes in the same article, 'because I never lacked company—the company of the great navigators.' "

"So Conrad trimmed his sails and headed through Torres Strait, for, instead of the expected 'rap on the knuckles,' his owners gave him the permission he desired, merely adding somewhat plaintively, that they supposed he knew the insurance would cost them more. 'It must have been a romantic day in the office of Messrs. H. Simpson & Sons,' says Conrad. It must, indeed, when hard-fisted owners would pay an increase of insurance premiums that one of their captains might take to dangerous waters merely to follow in the wake of an explorer dead two hundred years! More probably they thought him mad— as he was, with the madness of Columbus and of Drake—and were already planning how they could drop him from their service before he hatched further hare-brained schemes. But behind this request is to be found the master-key to Joseph Conrad? The Ulysses of Tennyson's poem, about to set forth on his last voyage, is made to exclaim:

> For my purpose holds
> To sail beyond the sunset, and the baths
> Of all the western stars, until I die.

"Conrad would sail beyond the sunset; he would follow in the wake of the great navigators, they who had marked out the earth, and the waters thereof. Yet, even as he entered Torres Strait he must have realized the second-hand nature of his adventure, and that the baths of all the western stars lay for him elsewhere. Already he had started on his own voyages, those voyages of the mind, of which each one of his books, each one of his short stories is the imperishable log. A power greater than himself, the power of that expanding imagination which had compelled him when a child to declare his intention of going to the Kongo, which had compelled him, when a youth, to go to sea—this power was already driving Conrad on to demand an ever larger, more colorful, and freer world, the world of the creative artist, which for him meant the world of letters. At first his writing had proceeded fitfully, and with many misgivings on his part. But when he had finished *The Nigger of the Narcissus,* he knew that he was done with the sea. 'After writing the last words of that book,' he says in the foreword to his American readers, 'I understood that I was done with the sea, and that henceforth I had to be a writer.' And it is evident from this confession, supplemented as it is now by the story of the incident of Torres Strait, that Conrad's evolution was determined from the outset; and his history is seen, not as two separated histories, but as one, the events of which, from forecastle to preeminence as a writer, were necessitated by his all-compelling imagination.''

What an attraction Conrad as a stylist has had for the younger generation of writers! He is a contradiction to the theory that no man can know two languages thoroughly. James Norman Hall, the author of *Kitchener's Mob,* an ace of the Lafayette Escadrille, and interesting writer of experiences in Iceland and the South Seas, is explaining in the *Atlantic Monthly,* why he prefers to live in Tahiti. He can live cheaply, has leisure for reading, has quiet for meditation, he can ''loaf and invite his soul''; when he reads he can read without interruption, mornings, afternoons, evenings, far into the night for a whole week.

During one of these orgies of indulgence he reread Conrad's *Lord Jim;* was it for the fifth or sixth time? He knew it so well that he could repeat much of it by heart.

''I had reached,'' writes he, ''that point in the

story where Marlowe tells of his visit to Stein, whom he wished to consult about Jim's case:—

'Late in the evening I entered his study, after traversing an imposing but empty dining-room very dimly lit. The house was silent. I was preceded by an elderly grim Javanese servant in a sort of livery of white jacket and yellow sarong, who, after throwing the door open, exclaimed low, "O master!" and, stepping aside, vanished in a mysterious way as though he had been a ghost only momentarily embodied for that particular service.'

"The magic of this chapter has always been potent for me, but on this occasion it was something more than magic. I was on my knees, in spirit, before the beauty of it. I realized that here was something perfect. Nothing in it could be altered except to its detriment—nothing omitted, nothing added."

Conrad himself says that he never kept a diary nor owned a notebook. This might lead one to think that with him writing was easy. But he is no exception to the rule that easy reading means hard writing. Experienced writers admire Conrad for the exquisite accuracy of his expression. The writing of *Lord Jim*, the book just mentioned, was not accomplished without blood and tears, as we learn in a letter to Galsworthy:

"The end of *Lord Jim* has been pulled off with a steady draft of twenty-one hours. I sent wife and child out of the house (to London) and sat down at nine a. m. with a desperate resolve to be done with it. Now and then I took a walk around the house, out at one door, in at the other. Ten minute meals—a great hush. Cigarette ends growing into a mound similar to a cairn over a dead hero. Moon rose over the barn, looked in at the window and climbed out of sight. Dawn broke, brightened. I put the lamp out, and went on with the morning breeze blowing the sheets of MS. all over the room. Sun rose. I wrote the last word and went into the dining-room. Six o'clock. I shared a piece of cold chicken with Escamillo (his dog) who was very miserable and in want of sympathy, having missed the child dreadfully all day. Felt very well, only sleepy; had a bath at seven, and at 8:30 was on my way to London.''

Polish was his native tongue; he knew French better than he knew English,—at least Ford Madox Ford tells us that Conrad often mentally formulated his sentences in French and then translated them into English,—and yet he chose English as his literary language. Why did he do this? Pierre Mille, a French critic, thinks there were two good reasons: He knew that there were about two hundred million English-speaking people and only about one-fourth that number using French as a native language; and then the English language was rich in nautical terms, and Conrad needed the language of sailors as his early novels dealt with the sea.

Fortunately we need not depend upon a critic to give us Conrad's reasons for choosing English. Conrad himself has told us, and he ought to be the best authority on the subject.

''The impression prevails that I made a choice between two languages,—the French and the English,—both of which were strange to me. This impression is inaccurate. . . . If I had found myself faced with necessity of making a choice between the two languages,—although I knew French fairly well and though this language had been familiar to me from my childhood;—I would have felt myself apprehensive at having to express myself in so perfectly a crystallized language. . . . The truth is that the faculty for writing in English is as natural to me as any other aptitude that I may have possessed since birth.

"I have the strange and profound conviction that it always formed an inherent part of me. The English language for me was never a question of choice nor of adoption. The simple idea of a choice never occurred to me. And as for an adoption! Oh, well, there was certainly an adoption, but 'twas I who was adopted by the genius of the language. . . . It would be as difficult to explain it as to attempt to explain love at first sight."

All stylists exercise the greatest of care in choosing their words. With Conrad, familiar with three languages, and writing in an alien tongue, the selection of the fitting word was sometimes the task of hours. When he was writing *Youth* he spent almost a whole day over one word while correcting the proofs. "And she crawled on, do or die, in the serene weather. The sky was a miracle of purity, a miracle of azure."

He and Ford Madox Ford talked about the proper word for almost a whole day. "Why not say simply 'blue'? Because really, it is not blue. Blue is something coarser in the grain; you imagine it the product of the French Impressionist painter—or of a house painter—with the brush strokes showing. Or you think so of blue after you have thought of azure. Azure is more transparent."

During his last years writing became more and more difficult because of failing health. Gout stiffened his writing hand so that he had to resort to dictation,—a practice he disliked. Galsworthy, giving in *Scribner's Magazine* his reminiscences of Conrad, has this to say: "I think I never saw Conrad quite in repose. His hands, his feet, his knees, his lips,—sensitive, expressive, ironical,—something was always in motion, the dynamo never quite at rest within him. His mind was extraordinarily active and his memory most retentive, so that he stored with wonderful accuracy all the observations of his dark-brown eyes, that were so piercing and yet could be so soft. He had the precious faculty of interest in detail. . . . Conrad's eyes never ceased snapshotting; and the millions of photographs they took were laid away by him to draw on. Besides he was not hampered in his natural watchfulness by the preoccupation of an egoistic personality. He was not an egoist; he had far too much curiosity and genuine interest in things and people to be that. I don't mean to say that he had not an interest in himself and a belief in his own powers. His allusions to his work are generally disparaging; but at heart he knew the value of his gifts; and he liked appreciation, especially from those (not many) in whose judgment he had faith. He received more praise, probably, than any other writer of our time; but he never suffered from that *parvenu* disease, swelled head; and 'I,' 'I,' 'I,' played no part in his talk."

LXXVII

THE SENSITIVENESS OF JOHN GALSWORTHY

ALTHOUGH John Galsworthy attained fame ten years after he began to write,—and he began his career as writer at the age of twenty-eight—, he never has been what is called a popular writer. But with the publication of *The Forsyte Saga*, that monumental history of an English family, followed by *The White Monkey* and *The Silver Spoon*, a continuation of the history of the same family, he has come perilously near to popularity. This writer of plays, essays, and novels can stand all the popularity that comes his way, for in his case his cultured maturity will prevent the cheapening of his seasoned art.

After attending Harrow and Oxford, he was called to the bar in 1890. He took up the law, because his father had done so before him, but the law as a profession had no attraction for him. "I read," he says, "in various chambers, practised almost not at all, and disliked my profession thoroughly."

As the elder Galsworthy was a successful man of affairs, a good judge of human nature, as well as a fond father, he encouraged his son to travel. For nearly two years John traveled, visiting Russia, Canada, Australia, the Fiji Islands, and

401

South Africa. It was during a sailing-ship voyage that he began an enduring friendship with Joseph Conrad.

In reading Galsworthy one gets the impression of a highly cultured, well-bred, sensitive personality. This quality has been well-expressed by St. John Ervine in an article in the *North American Review* which we are permitted to quote:—

"Mr. John Galsworthy is the most sensitive figure in the ranks of modern men of letters, but his sensitiveness is of a peculiar nature, for it is almost totally impersonal. . . .

"One thinks, too, of Mr. Shaw's lively interest in himself, and of Mr. Wells's eagerness to remold the world nearer to his heart's desire. And remembering these men, intensely individual and not reluctant to speak of themselves, one is startled to discover how destitute of egotism Mr. Galsworthy seems to be. It may even be argued that his lack of interest in himself is a sign of inadequate artistry, that it is impossible for a man of supreme quality to be so utterly unconcerned about himself as Mr. Galsworthy is. He has written more than a dozen novels and at least a dozen plays, but there is not one line in any of them to denote that he takes any interest whatever in John Galsworthy. The most obvious characteristic of his work is an immense and, sometimes, indiscriminating pity, but I imagine that the only creature on whom he has no pity is himself. Whatever of joy and grief he has had in life has been closely retained, and the reticence which was characteristic of the English people—I am now using the word 'English' in the strict sense—in pre-war times, but is hardly characteristic of

them now, is most clearly to be observed in Mr.
Galsworthy. And yet there are few among contemporary writers who reveal so much of themselves as he does. Neither Mr. Shaw nor Mr.
Wells, who constantly expose their beliefs to their
readers, do in the long run tell so much about their
characters as Mr. Galsworthy, who never makes
a conscious revelation of himself and is probably
quite unaware that he has made any revelations at
all. How often have we observed in our own rela-
tionships that some garrulous person, constantly
engaged in egotistical conversation, contrives to
conceal knowledge of himself from us, while some
silent friend, with lips tightly closed, most amaz-
ingly gives himself away. One looks at Mr. Galsworthy's handsome, sensitive face and is immediately aware of tightened lips! . . . But the lips
are not tightened because of things done to him,
but because of things done to others.

"I remember, more than ten years ago, reading
a notice of the first performance of *Justice* in an
English Sunday newspaper in which the critic,
who must have been terribly drunk when he wrote
it, attacked the play, making nine mis-statements
of fact about it in as many lines. Those were the
days when I took the field on the slightest provocation. An insult offered to a man of letters for
whom I had respect was an insult offered to me,
and I made much trouble for myself by smacking
faces with great ferocity for offences, not against
me, but against my friends and my betters. I
wrote a letter to that critic which created some
havoc in his sodden brain, and I then posted a
copy of it to Mr. Galsworthy. He thanked me
very civilly for what I had done, and added that

he never replied to criticism of any sort! I was astounded by this statement and a little dashed. My faith in those days was, crudely, two eyes for one tooth! Those who struck at me might expect two blows in return. Like Mrs. Ferguson, in my play, John Ferguson, I said to myself, "If anyone was to hurt me, I'd do my best to hurt them back and hurt them harder nor they hurt me!" I could not bring myself into line with the meekness of Mr. Galsworthy until I discovered in it a form of supreme arrogance! ... Now that I know him and his work better, I realize that I was wrong in my estimation of him both as excessively meek and excessively arrogant. His rule never to reply to criticism, however unfair, is a sign, not of humility or pride, but of complete indifference to himself. I can believe in him becoming furious with one who belittled a dog, but I cannot believe in him displaying any feeling over one who belittled him."

LXXVIII

SIR JAMES M. BARRIE, famous in fiction as the creator of *The Little Minister, Sentimental Tommy,* and in the drama still more famous as the creator of *Peter Pan, The Admirable Crichton,* and *Dear Brutus,* refused to appear as speech-maker either at banquet or at public assembly of any sort. This refusal persisted for many years, but after he was sixty-two years old he was persuaded to appear. He found the ordeal less disagreeable than he expected. Since then he has appeared several times.

In December, 1924, he revisited the old Scotch town of Dumfries—the neighborhood famous in the annals of Burns and Carlyle. Barrie had lived there as a boy; as a man he returned to receive the freedom of the city—in Scotch, a Burgess Ticket. His fellow Scotchmen, proud of Burns and Carlyle, desired to do honor to the man who as a schoolboy playing pirate in a Dumfries garden had got the idea that in later years developed into *Peter Pan.* The London *Daily Telegraph,* December 12, 1924, contains the speech delivered by Mr. Barrie when the Burgess Ticket was presented to him at Dumfries. The larger part of that speech follows:

"Mr. Provost, Ladies, and Gentlemen,—no, I claim my first privilege,—Fellow Townsmen: To be your youngest burgess—what does it feel like? I suppose I should be unreasonable were I to ask you to let me sit down now to think that out. I very nearly began by saying that the Burgess Ticket was the most agreeable document and Mr. McGeorge the ideal Provost. I see you think he is, but no one is perfect,—not even in Dumfries,— and even your Provost, my Provost, has his Achilles' heel. How easy it would have been for him, and what a relief to me, if the Burgess Ticket had on this occasion ended with some such beautiful words as these: 'Any reply by the new burgess is to be deprecated, and lest in his emotion he should break into speech, the town clerk is hereby empowered to append the common seal of the burgh to his mouth.'

"It certainly does not at this moment make me feel young. Too many loved ones who walked Dumfries in my time will not pass this way again —among them the brother who was far more fitten than I for the noble compliment you have paid me. It is not only faces one misses, but the aspirations, the fancies, the laughter, that in company with yours have long since been rolled down the Nith to the contemptuous sea. I am reminded to-day of a Spanish proverb: 'God gives us walnuts when we have no teeth to crack them.' . . . What was that saying about walnuts? That we get them after our teeth can't crack them. Only a half-truth. I think the five years or so that I spent here were probably the happiest of my life, for indeed I have loved this place. Instead of a set speech, let me tell you of a few of the walnuts

Dumfries has given me, whose taste is still sweet
to the tongue.

"The country round Dumfries! It is a lovely
spot, God wot. Criffel, the Nith frozen, the Nith
released, Torthorwald, Caerlaverock,—Lincluden,
the Solway,—the very names of them are music
to Scottish ears; when you and I were young they
were our partners at the ball. We must always
have something in common that others cannot
share if we have sat out a dance with the Cluden.
She was my favorite partner of all, and sometimes she sang to me, and sometimes I had a book
with me to improve her mind. Still I see

> the river dimple by
> Holding its face up to the sky.

"I wooed her in a canoe, but she was a capricious mistress, and often went off with the canoe,
leaving me in the water. I dare say she is carrying on the same diversions still—the Helens of
Troy never mend their ways. The next time one
of you goes in pursuit of her—in a canoe—I wish
you would give her my love and say that I never
think of her without feeling wet. I have a singular memory of the Cluden, and connected with it
is the first boy friend I made in Dumfries—a
friendship that began on my first day at the
Academy, which I am happy to say continues still.
He looked me over in the playground and said:
'What's your high jump?' And I said: 'Three
and a half. What's yours?' And he said: 'Four.
What's your long jump?' And I said: 'Six.
What's yours?' And he said: 'Seven. What's
your one hundred yards?' I said I didn't know,
but what was his, and he said: 'Five secs. less

than yours.' Then he said the one word 'Path-finder,' showing he was, like myself, luckily, an admirer of Fenimore Cooper. I replied with the same brevity, 'Chingachgook.' 'Hawkeye,' said he. 'The Sarpint,' I replied. 'I knew you had read about them.' he said, 'as soon as I saw you.' I asked him how he knew, and he said he knew by my cut. I was uncertain what cut was,—I am not sure that I know now,—but when he said he liked my cut I had the sense to say that so did I like his cut. He then took me aside and became more confidential. 'I wonder,' he asked, 'whether you have noticed anything peculiar about me?' Subsequent experience of life has told me that this is the one question which every person wants to ask of every other person. They all—all mankind—know that they are extraordinarily peculiar, and want to know if you have noticed it. I sometimes think that I must be the only person extant who is not peculiar. He explained what he meant. 'Do you remember,' he asked, 'how Pathfinder laughed?' And I said, 'Yes, he laughed so softly that no one could hear it.' 'Listen then,' said he; and when I replied that I could hear nothing, he said triumphantly, 'Of course you can't—that was me laughing like Pathfinder. I always do it that way now.' And so we swore friendship because we liked each other's cut, and any time we fell out after that was if I laughed like Path-finder. . . .

"I have never divulged to anyone what set me, a dour Scot, to the writing of plays, but to-day one seems impelled to tell everything, and to tell it truthfully—another unexpected and disturbing result of the Burgess Ticket. I think I should never have taken to it seriously but for pressure from two great Englishmen, Sir Henry Irving and Mr. George Meredith. Irving not only drove me to write my first three plays and found managers to produce them, but it was he who got me out of the way of writing them on the backs of old envelopes. Why Mr. Meredith wanted me so ardently to turn playright I could never quite understand, unless it was because he liked me to go down to his famous chalet and tell him about theatres without his having to go to them himself. Those two, however, had not the luck to be Dumfriesians, and so any further mention of them is barred. My first play was very properly written for the Dumfries Academy Dramatic Society, on whose boards I also made my only appearance as an actor. That was due to the histrionic enthusiasm of an Academy boy, certainly the best amateur actor I have ever seen, who, I am glad to know, is here to-day, and who blushes so easily— at least he blushed easily a century or two ago— that I shall cleverly conceal his identity under the name of Wedd. Never can there have been a more devoted follower of the Muse, or a stage manager with more ingratiating ways. During the winters of our existence his pockets were always bulging with stage directions, which fell on the floor as he was being caned, and all the time the masters were submitting him to drastic treatment he was considering how they would do for walking gentle- men. It is conceivable that he even had designs on Mr. Neilson. Our Wedd was truly great in low comedy, but not so convincing as a young lady with her hair attached to her hat, which was the sort of part for which he usually cast me.

"I may perhaps be allowed to tell you without unpardonable elation—so many years have elapsed—that at one of our performances at the Crichton a male member of the audience asked for an introduction. I think I did greatest credit to our admired Wedd on one occasion when the curtain rose on my husband and me about to partake of breakfast, and in his stage fright my husband pulled the table cover and its contents to the floor. How would a superb actress have risen to that emergency? I have asked some of them, Sarah Bernhardt and others, and none of them conceived anything equal to what that Adele did —Adele was my name; I was taken from the French; but the unworthy youth who played my husband would, to my annoyance, call me Addle. I went behind him, and putting my arms round his neck,—yet not forgetting even in that supreme moment to be wary about my hair and hat,—I said, 'You clumsy darling!' The house rose,—I don't mean they went out,—several of them cheered, led on by Wedd, who, when not actually on the stage himself, was always somewhere in hiding, leading the applause. Thus was a great comedienne lost to the world. The next time I saw that play was in London with Miss Irene Vanbrugh in my part. You may guess I was critical, and she was nervous. I told her I thought her good, but that she was lacking in some of my womanly touches.

"It was in order to escape from feminine rôles that I wrote for the Academy my first play, a staggering work, entitled *Bandelero the Bandit*. I was not Bandelero. I nobly gave up that to Tom Newhigging, because I thought one of the other

parts was better. It was the part of all my
favorite characters in fiction rolled into one, so
that I had to be constantly changing my clothes,
with the result that I was scarcely ever on the
stage. A disappointing kind of part. I foolishly
told Mr. Meredith about that play long afterward,
and when the fly came to take me from his house
to the station he used to announce in a manner
that would have set Wedd considering him, 'Bandelero's carriage stops the way.' . . .

"I did get two or three prizes at the Academy
—and I always knew that I could get the second
prize without working much, but that I could
never get the first however hard I worked. That
was because of a boy—I can't sit down without
saying a word about him. One day there was a
timid knock at the door of the Rector's room, and
a thin, frightened-looked boy, poorly clad and
frail, came in. No doubt we all promptly summed
him up as of small account, but I should not wonder, though, if he was the greatest boy that ever
sat on the forms of the old Dumfries Academy.
I don't mean merely as a scholar, though in
scholarship he was of another world from the rest
of us; so he shone, pale star that he was, when he
went to Glasgow University and afterward to Oxford, until—someone turned out that light. He
was too poor, was that brave little adventurer; I
think that explains it all. The other boys felt that
there was something winged about him, just as I
did. He couldn't play games, and yet we all accepted him as our Wonder One. That this could
have been so is a good mark for the Academy, and
is perhaps a proof, if one were needed, that Dumfries is a Scottish town. What was it about James

McMillan that has stayed with me for so many years, and can still touch me to the quick? I felt when we were boys that he was—a Presence, and I feel it still. Literature was to be his game, and what play he might have made with it! Your lost might-have-been!

> His spirit's bark is driven
> Far from the shore, far from the trembling throng
> Whose sails were never to be the tempest given.

"I think the shade of Burns was restless on the night the care-taker's boy died.

"Dumfries! So much vain blowing of fires that have burned themselves out. Even the ashes have gone cold. I feel as if I had popped out of the grave to show you some shivering, blackened piece of paper crumble in my hand. With your permission I shall now pop back again. I have sometimes been called elusive. After such a straight talk I can never be called that any more, can I? I thank you humbly for the great honor given me by inscribing my name in an illustrious list, in some cases so illustrious that it is almost strange to think that they have all to take the curb to make way for an Excise-man—among them belted earls and a' that, such as he liked, when the wind was in the east, to pour a molten fire upon, but every one of them now, we may be very sure, glorying chiefly in being burgesses of Dumfries, because he was one also. One half of Burns we can all fathom, for he was so Scotch that he was and is our blood relation, the one who lived more vividly than the rest. He was so frank about himself that we know that flame of life as we don't know even Dr. Johnson. All the miseries of him, his misdeeds, his follies, we understand, as we know some loving and erring son with whom we have sat up all night in the fields. That is the mortal part of him, and it is perhaps the one thing in all Scotland which we, his countrymen, ask outsiders to keep their hands off. There is also the immortal part, to which we don't belong, the part that is now a walnut tree for all the world. The errors and woes of Burns are perhaps too much harped upon. In his life even he too had his walnuts, and, by all the gods, he could crack them. To know how best to crack your walnuts! There have been many definitions of genius; I offer you that as another one."

LXXIX

THE CONCEIT OF BERNARD SHAW

IS Bernard Shaw conceited? Many have given an affirmative answer to this question, because Bernard Shaw has written very freely and frankly about himself. When he was criticized for writing excessively long prefaces to his plays, and told that Shakespeare had no prefaces, he replied that if Shakespeare could have written as good prefaces as he (Shaw) wrote, Shakespeare would have written prefaces. Such statements have given rise to the opinion that Shaw is excessively conceited. His admirers say that Shaw is not conceited, but that he writes as a detached critic, as one who can judge himself impartially, and that because a man talks about himself, evaluating his merits and defects, is no proof that he is necessarily boastful.

No, Shaw does not believe that he is a greater dramatist than Shakespeare. He admires Shakespeare; pities the man who cannot enjoy him; calls *Hamlet* "a great achievement," and of *Macbeth* says "no greater tragedy will ever be written."

At a time when mad wits were wildly discussing the authorship of Shakespeare's plays, he must have enjoyed the conclusive cryptographic proof that Bernard Shaw wrote the plays attributed to

BERNARD SHAW

Shakespeare,—discovered by Mr. S. T. James, of Leeds.

Mac	Beth
Oth	Ello
Comedy of Er	Rors
Merchant of Ve	Nice
Coriol	Anus
Midsummer Night's D	Ream
Merry Wives of Win	Dsor
Measure for Mea	Sure
Much Ado About Not	Hing
Antony and Cleop	Atra
All's Well that Ends	Well

Shaw himself in one of his prefaces disclaims originality. "I am a crow who have followed many ploughs. No doubt I seem prodigiously clever to those who have never hopped hungry and curious across the fields of philosophy, politics and art. Karl Marx said of Stuart Mill that his eminence was due to the flatness of the surrounding country. In these days of Board Schools, universal reading, newspapers and the inevitable ensuing demand for notabilities of all sorts, literary, military, political and fashionable, to write paragraphs about, that sort of eminence is within the reach of very moderate ability. Reputations are cheap nowadays."

Charged at one time with being conceited he replied: "No, I am not really a conceited man; if you had been through all that I have been through, and done all the things that I have done, you would be ten times as conceited." And at another time he said: "For ten years past, . . . I have been dinning into the public head that I am an extraordinarily witty, brilliant, and clever man. That is now of the public opinion of England; and no power in heaven or on earth will ever change it. I may dodder and dote; . . . but my reputation shall not suffer; it is built up fast and solid, like Shakespeare's, on an impregnable basis of dogmatic reiteration.''

That sounds very much like conceit, but perhaps Shaw differs from other celebrities not so much in his good opinion of himself as in the frankness with which he expresses that opinion. There was method in his madness. In the preface to *Three Plays for Puritans* he writes: ''I leave the delicacies of retirement to those who are gentlemen first and literary workmen afterwards. The cart and trumpet for me.'' He once related that during the nine years from 1876 to 1885 he earned exactly six pounds by his literary efforts. He then concluded that if he were ever going to earn a living by his pen he needed to attract attention, therefore, the cart and trumpet.

Mr. Shaw was certainly not conceited in regard to his ability as a novelist, although he humorously explains his inability to please as a novelist because his eye-sight was perfect, whereas the eye-sight of only about ten per cent of the population is normal. His mind's eye, like his body's, was normal; it saw things differently from other peoples' eyes, and saw them better.

He, therefore, quit novel writing and turned critic. In this he became immediately successful.

''It was as Punch, then, that I emerged from obscurity. All I had to do was to open my normal eyes, and with my utmost literary skill put the case exactly as it struck me, or describe the thing exactly as I saw it, to be applauded as the most humorously extravagant paradoxer in London. The only reproach with which I became familiar was the everlasting 'Why can you not be serious?' Soon my privileges were enormous and my wealth immense. . . . The classes patiently read my essays: the masses patiently listened to my harangues. I enjoyed the immunities of impecuniosity with the opportunities of a millionaire. If ever there was a man without a grievance, I was that man.''

Unsuccessful novelist, art critic, music critic, dramatic critic, Fabian socialist making a thousand speeches in favor of his political hobby, he at last turns to the writing of plays, his real success.

When he was asked what was his first real success, he replied, ''Never had any . . . what came to me was invariably failure. By the time I wore it down I knew too much to care about either failure or success. Life is like a battle; you have to fire a thousand bullets to hit one man. I was too busy firing to care about the scoring.''

In turning from novel writing to criticism, Shaw was following the familiar path described in those caustic lines of Pope:

> Some have at first for wits, then poets passed,
> Turned critics next, and proved plain fools at last.

But Shaw is a refutation of the witty climax; he won his laurels by passing from criticism to creative writing; he became a dramatist. Feeling that he was losing ground as a critic, that the well from which he drew the sparkling waters of his wit was in danger of running dry, he said to himself: ''I will begin with small sins; I will publish my plays.''

In 1892 *Widowers' Houses* was presented to the public in the Royalty Theater of London. "It made a sensation," writes Mr. Shaw, "out of all proportion to its merits or even its demerits; and I at once became infamous as a dramatist. The first performance was sufficiently exciting: the Socialists and Independents applauded me furiously on principle; the ordinary play-going first-nighters hooted me frantically on the same ground; I, being at that time in some practice as what is impolitely called a mob-orator, made a speech before the curtain; the newspapers discussed the play for a whole fortnight not only in the ordinary theatrical notices and criticisms, but in leading articles and letters; and finally the text of the play was published with an introduction by Mr. Grein, an amusing account by Mr. Archer of the original collaboration, and a long preface and several elaborate controversial appendices in the author's most energetically egotistical fighting style. The volume, forming number one of the Independent Theater series of plays, is still extant, a curious relic of that nine days wonder; and as it contains the original text of the play with all its silly pleasantries, I can recommend it to collectors of quarto *Hamlets,* and of all those scarce and superseded early editions which the unfortunate author would so gladly annihilate if he could.''

"I had not achieved a success; but I had provoked an uproar; and the sensation was so agreeable that I resolved to try again.''

Iago is nothing, if not critical; so Shaw is noth-

ing if not pugnacious. As an Irishman he has
found it easy to combat English institutions and
customs. During the Great War he aroused British indignation by writing articles that his critics
said gave aid and comfort to the enemy. Even his
admirers, while asserting that his war-time attack on British complacency was an act of courage, admit that it was a blunder.

Heywood Broun, the well-known American
journalist, has given us an interesting picture of
the soldier's point of view. At the front as a war
correspondent, he was thrilled one day, as looking
through the visitors' book at a certain château he
ran across the signature, "G. Bernard Shaw."
We read:

"The hand was tiny. In a sense Shaw is eco-
nomical of words. He writes many, but he writes
them small. This time economy was complete.
There was no preface to the signature, and no
handbook or footnotes. The visitor had simply
written 'G. Bernard Shaw' and allowed it to stand
without explanation or comment. The officers
supplied that.

"'Awful ass!'" said one who had met the play-
wright at the front. 'He was no end of nuisance
for us. Why, when he got out here we found he
was a vegetarian, and we had to chase around and
have omelets fixed up for him every day.'

"'I censored his stuff,' said another. 'I didn't
think much of it, but I made almost no changes.
Some of it was a little subtle, but I let it get by.'
"I inquired and learned that the blue pencil which
cut the copy of G. Bernard Shaw had not been preserved. It seemed a pity.

"'I heard him out here,' said a third officer,

'and he talked no end of rot. He said the Germans had made a botch of destroying towns. He said he could have done more damage to Arras with a hammer than the Germans did with their shells. Of course, he couldn't begin to do it with a hammer, and, anyway, he wouldn't be let. I suppose he never thought of that. Then he said that the Germans were doing us a great favor by their air-raids. He said they were smashing up things that were ugly and unsanitary. That's silly. We could pull them down ourselves, you know, and, anyhow, in the last raid they hit the post-office.'

" 'The old boy's got nerve, though,' interrupted another officer. 'I was out at the front with him near Arras, and there was some pretty lively shelling going on around us. I told him to put on his tin hat, but he wouldn't do it. I said, "Those German shell-splinters may get you," and he laughed and said if the Germans did anything to him they'd be mighty ungrateful, after all he'd done for them. He doesn't know the *Boche*."

" 'He told me,' added a British journalist, "when I want to know about war I talk to soldiers." I asked him: "Do you mean officers or Tommies?" He said that he meant Tommies.

" 'Now you know how much reliance you can put in what a Tommy says. He'll either say what he thinks you want him to say or what he thinks you don't want him to say. I told Shaw that, but he paid no attention.'

"Here the first officer chimed in again. 'Well, I stick to what I've said right along. I don't see where Shaw's funny. I think he's silly.'

"The officer who was showing the visitors' book turned over another page. 'There's Conan Doyle,' he said."

INDEX OF CITATIONS OF DESCARTES' WORKS